KINGS COUNTY
CAMPUS – WHC

Best wishes,

ALPHA STRIKE VIETNAM

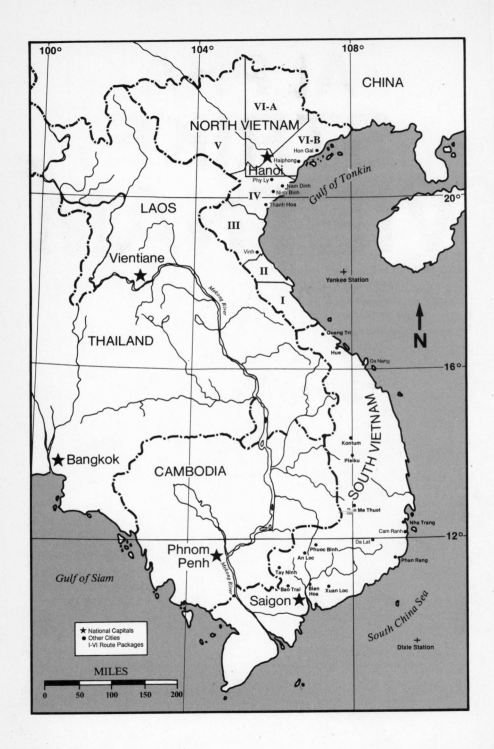

CHINA

NORTH VIETNAM

VI-A

VI-B

Hon Gai

Haiphong

Hanoi

Phy Ly • • Nam Dinh
Ninh Binh

IV

• Thanh Hoa

Gulf of Tonkin

20°

LAOS

III

Vientiane

Vinh •

II

Yankee Station

I

THAILAND

Quang Tri

Hue

Da Nang

16°

N

Bangkok

CAMBODIA

SOUTH VIETNAM

Kontum

Pleiku

n Me Thuot

Nha Trang

Cam Ranh

Da Lat

12°

Phnom
Penh

Phuoc Binh

An Loc

Phan Rang

Tay Ninh

Bao Trai

Bien
Hoa

Xuan Loc

Saigon

Gulf of Siam

South China Sea

Dixie Station

★ National Capitals
• Other Cities
I-VI Route Packages

MILES

0   50   100   150   200

ALPHA STRIKE VIETNAM

The Navy's Air War, 1964 to 1973

Jeffrey L. Levinson

★

PRESIDIO

To
Capt. John A. McAuley, USN (Ret.)
He, like many others, always gave his best.

Copyright © 1989
by Jeffrey L. Levinson

Published by Presidio Press
31 Pamaron Way, Novato CA 94949

Library of Congress Cataloging-in-Publication Data
Levinson, Jeffrey L.
  Alpha strike Vietnam: the Navy's air war, 1964 to 1973/Jeffrey L. Levinson.
    p. cm.
  Bibliography: p. 311
  ISBN 0-89141-338-3:
    1. Vietnamese Conflict, 1961–1975—Aerial operations, American.
  2. Vietnamese Conflict, 1961–1975—Personal narratives, American.
  3. United States. Navy—History—Vietnamese Conflict, 1961–1975.
  I. Title.
  DS558.8.L48 1989
  959.704′ 348—dc19
                                                              88–36994
                                                                  CIP

Photographs courtesy U.S. Navy.

Printed in the United States of America

Contents

Glossary

AAA. Antiaircraft artillery.

AI. Aviation intelligence officer.

Air wing. Mix of aircraft aboard each carrier, led by a senior commander.

Alpha strike. Large striking group involving virtually all of a carrier's offensive aircraft (attack, fighter), typically to one location and sometimes in coordination with other carriers. As the air war intensity increased, three alpha strikes a day were not unusual.

Ball (also "meatball"). Optical landing aid that guides pilots while landing aboard ship.

BARCAP. Barrier combat air patrol. Fighter patrol designed to protect an aircraft carrier. Flown 24 hours a day during the war, it was considered very boring work.

Battle E. Efficiency award. Given to squadron deemed the most combat effective.

BDA. Bomb damage assessment. Photos taken after bombing strikes to measure the effort's effectiveness.

Blackshoes. Surface or ship personnel. They wear black uniform shoes, whereas aviators wear brown shoes.

BN. A-6 or A-3 bombardier-navigator.

Bolter. Takeoff following unsuccessful (missed) arrestment aboard the carrier.

Bonnie Dick. Nickname for the aircraft carrier *Bon Homme Richard*.

Break. A rapid hard turn to avoid SAM or aircraft, or a prescribed pattern when an aircraft returns to the ship (heading into the break).

Bullpup. Air-to-surface missile fired and directed by radio control to the target. Normally fired pointing down.

Burner. Afterburner; provides a surge of power by feeding raw fuel into jet's hot exhaust. Used to gain maximum power for purposes of evasion or increasing speed or energy levels.

CAG. Commander air group (wing). Up until early 1960s, Navy air wings were known as air groups. Despite the change, the acronym was used in Vietnam and is still in use today. Vietnam CAG was a senior commander who'd already commanded a squadron.

CAP. Combat air patrol.

CARGRU. Carrier battle group staff.

CATCO. Carrier air traffic control officer. Directs all carrier aircraft off and on the ship when the weather is not VFR (visual flight rules).

CBU. Cluster bomb unit.

Check (your) six. Warning to pilot to look behind him for MiG or SAM activity coming his way. Refers to the clock system of scanning the envelope around the aircraft, 12 o'clock being straight ahead, 6 o'clock dead aft.

CIC. Combat Information Center. Nerve center for combat operations aboard a ship.

CINCPACFLT. Commander-in-chief, Pacific Fleet. In charge of all naval forces in the Pacific Fleet. Reported directly to CINCPAC, a Navy four-star admiral responsible for all U.S. forces in the Pacific.

CNO. Chief of Naval Operations. Top uniformed officer in the Navy.

CO. Commanding officer.

COMNAVAIRPAC. Commander, Naval Air Forces Pacific.

Connie. Nickname for carrier USS *Constellation*.

CTF. Carrier Task Force. CTF-77 directed Yankee Station activity, with several carrier groups (CARGRUs) under the command.

Daisy cutter. Pipelike extension placed on bombs so explosion occurs before the bomb hits the ground. Provides more of an air burst.

Det. Detachment. Not a full squadron, but a portion. As used in Vietnam, concept was combat attrition had converted the squadron to a det.

DFC. Distinguished Flying Cross.

Dixie Station. Point off South Vietnam in the Gulf of Tonkin designated for aircraft carrier operations in South Vietnam, Laos, and Cambodia.

FAC. Forward air controller. Pinpointed enemy concentrations to ground personnel or air strikes coming in. FAC usually flew in a light plane.

Fat bomb. World War II- or Korean-era 750-pound general-purpose bombs used in the early stages of the Vietnam war when ordnance was somewhat scarce.

Feet dry/feet wet. Feet dry meant a pilot had reached land, feet wet that he was back over water.

Flag. Admiral rank.

G-suit. Worn by pilots, comprises a system of air bladders which compress on fatty tissue (legs and abdomen) so the blood does not pool in the lower extremities during high performance maneuvers. Prevents loss of blood to the brain.

Hanoi Hilton. Nickname for the Hoa Lo prison, which housed the majority of American prisoners of war. Located in the middle of Hanoi, Hoa Lo was built by the French. Heavily guarded, the place was virtually escape proof.

Heartbreak Hotel. Located at Hoa Lo prison, Heartbreak was a receiving station for new shootdowns.

Huffer. Mobile device used to start aircraft engines aboard carriers.

IFF. Identification friend or foe.

In-country. Within South Vietnam.

Iron Hand. Missions against SAM sites.

Iron Triangle. Highly defended area between Haiphong, Hanoi, and Thanh Hoa.

Jink. Irregular flight path, constantly changing altitude and direction. Key was to prevent a regular flight pattern, making it difficult for gunners to track the plane.

JO. Junior officer, lieutenant and below.

Karst. Irregular limestone rock formations much like pinnacles but on a grander scale and covered in many cases with dense jungle. A familiar term for pilots was "hanging around the karst," since some karsts by virtue of their familiarity became rendezvous points.

KBA. Killed by air.

Lay-down ordnance. Ordnance designed with retardation device, allowing for low-level delivery without the pilot blowing himself out of the sky.

LSO. Then known as landing signal officer (now landing safety officer), the individual responsible for bringing planes aboard ship.

MACV. Military Assistance Command, Vietnam.

MERs. Multiple-ejector bomb racks; add-on device designed for carrying multiple weapons on a single bomb rack.

Must pump. Aviation candidates pushed through the training command as fast as possible, as the need for pilots increased during the war.

Nuggets. First-tour aviators.

Over the beach. Over land, feet dry.

PACAF. Pacific Air Force.

Pipper. Center dot in gun sight.

POL. Petroleum-oil-lubricants.

Pop-up point. Geographic point at which a pilot started his climb in order to gain altitude for dive (bomb) delivery.

RAG. Replacement air group. Outdated term, but still used, for training squadron. Today called fleet replacement squadron (FRS).

RAN. Reconnaissance attack navigator. Backseater in RA-5.

Recce. Reconnaissance flight.

RESCAP. Rescue patrol.

RIO. Radar intercept officer. Backseater in the F-4 Phantom.

ROE. Rules of engagement.

Route packages. Geographic areas established in North Vietnam for purposes of greater control of strike prosecutions by U.S. forces.

SAM. Surface-to-air missile.

SAR. Search and rescue.

Shrike. Anti-radar missile fired at SAM sites. Shrike missions were considered among the toughest of the war. The only Medal of Honor presented a jet pilot in a combat role went to Lt. Cmdr. Michael Estocin, shot down while flying a Shrike mission.

Spad. Nickname for Douglas A-1 Skyraider.

TACAN. Tactical air navigation system.

TARCAP. Target combat air patrol. Air patrol conducted over top of target area during air strike.

Tico. Nickname for aircraft carrier USS *Ticonderoga*.

Up North. Common phrase used to designate North Vietnam.

VA. Attack squadron.

VAW. Carrier airborne early-warning squadron.

VC. Composite utility squadron.

VFP. Photo-reconnaissance squadron.

Viggie. Nickname for RA-5 Vigilante.

VRF. Aircraft ferry squadron.

VSF. Squadron designated to provide fighter protection to antisubmarine (ASW) carriers.

VT. Training squadron.

Walleye. TV-guided air-to-surface glide bomb. The pilot could see his target through the missile's TV eye. Introduced in March 1967.

Yankee Station. Position in the Gulf of Tonkin south of Hainan Island for carrier strikes into North Vietnam.

Zoo. Nickname for POW compound in the North Vietnam prison system on the southwestern edge of Hanoi.

Prologue

In 1987, two naval aviators with together more than fifty years of service and 925 combat missions in Southeast Asia called it quits.

Commander Randall Cunningham's retirement received tremendous media attention, specifically because Cunningham—a U.S. Navy fighter pilot—and his radar intercept officer had accomplished a feat no other sea-going aviators had matched during the Vietnam conflict. They shot down a total of five North Vietnamese MiGs.

Captain Denis Weichman's retirement, which culminated thirty-two years of naval service, received no substantive fanfare, despite his having flown 625 missions over Vietnam—more than any other fixed-wing naval aviator.

Why the contrast? Cunningham flew fighters, while Weichman was an attack pilot, a practitioner of the unglamorized and relatively under-publicized air-to-mud business. Fighter pilots have long held the attention of aviation enthusiasts and the American public, a fondness dating back to the days of the dramatic exploits of the Red Baron in World War I. But attack pilots, except for brief moments of public glory—the Korean War film, *The Bridges at Toko-Ri,* is one notable example—have been relegated to plodding unnoticed in the aviation trenches.

Vietnam, however, was an air-to-ground war. Yes, there were many duels in the skies over North Vietnam, and, yes, the exploits of MiG killers have been well documented. But those aerial duels were just a thin slice of the air-war pie. The bulk of naval air activity consisted of A-1 Skyraiders, A-4 Skyhawks, A-6 Intruders, and A-7 Corsairs (joined on occasion by F-8 Crusaders and F-4 Phantoms), dropping bombs and firing rockets and bullets on the fields, factories, and bridges of North Vietnam.

Alpha Strike Vietnam is the story of twenty-three attack pilots, who share the bond of having flown over North Vietnam between 1964 and 1973. All but one of the interviewees made the Navy a career; twenty of the twenty-three flew from Lemoore Naval Air Station (NAS), the

Navy's newest air station (home to the Pacific Fleet's light attack squadrons) situated in the relative isolation of California's San Joaquin Valley; and to a man—despite the death, destruction, and senseless waste of material resources—all no doubt consider the war as the zenith of their military careers.

Today these men live throughout the country. During two years of research and writing, Washington, D.C., Atlanta, Georgia, Flint Hill, Virginia, Needles, San Diego, and Oakland, California, were all on my travel itinerary. Each person was selected for one of several reasons: timing, relationship to another pilot, and the ability to communicate experiences effectively. There were forty interviews in all. All but one allowed use of their names; that individual requested anonymity for purely personal reasons.

The remembrances are poignant, descriptive, and informative; yet they must be kept in perspective as subjective accounts. As one individual wrote following our interview, "After I talked to you I reflected back on some of the not-so-good aspects—there are many of our own work and some of the things that [just] happened. We all block these out to the point of forgetting them completely. So take that into account—after 20 years much of this is gone and forgotten, and we only talk and remember the good, fun and heroic times."

Alpha Strike Vietnam is obviously not a definitive history of the naval air war in Southeast Asia. But it does reveal a segment of American history that—in whatever form—should never be forgotten for fear the United States will make the same mistake again. The book also stands as a tribute to all who fought—those who survived and those who did not.

Part One
1964

One thing we're going to have to do is make up our minds that we are going to win. . . . We should win as easily as possible, and with the best tactics available. I don't think it would take a large number of troops. We could use small detachments. . . . If we make up our minds that our troops are really going to fight . . . we will win.

Admiral Arleigh Burke, USN (Ret.), former Chief of Naval Operations and then director, Center for Strategic Studies, Georgetown University. Interview, *U.S. News & World Report*, 13 July 1964.

Introduction

United States President Lyndon Baines Johnson, even in his worst nightmares, could not have envisioned the tragedy, despair, and destruction that loomed on the Southeast Asian horizon with the onset of 1964. Military activity authorized by the administrations of Dwight D. Eisenhower and John F. Kennedy had steadily led to an increased presence in Southeast Asia in an effort to stem the growing tide of communism in Laos and South Vietnam. But the buildup was comparatively small in nature and of little consequence from a national perspective.

Direct American aid to the Republic of South Vietnam and the training of troops had begun in 1955. The first American fatalities occurred three years later when American advisors Major Dale Buis and Sgt. Chester Ovnand fell victim to guerilla fire on July 8 at Bien Hoa. February 1962 witnessed the formation of the American Military Assistance Command, and by mid-year, 12,000 advisors were on hand in South Vietnam to stem the tide of North Vietnamese aggression. As 1963 came to a close, 15,000 advisors were in-country, and South Vietnam had benefited that year from $500 million in American aid.

These latter figures would pale by comparison to the final statistics of the conflict Johnson "officially" initiated with the Gulf of Tonkin reprisal strike in August 1964. Nine years later, roughly 3.4 million men and women had served in Southeast Asia. The conflict would directly cost U.S. taxpayers between $141.3 and $171.5 billion, with indirect costs in the range of $900 billion.

But such astronomical escalation seemed impossible in 1964 when LBJ made the decision to authoritatively punish the government of Ho Chi Minh for guerilla activity in South Vietnam. America represented the best and the brightest, while Ho and company were certainly nothing more than ragtag, barefoot revolutionaries. Or so it seemed.

Chapter 1
The Beginning

Daniel Robert White banked the C-123 sharply to the right and began his final approach to the drop area. The location was somewhere over a darkened North Vietnam jungle, the time June 1964, and the cargo South Vietnamese mercenaries procured by the Central Intelligence Agency (CIA) and U.S. military to carry out sabotage missions in the heart of North Vietnam.

A naval aviator by profession, White (then a lieutenant) had volunteered to fly the highly secretive missions during the first of five Vietnam tours he would complete. By war's end he was bombing "up North" from the cockpit of an A-7B Corsair light attack jet assigned to the aircraft carrier USS *Oriskany*. But long before Vietnam became an American household word, White transported mercenary teams into North Vietnam and resupplied them.

These aerial missions represented one small element of Operation Plan (OP) 34A, a varied program of covert military operations conceived by the administration of President Lyndon B. Johnson. Administration officials had developed the program to intimidate the North Vietnamese, hoping the reality of a backyard war would curtail the Communists' ever-increasing activities within troubled South Vietnam. As with many decisions about Vietnam to follow, the White House was far off the mark, thanks in part to the chaos that had enveloped the South Vietnamese leadership following the U.S.-backed overthrow of President Ngo Dinh Diem in November 1963.

Former President Richard M. Nixon in his book *No More Vietnams* succinctly recalled the abysmal state of South Vietnam's leadership, labeling the gate of the Presidential Palace there a revolving door: that country endured ten new governments during the two-year period after the overthrow of Diem and even more changes in the military high command. "During one chaotic week, a new government took power, one faction suppressed the attempt, and then the suppressors of the coup ousted the commander in chief. Every time I visited South Vietnam in that period, I found a new president or prime minister in power. I have never met more pitiful incompetents."

Operation Plan 34A began three months before White's arrival in South Vietnam in May. The effort included destroying railroad and highway bridges in raids from the sea, flying U-2 spy planes over North Vietnam, parachuting sabotage and psychological warfare teams into the North, kidnapping North Vietnamese officials for intelligence information, and using PT boats (patrol torpedo gunboats) to bomb coastal installations.

The aerial insertion assignment was hampered—if not made useless—by the unenthusiastic pay-for-play participants. The mercenaries, thugs according to White's frank description, would sometimes not show up for scheduled missions, or deliberately arrive drunk to avoid going. Others had to be literally forced out of aircraft at gunpoint over the jump areas.

White's specific role involved transporting the twelve-man mercenary teams into North Vietnam in the twin-engine, Fairchild C-123 Provider cargo plane. He wore civilian clothing; used an alias; flew with a Third World crew; and was well aware that if he were forced down because of enemy fire or mechanical difficulties, the odds of survival were indeed slim. Even though the consequences were certainly deadly, White, who at six feet, four inches literally towered over his Asian counterparts, enjoyed his fourteen months in-country, relishing the excitement and independence of flying secret missions throughout Southeast Asia.

Flying had been the specific factor in White's 1957 decision to leave the University of Illinois and join the Navy. "I was taking a flying course, that's what got me interested," said the soft-spoken son of an air conditioning repairman. "Several buddies had gone into the Navy and written, 'Hey, this is the thing to do, come fly off these ships.'" He did; entering flight school through a program designed for prospective aviators with only two years of college experience.

Assigned to the Special Operations Group of the Military Assistance Command, Vietnam (MACV), White also flew the propeller-driven, single-seat Douglas A-1 Skyraider, nicknamed the Spad, as cover for commando teams racing their patrol boats back from North Vietnam missions. This Spad background provided the catalyst for bringing him face-to-face with the future aviators of South Vietnam.

"My first fleet tour was with VA-25 [Attack Squadron 25], a Spad squadron based at Alameda Naval Air Station [California]," noted White; it was followed by duties as an A-1 instructor with Training Squadron 30 (VT-30) at Corpus Christi, Texas, in the early 1960s. "That's where I first became tangled with the Vietnamese."

I was the squadron safety officer, and the job was pretty much of a challenge because we had an accident continually running, or an incident going, the entire two-and-a-half years I was there. Now, the accidents involved everybody, but more so the several hundred South Vietnamese that came through.

They were pretty intelligent, really; I think the cream of the crop; but there was no aviation background or mechanical experience. Basically the South Vietnamese were afraid of the airplane; it was a big airplane for somebody who'd hardly even driven a car. Because of their size, all the Vietnamese pilots had to have big pads, so they could reach the pedals of the airplane.

The squadron was also instructing U.S. Air Force officers who were going over to South Vietnam as advisors, and that fact really rubbed me the wrong way. I figured since these Air Force guys never even knew how to fly the airplane, why not take Navy people over there to be the advisors. So I was complaining about that and saying I'll go over.

I asked the commanding officer [CO] of the squadron for his support in getting me over there, and his reply was "You don't want to do that, it's bad for your career." I said, "Yes, I do." The CO left the squadron and went to Washington, D.C., and a couple of weeks after talking to him I got a call one night asking if I could be ready to go in two weeks.

"Go where?"

"Can't tell you."

"Is it across the pond?"

"Yes, it is."

"I can be ready to go in two weeks."

Two weeks later I was on my way.

A Marine captain and I initially spent a month at the MACV complex located in the Chinese section of Saigon. The place was like a fort, with all these buttons to push and code words. From there, we were assigned to the flight detachment up in Nha Trang.

Our airplane was the C-123, which the two of us had never flown. We were single-engine guys, and all of a sudden, we're told, fly the C-123. An Air Force captain who knew how to fly the airplane checked us out. I had three rides in the right seat, three in the left, and became an airplane commander.

The C-123 was a cargo plane designed to look like a baby C-130 with two engines. Certainly the 130 would have been better for our purposes because it carried more and could get to the drop area faster, but [Secretary of Defense Robert] McNamara said here's four or five 123s, go do it.

We'd always amaze the Air Force, landing at Tan Son Nhut Air Field and parking right next to their C-123s. Ours were all black, and we could put a tag from any Southeast Asian country on the side of the airplane depending on where we were. We flew under the name of China Airlines, which is an actual airline that operates out of Taipei [in Taiwan]. Matter of fact, we'd fly the birds over there once a month—those that were shot up pretty badly—to get [them] fixed.

The experience, the mission, was different. I was the only American aboard; everybody else was Third Country. The copilot and crew were [Nationalist] Chinese, and they weren't supposed to be in-country. The company kept those guys under wraps and wherever we went, safe houses were provided. We did have about three Vietnamese crews, but the Chinese were much better than the Vietnamese as far as flying.

Lou, the Marine captain, and I ran the whole show, flying virtually seven days a week and planning our own routes with hardly any rules or regulations. Going up the back door, we'd head through Laos, and up that way. Sometimes we'd go to Da Nang, jump off and come out over the water, and penetrate way up into North Vietnam.

We worked primarily through the embassies, whether it was Hong Kong, Nationalist China, or Laos. We usually had to brief the U.S. ambassador to South Vietnam on the routes, and it was interesting to see the difference in the ambassadors. [Henry Cabot] Lodge was the kind of guy who said, "I don't want to know anything about it. Just do it, don't get in trouble and don't get caught." [Gen. Maxwell] Taylor, you had to more or less take him along the entire route, show him everything. He was interested, he knew more, plus he was a military man and wanted to know about the mission. I also met [Air Vice Marshal, and future President, Nguyen Cao] Ky, a little wise guy, a banty rooster. He swaggered around with that six-gun on his hip, and all of his pilots tried to imitate him. They were just a bunch of kids, laughing and scratching, and whatever General Ky wore, they'd show up with the next day. The group all had a cowboy hat, boots and a big gun belt.

Ky's personal pilot flew with us, and, as a matter of fact, he flew into a mountain by Da Nang one night, planting the C-123 and killing himself and everybody else, about thirty-four in all.

The 123s took a lot of hits, and that made the job interesting. We had ECM [electronic counter-measure] gear in the airplane, a commercial brand that was just exceptional. You could tell what was coming, pinpoint it, and also zap it. We were fired at by AAA [antiaircraft artillery], and sometimes even SAMs [surface-to-air missiles]. Low and slow and still getting SAMs, all very colorful at night. Our routes were planned to stay away from the known sites, and we were well protected: [flying at a] low level; down below the mountain tops; in the valleys; and all of this was at night, so there usually was moonlight to see by. Really sort of exciting.

We knew the location of the teams because the Marine and I [had] put them in. We were in radio contact, and when they needed something, a regular drop would be set up. The radios were rigged with a low power beacon, so you could home in on them from about ten miles out. The drops included whatever was needed to carry on the counterinsurgency program: sometimes food; sometimes ammunition; and in some cases, medical supplies.

The people dropped up North weren't of the best quality. They were a cutthroat bunch. Basically thugs, but the best thugs money could buy. They liked watches and radios, that was a big incentive. Sometimes we needed armed guards on the airplane to get them to even jump out. One flight (and I wasn't on it, Lou was), a shootout took place in the back of the airplane. The thugs just didn't want to jump.

On the ground, we were never sure when coming in for a drop, who was down there. The thugs were getting caught, probably even giving up, although I don't know that. In a couple of incidents, all the signals were right but planes were shot down.

At times I felt there was a purpose to what we were doing, but other times I felt the job wasn't done well enough. More sabotage could have been done on the railway system—basically the reason for being up there—and in gathering intelligence. We really weren't getting our money's worth from the operation.

34A had the air ops and a mar [maritime] ops—little swift boats and nastys that ran up North and which really caused the war, in my estimation. The PTs had to be back across the DMZ [demilitarized zone] before daylight, and if [they were] chased, we'd pounce on the chase boats in the A-1s. The A-1 flights were intermingled with the C-123 missions, and the A-1 was more fun because I got to shoot back. Sometimes we'd also have regular strikes in the A-1; really neat work, fun work—

if you can call war fun—because it did get tiring driving those C-123s around.

The Spad missions were flown in conjunction with the South Vietnamese Air Force out of Nha Trang, Da Nang and Tan Son Nhut, so we always had to contend with coups. If there was a coup going on in Saigon, we could not rely on them [the South Vietnamese pilots] to fly their missions. They would all go to fly in the coup, depending of course, if they were all on the right side. Since the coups had priority, it was shaky as to whether the South Vietnamese pilots were going to be available all the time.

The Vietnamese, the fighting ones, weren't all that aggressive. Basically, they knew the U.S. forces were going to do it for them, and in many cases they just sat back, realizing the U.S. would pick up the slack. Maybe we didn't allow them to do enough. I don't know.

A good example was our practice day-drops with the Vietnamese in the C-123. We'd put them into little fire fights, their baptism of fire with the A-1s as fighter escorts. The A-1 in front would draw the fire, and the second, pounce. You could always tell who was flying the lead A-1, American or Vietnamese. The Vietnamese would be way high. American pilots flew down low, right where they were supposed to be. The [Vietnamese] were also afraid of napalm, thinking the plane would incinerate if hit from the ground. Napalm should be dropped low, and they'd drop it around two thousand feet.

I don't think the Vietnamese officers or noncommissioned people were good leaders. They reminded me of kids a lot, fooling around, joking and just having a good time. That attitude could be picked up in the special forces camps when we would land in there and talk to the advisors. They were, at times, disgusted with their little people.

When the U.S. got into it, the enthusiasm picked up, like we're in it and maybe the job will get done right. That was a mistake. But I know we could have taken care of it in a hurry had they let us.

Chapter 2
The *C. Turner Joy* and the *Maddox*

Like a good many of his Navy contemporaries, John Nicholson was fairly oblivious to the growing turmoil in Southeast Asia when the aircraft carrier USS *Constellation* departed San Diego Bay on 4 May 1964.

"I really didn't know much about Vietnam," recalled Nicholson, then a lieutenant commander with Attack Squadron 144 (VA-144), an A-4C Skyhawk squadron assigned to the *Constellation*'s Carrier Air Wing 14. "It had never been a significant area as far as I was concerned, but all of a sudden we were operating in the South China Sea. And we felt it might get interesting when we had an F-8 photo plane shot down."

Air Force and Navy photoreconnaissance jets had been authorized in May to gather intelligence information supporting T-28 bombing raids against North Vietnamese and Pathet Lao troops in Laos. Navy participation began on 21 May with a flight of two RF-8A Crusader photo-reconnaissance planes from the deck of the carrier USS *Kitty Hawk*. By 9 June, 130 flights had been carried out, confirming the existence of a North Vietnamese infiltration system in the southern panhandle.

The first Navy casualty took place on 6 June when Lt. Charles F. Klusmann, an RF-8 pilot attached to VFP-63, was shot down while photographing Pathet Lao installations in Central Laos. Klusmann was taken prisoner but escaped eighty-six days later.

Twenty-four hours after Klusmann's loss, escort aircraft were added to the reconnaissance missions with orders to retaliate against AAA sites firing on American planes. One escort aircraft, an F-8D piloted by Cmdr. Doyle W. Lynn of Fighter Squadron 111 (VF-111), was shot down that same day over Central Laos. Lynn was rescued on 8 June but, ironically, would die the following year, killed during a bombing run over North Vietnam.

Lynn's '64 shootdown, combined with a growing tide of pilot complaints, generated a readjustment of tactics. Navy recon flights were continued on 19 June but at a higher altitude—ten thousand feet and up—and away from the hot areas of Laos. Through the remainder of 1964 and without additional losses, the Crusaders, joined by the RA-3B Skywarriors and RA-5C Vigilantes, continued to carry out the aerial photoreconnaissance of Laos from carriers in the South China Sea.

"From the time we arrived in the South China Sea, the latter part of June and all of July, what we were doing was escorting either as a tanker or just as a buddy, the photo planes and the reconnaissance aircraft way up into Laos and China," stated Nicholson. "I'd go along for the ride, marking the point where we might get shot at—or whatever the hell might happen."

A future skipper of the aircraft carrier USS *Ranger,* Nicholson had never set foot on U.S. soil until he was fifteen years old.

My Mom and Dad were with Goodyear Tire and Rubber Company, and we traveled extensively. I was born in Bombay, India, and ended up living in South Africa. We got caught down there when World War II broke out, and I left in 1945 by jumping on a Liberty Ship and sailing without my family across the Atlantic.

It was very important to my family that I be in America. Understanding what this country is all about is very difficult if you've always lived here. But having come from South Africa where racism was so rampant—and my parents were pointing out to me it was wrong—and being different myself with an accent, I saw what this country was all about. I could see people dress in certain ways if they wanted to; they had a choice in taking classes; and there was an openness and friendliness. I really loved the country right off the bat.

By midsummer 1964 events were taking place in the Gulf of Tonkin that would lead to the first clash between North Vietnamese and American forces, and present Nicholson the opportunity to defend the interests of the country he had come to love.

In late July the destroyer USS *Maddox,* on patrol in the gulf gathering intelligence for OP 34A, had become the object of Communist attention. For two consecutive days, 31 July–1 August, the *Maddox* cruised unencumbered along a predesignated route off the North Vietnamese coast. In the early morning hours of 2 August, Capt. John Herrick, commander of Destroyer Division 192, learned from intelligence sources of a possible attack against the destroyer.

The attack by three North Vietnamese P-4 motor torpedo boats (PT boats) materialized just after 4:00 P.M. on 2 August. The *Maddox* fired off three warning volleys, then opened fire. Four F-8 Crusaders led by

Cmdr. James B. Stockdale, from the aircraft carrier *Ticonderoga,* also took part in the skirmish. The result of the twenty-minute affair saw one gunboat sunk and another crippled. The *Maddox,* ordered out of the gulf after the incident concluded, was hit by one 14.5-millimeter shell.

A day later the *Maddox,* accompanied by the destroyer USS *C. Turner Joy,* received instructions to reenter the gulf and resume patrol. The *Constellation,* on a Hong Kong port visit, was ordered to join the *Ticonderoga,* stationed in the South China Sea, at the mouth of the gulf. The two destroyers cruised without incident on 3 August and in the daylight hours of 4 August moved to the middle of the gulf. Parallel to the movements of the *C. Turner Joy* and *Maddox,* South Vietnamese gunboats taking part in OP 34A operations launched attacks on several North Vietnamese radar installations. These attacks bothered Herrick, who reported to superiors his fear the North Vietnamese would believe the destroyers were also involved in the raids. Herrick's concern was justified.

At 8:41 P.M. on 4 August both destroyers reportedly picked up fast-approaching contacts on their radars. Navy documents show the ships changed course to avoid the unknown vessels, but the contacts continued intermittently. At 10:39 P.M. when the *Maddox* and *C. Turner Joy* radars indicated one enemy vessel had closed to within seven thousand yards, Captain Herrick ordered the *C. Turner Joy* to open fire; the *Maddox* soon followed. For the next several hours, the destroyers, covered by the *Ticonderoga*'s and the *Constellation*'s aircraft, reportedly evaded torpedoes and fired on their attackers. The entire engagement saw the *Maddox* and *C. Turner Joy* fire 249 five-inch shells, plus four or five depth charges.

Were the destroyers actually attacked? Historians have debated and will continue to debate the issue. Most of the pilots flying that night spotted nothing. Stockdale, who would earn the Medal of Honor for heroism as a prisoner of war, says in his novel *In Love and War* that the gunboat attack did not occur.

> I had the best seat in the house from which to detect boats—if there were any. I didn't have to look through the surface haze and spray like the destroyers did, and I could see the destroyers' every move vividly. . . . When the destroyers were convinced they had some battle action going, I zigged and zagged and fired when they fired. . . . The edges of the black hole I was flying in were still periodically lit by flashes of lightning—but no wakes or dark shapes other than those of the destroyers were ever visible to me.

Commander Wesley L. McDonald (later to become a four-star admiral), skipper of the *Ticonderoga*'s VA-56, says he didn't see anything that night except the *Maddox* and the *Turner Joy*. And I think the *Maddox,* basically, was in disarray as far as the [Combat Information Center (CIC)] controller was concerned in trying to get us to attack PT boats that were imaginary. I didn't see any wakes, I didn't see anything.

What happened on August 4 is something that still remains to be uncovered. Possibly it was some spurious radar signals that created a lot of imagination, sometimes you can get that to happen. Whatever it was, I didn't see a damn thing, and that's not to condemn the president for his decision or to say anybody else was fabricating a story. It's just that I didn't see it, that's all.

Nicholson, who arrived at the "battle scene" leading two other VA-144 pilots, seconds McDonald's assertion that the men of the *C. Turner Joy* and *Maddox* believed they were in imminent danger.

"There is no doubt in my mind those two ships were under stress, judging from the voice of the guy at the [CIC] control. Whether he was an ensign or captain, his voice was very tense, he had his headings completely screwed up, and there is no doubt in my mind the crew felt they were under attack and in peril."

The *Constellation* had been at sea less than ten hours on 4 August when Nicholson, as VA-144's operations officer, received a call shortly after dinner to man three aircraft.

We were watching a movie after dinner, and I'll never forget its name, *The Night Has A Thousand Eyes,* a B-rated movie where the Indians run around in tennis shoes and you can see contrails in the sky. One of the real classy pictures they used to give to the fleet.

The phone rang and it was the duty officer, and he said the flag [admiral] wanted to see three attack pilots immediately for a briefing. I went back to the ready room, where the movie was being shown; sitting on one side was Ronnie Boch and on the other side Everett Alvarez. I just grabbed those two guys and said, "Let's go down and get in our flight gear."

These were typical flight drills and always routine. You'd get all suited up; go up to flag intelligence and get a briefing; pick up a frequency card; go on deck and man your aircraft; start it up; shut down; and then go back and watch the movie. That's exactly what was going through my mind, and I was a little torqued we had to go through this routine so soon out of port.

Up in the flag spaces, there seemed to be just a little more activity than normal, and I thought, boy, these people are really playing it to the hilt. We were assigned a frequency and call sign to check in with, and found the ship's position on the west side of Hainan Island [Chinese territory]. Our assignment said fly to the Gulf of Tonkin, meaning we had to go way south, do a dogleg, and then go up. I didn't think anything about it because I was sure we weren't going to fly the mission anyway.

Up on the flight deck, rain was coming down like hell, with lightning and thunder. Soaking wet, we all got into our cockpits, and my crewman was complaining about the drill because of the rain. The plane cranked up, as usual, but this time the three of us were taxied onto the catapult, which had never happened before. All of a sudden I had this sinking feeling in my stomach, that "What if it really happens," and then I was airborne, and frantically trying to recall just where the ship's position was.

I was the first one off, right into the thunderstorm's lightning and everything else, and finally found sort of a VFR [visual flight rule] holding spot. Boch was the second off, and he joined up right on me. Way later, for whatever reason, came Alvarez. He took forever getting off the ship; finally launched, [he] comes on the air and says, "I've got vertigo." I could see his lights, so I told him to climb up, and Ronnie and I joined on him. He popped his eyes out and all three of us climbed out.

Moving south, we left the rain squalls; the moon was out, a real bright moon. Approaching the dogleg, I switched to our assigned frequency, still unaware of the *Maddox* and *Turner Joy* incident; the first words over the air were "torpedo bearing." I recall that very vividly because the three of us are airdales and all of a sudden we're listening to "torpedo bearing." I thought, What the hell is going on now, as we picked up the Tico [*Ticonderoga*] air wing—CAG-5—busy working with the ship. CAG-5 aircraft were just leaving as we arrived in the area, and immediately I asked for an update. "Where are we and what are we doing here?" The briefing came from a high-pitched voice in the CIC, telling us they were under attack from PT boats.

We began searching for ships, and I saw two high-speed wakes heading 180 degrees, heading south. The guy in the CIC said, "That's not us, we're heading 000," and I recall him calling that heading because 000 is 360. Aviators use 360 and blackshoes [surface ship personnel] 000. Boch was with me, and he said, "Roger, I've got the two wakes; they're heading 180." The voice in the CIC said, "Those must be the PT boats, take them under attack." We armed, and I said, "One in," as we went into our run, and all of a sudden I heard, "Hold fire, hold fire"—it was the two destroyers heading 180—and the attack was broken off.

Talk about history being made; we were within split seconds of dumping on those two tin cans—I mean split seconds. From that point on, I lost total faith in who the hell was controlling down there. We continued to circle overhead, when Alvarez thought he saw something in the water. Alvarez had the flares, Boch and I the rockets, and he [Alvarez] went down and lit up whatever he thought was in the area. I didn't see anything, but we were getting low on fuel and needed to get rid of our ordnance. I thought, The hell with it, let's fire into this general area. That's what we did: fired off our ammunition into this flared area.

For the first time at night, I fired off two pods of 2.5 [-inch] rockets, eighteen to a pod, and that was sort of the thrill of the evening, watching the stuff off. You get night-blinded fast when two loads of those things go out.

No one relieved us on-station, and I told the destroyer we were in a low fuel state and had to get going to make the dogleg back. So we started climbing for altitude, and one of the two, Alvarez or Boch, called in and said they were really low fuelwise, almost down to nothing. I made a decision, and we cleaned our wings—dumped tanks, ordnance pods, everything—and climbed to a great altitude. But there was no way we were going to get back to the ship by taking the dogleg, so everything was lights out, and right across Hainan we went.

At landing, the fuel states were extremely low, like one pass and you better make it or trouble's coming. It was still rainy and windy, the ship was into the wind, and the three of us went straight in and landed. Of course, there was all kinds of activity going on: aircraft were launching, people briefing. The time was 1:00 or 2:00 A.M., and we were rushed up to the admiral's quarters for a briefing. We had to write exactly what happened, and the explanation given to us was our comments were going to be used for the United Nations or something like that.

I was bothered by the drill concept of the mission when it wasn't a drill. It shook me; I hadn't put the energy into it that I really should have. While the mission was happening, I sensed something spectacular might be occurring, historically. And of course, after the debriefing and writing the letters to the U.N. and all that garbage, I knew something was going to happen that was pretty important.

Chapter 3
Reprisal

Because of the twelve-hour time difference, military and political leaders in Washington, D.C., first learned of the *C. Turner Joy-Maddox* engagement at 11:00 A.M. on 4 August. The Joint Chiefs of Staff began selecting possible reprisal targets from a list of ninety-four drawn up at the end of May. The suggestion of Adm. U. S. Grant Sharp, commander in chief of U.S. forces in the Pacific (CINCPAC), was to bomb coastal bases in pursuit of torpedo boats.

At 4:49 P.M. formal execution orders for reprisal strikes reached Admiral Sharp in Honolulu. The carriers *Ticonderoga* and *Constellation* were authorized to attack four torpedo boat bases, plus an oil storage depot near Vinh. President Johnson met two hours later with congressional leaders from both parties, telling them of the so-called unprovoked attacks on the destroyers and his decision to launch reprisal strikes.

Just after 11:30 P.M. Secretary of Defense Robert McNamara learned from Sharp that at 10:43 A.M. Vietnam time on 5 August the *Ticonderoga* had launched her aircraft, and that they were expected to arrive at their targets in about one hour and fifty minutes. Both carriers had needed more time to get into launching position than the execution order envisioned, and the *Constellation* was not able to launch her planes for several more hours.

President Johnson, seemingly more concerned with prime time publicity than with the lives of American airmen who might fly into the guns of a waiting enemy, went on national television at 11:36 P.M. to tell the nation and world of the sixty-seven-plane reprisal strike, code-named Operation PIERCE ARROW.

> My fellow Americans, as President and Commander in Chief, it is my duty to the American people to report that renewed hostile actions against U.S. ships on the high seas in the Gulf of Tonkin

have today required me to order military forces of the United States to take action in reply.

The initial attack on the destroyer *Maddox* on August 2 was repeated today by a number of hostile vessels attacking two U.S. destroyers with torpedoes. The destroyers and supporting aircraft acted at once on the orders I gave after the initial act of aggression.

Repeated acts of violence against the Armed Forces of the United States must be met not only with an alert defense but with positive reply. That reply is being given as I speak to you tonight. Air action is now in execution against gunboats and certain supporting facilities in North Vietnam which have been used in these hostile operations.

In the larger sense, this new act of aggression aimed directly at our own forces again brings home to all of us in the United States the importance of the struggle for peace and security in Southeast Asia. Aggression by terror against the peaceful villages of South Vietnam has now been joined by open aggression on the high seas against the United States of America. The determination of all Americans to carry out our full commitment to the people and to the Government of South Vietnam will be redoubled by this outrage. Yet our response for the present will be limited and fitting.

Sixteen aircraft from the *Ticonderoga,* led by Commanders Stockdale and McDonald, struck the Vinh petroleum storage complex at 1:30 P.M. (Vietnam time) on 5 August. Other *Ticonderoga* flights attacked enemy Swatow gunboats (Russian-built PT boats) or other PT boats at Quang Khe and Ben Thuy.

A-1 Skyraiders and A-4 Skyhawks from the *Constellation,* reaching their first target at 3:40 P.M., bombed and strafed North Vietnamese naval craft near their bases at Hon Gai and near the Lach Chao Estuary.

The results saw 90 percent of the storage facility at Vinh go up in flames while at the nearby Ben Thuy Naval Base, three craft were sunk. One boat and five others were damaged at Quang Khe; at Hon Gai's inner harbor, the *Constellation* aircraft sank or disabled six Swatows or P-4s, and en route to Lach Cho Estuary, Connie airplanes damaged five naval craft near Hon Me Island.

Aircraft from VA-144 made a fast approach to Hon Gai from the southeast, attacking boats in the harbor with rockets and 20-millimeter cannon fire. Enemy gunners, presumably well aware the Americans were coming, responded from the craft under attack and shore batteries. Twenty minutes later, one Swatow was aground and burning in the harbor, another burning but underway, and one P-4 burning and slowly circling. Three other vessels were either damaged or sunk.

All totaled, thirty-three of the thirty-four coastal fleet North Vietnamese PT boats or Swatows were struck by Navy rocket or cannon fire. Seven were sunk, ten severely damaged and sixteen received lesser damage. The Navy lost two aviators, Lts. (jg) Everett Alvarez from VA-144 and Richard C. Sather from VA-145, an A-1 Spad squadron. Alvarez earned the dubious distinction of being the first naval aviator captured by the North Vietnamese and spent eight-and-one-half years in captivity. Sather, in a sense, was less fortunate, becoming the Navy's first pilot killed during the conflict. It would take twenty-one years for his remains to be returned.

On board the *Constellation* the morning of 5 August, John Nicholson's emotions were touched with seriousness and anticipation. He was only hours from firing his first shot in anger.

I woke up at 6:30 or 7:00 and Boch was already in the ready room preparing for a test flight. A group of us were soon called up by air intelligence for a briefing, and this time I wasn't playing any more games.

We were told of the retaliatory strikes and assigned targets. One was the Hon Gai port area, while my flight was given an ocean target right on the border with China, a port facility where the Chinese border meets North Vietnam. The plan was to launch the two goes simultaneously, and the brief was for one run at each target.

We'd never flown in the area, so there was no knowledge of our target, and I was nervous because the briefers emphasized it was paramount that we not come anywhere near dropping on Chinese soil. Yet looking at the map, if you sneezed or did something wrong, the bomb could end up in China with no trouble at all.

While up on the flight deck and manning the aircraft, we were told President Johnson was either on the air or about to go on the air indicating the U.S. was now in the process of making retaliatory strikes. That sort of disturbed me, knowing this speech was happening before we even launched.

As a group, there was a hype of dropping ordnance in anger for the first time. I'd been in Lebanon; I'd been off the Suez Canal; I'd been off Formosa and practiced at Fallon [home of a Nevada bombing range] and all that, but I'd never dropped anything for real. The adrenaline was flowing liberally.

Just before launch, our target was changed to Hon Gai. We had to regroup and frantically look on the map to [see] what this damn Hon Gai looked like. There really was no time to study the target; and then off we went in this mass gaggle. The flight leader did brief us on the way, saying the target would be PT boats tied up at the southeast pier, or wherever the hell it was.

We started up into the gulf, moving close to land, and I remember what impressed me most was the mountains. I'd always looked at Chinese art as being so out of proportion, the mountains always went straight up and [down] into the water, and everything seemed to be so pinnacled. But as we came up into that gulf, all of a sudden I looked over at the coast, and damn if the mountains didn't go straight up and straight down. It was, I guess, just a moment of thinking about other things.

The boats at Hon Gai weren't visible as we approached, and the lead called up and said, "I see no PT boats tied to any pier," and we were now a mass of planes in enemy territory. Alvarez came up and said, "The boats are out in the bay. They're anchored in the bay." We all looked, and there were all these PT boats anchored in different directions.

We rolled in as a mass gaggle on the second pass, the call was, "One in," and away we went. I was in the middle of the group somewhere, and rolled in on a large Swatow. Coming down the chute, my rockets were going off, hitting in the water, and I had this guy bored in. Really target fixation, I had to get in-in-in, and finally dropped my bombs way too close. There was no time to watch where the ordnance went because I had to get out, and what do I do but pull out to the left. At the briefing, we decided to break off to the right. Navy pilots are notorious for breaking off to the left, so we were going to outsmart the bad guy and turn to the right. I remembered as soon as I pulled off—you idiot, everybody else went right and you went left.

Pulling off the target, what impressed me, stuck in my mind, was this area had a lot of smog in it, really two layers of smog. Well, the two layers was the AAA going off, two very distinctive layers, and I mean the North Vietnamese were really letting it go in every direction. For the first time I realized they're shooting at us, and just about that time Alvarez was hit.

Four-eleven was his call sign, and he came up on the air and said, "411, I'm hit," then followed with "I can't control it, I'm ejecting." I came on the air real fast and said, "Okay 411, you know what to do." It's the most stupid thing in the world to say except to let him know that we knew he was hit. About that time the emergency beeper went off, and I circled a couple of times trying to look for him. I didn't see his airplane go down, or anything that looked like a chute. I don't know how long I spent in the area, maybe three or four orbits, and then we had to come home because of our low fuel states.

Losing Alvarez was very sobering. We came back quiet; a lot of people were just thinking, just amazed a jet was getting shot down in combat. People were saying, "How the hell could that happen? How can a pilot in this day and age get shot down by guns?" Of course, there were pilots on the ship who had been flying the F9F2 in Korea, and they said, "We're learning the lesson all over again. The North Koreans shot us down with no problem [when we were] flying the F9F2, and we learned you don't go below thirty-five hundred feet. And here you kids are practicing low and slow maneuvers." Ask any pilot training at Lemoore Naval Air Station in the early 1960s. We were practicing low and slow, half flaps, two hundred and some miles per hour. Hell, they were going to shoot us out of the sky with a slingshot. Somehow in our crazy minds we lost the lessons of Korea, and they knocked Alvarez down. By 1968 no one, and I mean no one, was going below thirty-five hundred feet. To do that was the kiss of death, and those were hard lessons to learn. We lost a lot of pilots, and a lot spent many hours in the Hanoi Hilton [Hoa Lo Prison] because they went below thirty-five hundred.

The loss of Alvarez sat with me throughout the war. Why him? It could have been me, it could have been anyone else. Believe me it was sheer luck. And when Alvarez went down I almost—no it wasn't almost—I did have a guilt feeling, it shouldn't have been him, it should have been me. Why did I cut my Master's program short at Monterey [U.S. Naval Postgraduate School] in 1966? I had every excuse to live in that beautiful climate, read books, and have a wonderful life. Why did I cut it short? Why did I volunteer to go back to Vietnam every year during the 1960s? The answer is Alvarez was sitting in a prison camp; I know that was a determining factor. I could not sit still with that on my mind.

Part Two
1965

To the gang down in that flak site
when their radars start to shine,
their 85's are breaking up that old
flight of mine.
When the bursts start getting closer
that's a very certain sign,
those 85's are breaking up that old
flight of mine.
There goes Sam, there goes Mac
it really is a shame,
now I don't have to pay my debt
from last night's poker game.
Now the leader's plane is burning
and he says it's punch out time,
those 85's are breaking up that old
flight of mine.

Sung to the tune of "Those Wedding Bell Blues,"
from the songbook of Attack Squadron 72.

Introduction

Nineteen sixty-five quickly witnessed a new fervor to the American military commitment in Southeast Asia.

Less than seventy days into the year—on 8 March—some sixteen hundred U.S. Marines, the first units of American combat troops ordered to South Vietnam, landed at Da Nang. Their orders were to protect nearby American aircraft. By year's end, nearly two hundred thousand U.S. troops were in-country.

In the air, two February retaliatory strikes soon led the way to a much more substantial effort, a sustained air war against North Vietnam, code named ROLLING THUNDER. It debuted 2 March 1965, kicking off a bombing program that spanned more than three years. Involving Navy, Air Force and Marine Corps aircraft, ROLLING THUNDER grew from a sequence of single-mission, retaliatory strikes into a massive strategic air campaign.

The Johnson administration's original intention with ROLLING THUNDER centered on breaking the will of North Vietnam. Ho Chi Minh and company, however, did not respond to the message. By summer the direction of ROLLING THUNDER shifted. American pilots were called on to destroy the logistical capability of North Vietnam, in order to limit the flow of men and supplies into the ever-expanding war down South.

ROLLING THUNDER initially concentrated on attacking infiltration routes into the South from southern North Vietnam. Targets were designated on a weekly basis by the nation's top military leaders, the Joint Chiefs of Staff, and approved by the Office of the Secretary of Defense, the State Department, and most significantly, the White House. Admiral U. S. Grant Sharp in his book *Strategy for Defeat* said the final decision on targets "to be authorized, the number of sorties allowed, and in many instances even the tactics to be used by our pilots was made in a Tuesday luncheon in the White House attended by the President, the Secretary of State [Dean Rusk], the Secretary of Defense [Robert McNamara], Presidential Assistant Walt Rostow and the Presidential Press Secretary (first Bill Moyers, later George Christian). The significant point is that no professional military man, not even the chairman of the JCS, was present at these luncheons until late in 1967. The omission . . . was in my view a grave and flagrant example of his [McNamara's] persistent refusal to accept the civilian-military partnership in the conduct of our military operations."

As ROLLING THUNDER expanded in 1965, target areas authorized for operations included most of North Vietnam. By summer, American pilots were striking slightly north of Hanoi, hitting airfields, supply depots, and military barracks around the 21st Parallel. New targets were authorized in packages covering two-week periods. A small power plant below the 19th Parallel was attacked in June, and in late July and August, a larger one near Thanh Hoa was struck. This period also saw explosives factories hit, as well as certain dams and waterways in the Red River delta, and the number of planes involved in bombing missions almost doubled. In late August about sixty-five planes were participating daily in strikes against the North, and by the next month, the figure totaled 120. That fall, major transportation routes between Hanoi and Haiphong came under attack and in December the large Uong Bi Power Plant, fourteen miles from Haiphong, was struck three times. The plant was reported to supply 15 percent of North Vietnam's electrical power, including one-third of the power supplied to Haiphong and one-fourth of that supplied to Hanoi. During the year no attacks were permitted within a thirty nautical-mile radius of Hanoi, within a ten nautical-mile radius of Haiphong, and within a buffer zone along the Chinese border.

When President Johnson called a thirty-seven-day bombing halt on 23 December 1965, Navy pilots alone had flown thirty-one thousand combat and combat-support sorties, with each sortie representing one plane flying a single mission. Attack and fighter aircraft dropped 64,000 bombs and fired nearly 129,000 rockets during that initial year.

The Navy's aerial command structure placed all carriers operating in the South China Sea and the Gulf of Tonkin under the leadership of the Seventh Fleet, specifically the Commander, Attack Carrier Striking Force (Task Force 77 or CTF-77). Carriers were deployed at Yankee Station off the northern coast of South Vietnam, and during 1965–66, at Dixie Station. The latter imaginary site, some one hundred miles southeast of Cam Ranh Bay, provided an orientation period for the majority of carriers and their personnel, an opportunity to operate in the less hostile environment of South Vietnam before moving north.

Carrier deployments in the early ROLLING THUNDER time frame typically ranged from seven to ten months, although many went on longer as the tempo of the air war increased. A carrier would stay in a combat mode (known as a line period) from twenty-five to thirty-five days or longer, then pull back to the Philippines, Hong Kong, or Japan for rest and relaxation periods. Standard procedure found a carrier completing four line periods before heading home, although exceptions were certainly the rule. In late 1964 and early 1965, the *Ranger* spent 117 out of 125 days under way, with one stretch of seventy days continuously at sea, while the *Coral Sea* in 1965 was in a combat cycle of eight out of ten-and-one-half months. This hectic pace would eventually take an unmeasurable toll on officers and enlisted personnel.

Throughout 1965 three to five Task Force 77 carriers could be found operating in the gulf. On each ship, the carrier's air wing consisted of some sixty to ninety aircraft, with the exact number dependent on the size of the carriers, which ranged from the large-deck, nuclear-powered USS *Enterprise,* then the world's largest warship, to the 33,000-ton, World War II Hancock-class ships.

Command of the carrier air wing, a prize plum in the small and close-knit fraternity of naval aviators, went to a senior commander, known on the ship as CAG, an outdated acronym from the days when the wings were called Carrier Air Groups.

While fighting the in-country war was certainly the focus aboard each carrier, on many occasions there was also another kind of conflict. Each Yankee Station carrier sought to outperform its on-station counterparts by launching more combat missions or sorties over the beach, a well-documented drive that played a significant role in the future promotion of ship captains, air wing commanders, and squadron skippers.

The Navy's strike aircraft during ROLLING THUNDER, and primarily throughout the war, included the maneuverable A-4 Skyhawk, propeller-driven A-1 Skyraider, A-7 Corsair II (introduced in late 1967), and the all-weather, day-night A-6 Intruder which appeared first in July 1965. The F-4 Phantom provided attack support, although its specific Navy purpose was air-to-air intercept, a function also handled by the F-8 Crusader.

Attack and fighter aircraft carried a vast array of ordnance, from World War II-era "fat" bombs to advanced missiles and precision-guided munitions. For strikes in North Vietnam, Laos, and South Vietnam, the load might include 250-, 500-, 1,000-, and 2,000-pound general purpose bombs (Mark 81, 82, 83, 84 series); napalm bombs; cluster bombs (CBUs) containing steel pellets especially effective against personnel; magnetic mines; and 5-inch Zuni and 2.75-inch rockets. Carrier-based aircraft also utilized Bullpup AGM (air-to-ground) guided missiles, the newly developed Walleye TV-guided missile (a television camera was attached to the nose of the bomb and the bomb directed to the target by the pilot), and the AGM-Shrike anti-radar missile. Fighters were equipped with Sidewinder and Sparrow air-to-air missiles and 20-millimeter machine guns.

ROLLING THUNDER suffered from the whims of weather, as did any Southeast Asian air campaign. Many a mission was cancelled due to poor visibility; and numerous aircraft recoveries, a challenging chore under normal circumstances, became an exercise in gut-wrenching futility as visibility dwindled to a precious several hundred feet.

During the periods of the Northeast (winter) Monsoon from November to March, the weather in the Gulf of Tonkin and over most of North Vietnam is characterized by heavy clouds and a high amount of rainfall. Conditions are especially harsh when a weather phenomenon known as "crachin" occurs, characterized by thick clouds and ceilings as low as five hundred feet in combination with fog and persistent drizzle. Conversely, during the Southwest (summer) Monsoon from May to September, skies are clear and dry. These general weather patterns are almost reversed in South Vietnam and Laos.

Chapter 4

FLAMING DART

Commander Paul Peck could not believe his orders.

"Your signal is jettison your bombs and return to the ship," barked the commander from the aircraft carrier USS *Ranger*.

Peck, skipper of Attack Squadron 94 (VA-94)—the "Mighty Shrikes"—was devastated. His first taste of combat, or what should have been his initial experience after sixteen-and-one-half years of naval service, had come up empty. Instead of striking the North Vietnamese staging base at Vit Thu Lu, or the possible secondary target of the army compound at Dong Hoi located twenty miles north of the DMZ, Peck had just been ordered to dump the strike group's bombs and rockets into the winter waters of the Gulf of Tonkin.

"That's what we did," noted Peck in remembering the events of 8 February 1965. "We dumped everything into the ocean. And of all the incidents on that cruise which strikes home the most, dropping those bombs in the ocean was it."

Peck, his squadron, and the remaining pilots of the *Ranger*'s Air Wing 9 had deployed to Southeast Asia on 5 August 1964, the day of the Gulf of Tonkin reprisal strike.

"Quite frankly, I thought it was a tempest in a teapot, that it wouldn't turn into anything," reflected Peck about the retaliatory mission. "Although I got my wings in 1948, I had missed Korea, so I'd never been at war; we'd been through a lot of crises, some that seemed much more important than that little Tonkin Gulf crisis."

Peck, obviously, was quite mistaken, for there was nothing little about the magnitude of events taking shape in Southeast Asia. The political and military structure of South Vietnam was rapidly deteriorating, thanks to pressure from Communist guerrilla activity in the south and high-level government corruption. Support from the administration of President Lyndon B. Johnson, by way of military advisors and covert operations, was doing little to stem the Communist tide or to shore up the South Vietnamese government.

By early January 1965, following two significant military defeats at the hands of North Vietnamese guerrilla forces, the Army of the Republic of South Vietnam was near collapse; U.S. options were either to leave the country or increase its military activity. President Johnson, the man who had defeated arch-conservative Barry Goldwater in the 1964 presidential race by promising to keep American boys out of Vietnam, chose to escalate. Plans were authorized for a "limited war" that included a bombing campaign in North Vietnam.

The first major air strike over North Vietnam took place in reaction to Viet Cong mortaring of an American advisor's compound at Pleiku in South Vietnam on 7 February 1965. Eight Americans died in the attack, more than one hundred were wounded, and ten aircraft were destroyed.

Johnson immediately convened his national security advisors, bellowing he'd "had enough of this." Within hours, FLAMING DART I was under way. The carrier *Ranger* launched a thirty-four-plane strike against the Vit Thu Lu staging area, fifteen miles inland and five miles north of the DMZ. Poor weather prevented carrying out that attack, and the *Ranger* aircraft were not allowed to join the forty-nine planes from the carriers USS *Coral Sea* and USS *Hancock,* which struck the North Vietnamese army barracks and port facilities at Dong Hoi.

"At this stage of the war," said Rear Adm. H. L. Miller, then commander of Task Force 77 (CTF-77), under whose immediate direction the strike fell, "attack groups were assigned a specific target, as in this case for the *Ranger.* If that target was closed at the time of attack, there was no recourse but to drop the ordance in the water."

Judged at best an inadequate reprisal, the strike accounted for sixteen destroyed buildings. The cost? One dead A-4E Skyhawk pilot from the *Coral Sea,* Lt. Edward A. Dickson of VA-155, and eight damaged aircraft. Dickson's demise was indeed ironic, or possibly just symbolic of the deadly business of naval aviation. One year earlier, Dickson had narrowly evaded death after ejecting from an A-4 during a training exercise over the Sierra Nevada range in California. His parachute failed to open, but Dickson landed in a thirty-foot snowdrift and survived.

FLAMING DART II unfolded 11 February one day after the Viet Cong blew up a U.S. enlisted men's billet at Qui Nhon, killing twenty-three men and wounding twenty-one others. Nearly one hundred aircraft from the carriers *Ranger, Hancock* and *Coral Sea* bombed and strafed enemy barracks at Chanh Hoa. Damage assessments revealed twenty-three of the seventy-six buildings in the camp were damaged or destroyed. American losses were three planes and one pilot, Lt. Cmdr. Robert H. Shumaker of VF-154, who became the second Navy airman to become a prisoner of war. Shumaker would reveal to POW compatriots that he shot himself down, a victim of his own rocket's frag pattern.

The statistical tally board—a prominent feature of the soon-to-be expanding Johnson air war—saw 267 FLAMING DART I and II sorties or individual strikes damage or destroy 69 buildings from a total of 491.

Defense Secretary Robert McNamara summarized the Washington, D.C.–orchestrated raids as satisfactory because our "primary objective, of course, was to communicate our political resolve." However, he stressed future "communications of resolve . . . will carry a hollow ring unless we accomplish more military damage than we have to date." McNamara's future "communications" started one month later with the advent of the ROLLING THUNDER campaign.

For the pilots taking part in the early Vietnam excursions, the war, the first combat endeavors for virtually all but a few of the senior operational pilots, was long awaited. At least Paul Peck felt that way.

Everybody was very enthusiastic. The pace was exciting; something most of us had been training to do for years and now we were doing it. I think everyone was pitching in and working real hard, and I really didn't have much time to stand around and hold pep talks, nor did I need to.

Our concentration was focused on the target we intended to strike, the ordnance load, and the tactics to be utilized. And the rules of engagement, which became very onerous as the war progressed, weren't that bad in the early stages.

I took command of the squadron in December of 1964, while the *Ranger* was under repair in Yokosuka, Japan. When the repairs were through, we immediately headed for the Gulf of Tonkin. The *Coral Sea* and *Hancock* had been stroking, double stroking while we were in the shipyard. We were at sea seventy consecutive days, and during that stint the initial raids of the war took place, which the air wing took part in. We pretty much kept a high tempo of operations for the remainder of the cruise, which ended in about June.

The squadron started out with twelve pilots and thirteen airplanes, really at a low point in that regard. I only received two more pilots and finally ended up with fourteen airplanes and fourteen pilots. We ran 100 percent availability for forty-five days on the line at one point, and had no trouble with the A-4C Skyhawk. Our planes were still relatively new and all in damn good shape. We flew everything they would let us fly, and two or three missions a day were not unheard of. I totaled sixty, seventy combat missions in that period.

Our first strike was memorable. We had been milling around in the gulf for about a month, planning strikes at different targets in North Vietnam. When the call came, the target was Vit Thu Lu, a small training or staging base for the resupply of troops into the south and the foothills. We'd never heard of it.

The weather at launch was not good; I'd say the ceiling was probably two thousand feet, maybe a little more. Later in the war, the wing would not have gone, but that day we charged out and, of course, as soon as we got to the foothills the overcast was right down to the ground, and we couldn't make it. I was leading, and devastated, like, My God, we've *got* to make it in. Boy, we tried everything and just couldn't do it.

Coming back, I saw the *Coral Sea* air wing striking a barracks by Vinh. I called in and said, "We're unable to reach our target and plan to divert and hit the barracks Air Wing 15 is already hitting."

The reply was "Negative, your signal is jettison your bombs." I thought you've got to be kidding me, there's a target down there, and I've got more bombs than I've ever dropped in my entire life. But that's what we did.

Despite the outcome, the first combat mission was quite special. I had been flying for close to twenty years, and training for just this type [of] event; we'd briefed and planned it as thoroughly as you can in twenty-or-so hours.

The weather kept us low; I don't think I've ever been that low with that many airplanes. The ceiling was no more than one hundred feet when I finally decided we can't do it, and pulled up through the clouds. In retrospect, all of that was dumb. But that's what happens when you run a war from 4,000 or 5,000 miles away—you lose grasp of what's going on.

All of our targets during the cruise were in North Vietnam, we didn't hit anything in the South. I can't even remember going down South.

We didn't lose anybody in the squadron, although the air group lost some folks. We took several good hits, yet nobody went down. Charlie Baldock, who ended up a prisoner of war on the next cruise, took a hit in the tailpipe about twice the size of my fist. He flew that darn thing down to Da Nang and landed, then took off and flew to the carrier. I could have killed him for that, but he made it.

Overall, we were meeting little opposition relative to what the squadron met the next cruise, and my cruise as air wing commander. A lot of AAA and automatic weapons and that kind of thing, but the missiles had not yet been introduced. There was essentially no fighter opposition aircraft at all, so we didn't have any problem with that. The first time I went over the Hanoi area, I never even drew a shot. There is no question we could have done anything we wanted to in those first four-to-six months.

After the initial raids in 1965, several weeks went by before ROLLING THUNDER started with two or three missions a week, and the pace gradually increased in tempo.

The flying primarily consisted of four-plane division and two-plane section activity, mostly smaller efforts for interdiction. It was not well prosecuted because we didn't go where it would hurt [the North Vietnamese], and did go to places where it wasn't going to hurt them at all.

We learned as we went along, and in retrospect, the things we did and got away with I would never have stood for later on. Tactics like low and slow, or even low and fast.

All in all, the first cruise was the honeymoon phase. I think morale was very high, and we were pleased with our accomplishments, and there were some. We had taken every target and done pretty well with them. But I also think there was a feeling of concern expressed by the whole air wing—"You know, somebody doesn't understand how to fight a war, at least from the aerial viewpoint." We put together an air group plan on how we thought the air war ought to be prosecuted, sent it off, and that was the last I ever heard of it. In essence, the message said we need to be more aggressive, go after more crucial targets, rather than nibble away at the outer edges of the problem.

Coming home was very interesting. We and VA-93 both flew in to Lemoore Naval Air Station, the first combat squadrons to get back. I don't think I'll ever forget crossing the foothills and seeing the familiar brown of the San Joaquin Valley. It looked so different from the lush tropics we had been flying over, but yet, of course, so very familiar. That return home, as all my returns to Lemoore, was nothing but pleasant. There were no anti-war indications whatsoever, everybody was red-hot for the war and treated us like the conquering heros. Quite frankly, I didn't feel that we had more than a fair chance of going out to do any more combat. Of course, I was wildly wrong on that one.

The squadron was slated for a nine-month turnaround, but ended up heading back out to Vietnam in three-and-a-half months. About four or five weeks after getting home, the word came we'd be cross-decked to the USS *Enterprise* based in Norfolk. So, the squadron was back out again in October, and on-the-line that first week in December.

Chapter 5
Shootdown

Commander Harry Jenkins heard the 37-millimeter gun fire, saw the tracers rising from the countryside below, and quickly pulled back on the stick of his A-4 Skyhawk. He sought the safety of cloud cover overhead, safety that would never come. A well respected seventeen-year veteran of the perils of naval aviation, Jenkins was in the midst of the last seconds of his final combat mission.

One hundred and one naval aviators became combat statistics in 1965, the majority falling victim to small arms, antiaircraft guns and surface-to-air missiles fired from the jungles, rice paddies, villages, and cities of North Vietnam. Forty of these well trained, highly motivated pilots were rescued by friendly forces. The remainder were less fortunate. Most were mourned by their families, who forever remember them as gallant warriors taken long before their time. The others began a torturing nightmare, exchanging carrier staterooms for less hospitable quarters at the Hanoi Hilton and its like.

Jenkins fell into the latter category. He was the victim of a solitary antiaircraft gun site while flying his 133d combat mission in Southeast Asia. The date was 13 November 1965, some six months after Jenkins had led his squadron, the Saints of Attack Squadron 163 (VA-163), into combat as an integral component of Air Wing 16 aboard the carrier USS *Oriskany*.

Jenkins was the lone American pilot shot down in North Vietnam that day. He would not see his wife Marjorie and their three children until a cloudy, San Diego afternoon some eight years later. A 1945 high school graduate, the slender, tallish Jenkins—readily identifiable by his prominent nose and protruding ears—had marveled at the wonders of naval aviation while growing up in the Washington, D.C., area. He earned his wings in 1948 and reached the pinnacle of operational success, command of a carrier-based squadron, on 30 December 1964. Less than a year later, gunfire and fatigue had taken their toll.

Most aviators are very gung ho, aggressive people, and even if they know they're tired, they're reluctant to say so because of that desire to get out and do some more. But when you're worn out, there's very little realization of just how tired you are.

I can remember one instance when the squadron, ready to leave the line, had one final mission to bomb oil tanks in an area by Vinh. We expected the target to be fairly difficult, and my executive officer [XO], Wynn Foster, led the raid. I manned the spare, and got on the flight because another plane went down, one of the rare times when Wynn and I flew together because our policy was not to have the XO and CO fly in the same strike. After the flight, I couldn't get out of the airplane— I was just beat. I sat there a few minutes, and the crewman climbed up to see if I was okay. I was, just very tired. But at that moment, it dawned on me I'd been pumping all my energy up to the moment of leaving the line, and then it was all gone.

On the day I was shot down, if that had been one of my earlier missions, there is no way that gunner would have gotten me. I'd just seen so much flak, and had been hit several times. I was just tired, I guess, and not thinking.

The *Oriskany* and my squadron left San Diego in April, arriving at Dixie Station in early May. I was just proud as hell. Up to that time, I'd spent about twenty years getting ready and training to fight. That's the sole purpose of the military, to fight. If you don't face that prospect, there's no sense in having a military. So I was ready, anxious to get over there, and really do something, and I think my whole squadron felt the same way. And I did have a good squadron.

We got over there and started right in. Our planes ran better than any on the ship, and we were taking flights that the other A-4 squadron couldn't make. The air wing started in at Dixie Station, flying nothing but daylight operations. Certain flights were at night, but that was just to keep our hands in them. There were no operations inside of South Vietnam at night.

Initially, there was some discouragement about our missions. Very few targets could be seen, a lot of the time was spent dropping bombs in the jungle in support of the forward air controllers [FAC]. We'd get back to the ship to glowing kill and damage reports, and the kill quota was really big for McNamara: How many VC [Viet Cong] did we kill today? I imagine a lot of those figures were inflated guesses because nobody really went in to add them up.

We did have some good times during the month down South, plus there were no losses except for an airplane casualty. One of my pilots flew through the frag pattern of his bombs, and that's something, I think, which comes slow in any war. Peacetime practice is with dummy bombs, and you get in the habit of pressing a dive at your recovery point, and maybe even lower, to get a good hit. The problem with dummy bombs is you forget about the frag pattern, until it becomes real.

On another occasion, I was working a river and the FAC called up and said there's a boat, a big canoe, with three Viet Cong in it. Don't ask me how he knew they were VC, but he called us down and said the boat is stuck on a sandbar and the three VC have run into the woods. I put some bombs along the treeline on the river bank, and the FAC asked if we could break up the boat. I made a strafing run, really laying it in with an explosive-type bullet. Chunks were flying all over the place, and somehow it dawned on me that I was awfully low. I recovered—pushing through this wall of muddy water my ordnance had thrown up—and this wall of mud kind of sobered me to the fact that if the boat had blown up, if there had been something in it, and I really hit it, I'd have been in deep trouble. You learn slowly in war about things like that.

Wynn, my XO, had combat experience in Korea and was constantly giving the squadron pilots advice. One of the points he drove home over and over again—never duel with a flak site. When we went up north, one of our targets was the Ha Tinh Army Barracks. We'd hit it once and hadn't been able to burn it, and the napalm was giving us trouble because it wouldn't ignite. So I planned a mission to go in and napalm the barracks, followed by hard bombs to ignite the remaining napalm.

The plan worked well, a good mission, and I was assessing the damage in the air and noticed there were a couple of flak sites sitting up on a hill, not doing anything. So I called my wingman and said let's make a strafing pass at those flak sites; we'll see if those guys have any hair on their balls. The wingman went in, laying it on one site, and all of a sudden a guy at another site opened up on me. I hadn't seen him, and a shell blew the canopy off, went in forward of the instrument panel, exploded, and blew out all my instruments. I limped back to the ship and had to tell the squadron Wynn was right—don't duel with a flak site. It was a hard lesson and expensive. The airplane was ruined; the shell hit right on the reinforced area of the canopy, which deflected the round forward of the instrument panel. I went down and laid a broom handle up the hole the crease had made, and had it [the shell] not deflected, it would have gone right through my headrest. I wasn't hurt, but the next day I was putting on my G-suit and noticed there was a hole in the pocket. I reached inside and found shrapnel had penetrated my G-suit, but hadn't reached the inner lining.

After a month down South, we moved North. At the time, the only carriers out there were the *Coral Sea* and ourselves, although that soon changed. The war up North was very controlled. Down South, you were assigned a FAC, and wherever he placed you, that's where you'd go. Up North, the routes were picked for us and the targets did not extend beyond the highway. We ran the roads looking for trucks and if there was nothing, dumped our ordnance on a place called Tiger Island. Gradually these controls were expanded to anything that looked like a military target, although it might not be on the road but in our package area. Slowly this was changed to hit anything of significance in the area. Still, we were initially limited to an area south of Thanh Hoa.

We went against the bridge at Thanh Hoa a number of times, including one occasion where I opened a girder with a Bullpup B missile. As a prisoner [later on], I crossed the bridge and that girder was still wide open, although I didn't bother to tell them who laid it open.

We flew day and night up North. The *Oriskany* would operate from midnight to noon, and the next carrier would take over at noon or vice versa. We developed what we thought was a fairly proficient night tactic involving a flare plane, carrying flares and some bombs, and an A-4 with just bombs. The flare plane would go low, drop the flares, and the other plane would hang back.

Normally we couldn't see each other as all lights would be off. But we had an air-to-air TACAN [tactical air navigation system] that by keying a mike gave us a distance on the other plane. Our strategy was to pre-brief points A, B, C; and the low plane would say I'm at a point B, turning, and that would give the wingman a perspective.

We didn't get a lot of business at night. My wingmen and I caught a truck one night, blew it up, and started a fire; and Bill Smith, a lieutenant commander in the squadron, stopped a whole string of trucks one night. In the main, we didn't see a whole lot at night, and not a thing in the daytime. Usually we wound up dropping a bridge or blowing up what looked like a military target. As the war progressed north, moving north of Thanh Hoa, we began to spot trucks and such on the road, initially I'm sure because they didn't expect us to be there.

As a prisoner, I found out how much truck traffic really moved at night, and the amount was unbelievable. On my way to Hanoi, we traveled only at night, sometimes in convoys of trucks moving crude service weapons from place to place. The trucks had a low light under the hood, and were guided by painted stripes or plastic strips on the road about every thirty feet. Every five miles or so there'd be a guy in what could be described as a phone booth. He'd say something, and sometimes the truck would stop, and you could hear airplanes up ahead, and then we'd move on. Sometimes the truck would stop, and we'd get out and hide in a ditch, maybe a quarter of a mile from an intersection. Up ahead the planes would be dropping flares, looking for targets, and there'd be nothing to hit because the pilots were looking in the wrong place. I also noticed it was difficult to hear a jet while on the road, and in many cases, that first indication was the cartridge which fired to release the flare. There'd be a flash, and about twenty seconds would pass until the flare reached workable brilliance. In that time, you'd get out of the truck and under the trees or in a ditch. Several nights we sat in a ditch as long as a half hour while a guy spit out flares, and only once was my truck attacked while heading to Hanoi. We started out before dark one night, and just at twilight, a pod of rockets went off from this jet nobody heard. The pilot, however, missed the mark.

Initially, there was no MiG activity and very little SAM activity, although we knew SAM sites were around based on [our] electronic indications. Everybody was anxious to get that first SAM site kill, and tactics were developed along that line. Our SAM hunts were carried out with two planes high and two low with the intent of trying to locate the site. SAMs came up, but the low planes never could locate the sites.

In the early days of the war, SAM kills probably came because pilots really weren't expecting them. Once you're looking for SAMs, they weren't hard to pick up, and once the missile is spotted, they can be avoided. SAMs are controlled to pick an intercept point, a collision point; and our tactic was to go in high when the SAM came up, dive for the ground; that tactic would place the collision point on the ground, and the SAM would drive itself into the ground. All the hard strikes had a division assigned for SAM suppression. If the SAMs didn't come up, the suppression people would be the last on target to unload.

At one suspected SAM site near Kep Airfield north of Haiphong, I took a recce [reconnaissance flight] in to verify prestrike photography, with a strike group in the air and another on the deck waiting. The plan was I'd fly across the site at six hundred knots, and if the site looked like the photograph, I'd call in the strike group. Well, I did, and the thing turned out to be the world's biggest flak site. Both groups hit it, and while nobody was lost, a couple of planes were really shot up. One guy, Charlie Stender, took a 57-millimeter shell through his intake. It knocked off the generator, went through the engine, and out the other side. The shell didn't explode because it [the plane] was so close to the muzzle, the round hadn't armed. Obviously he was low. Stender made it back to the ship, despite the plane burning, and got aboard on the first pass. The plane was so hot nobody could touch it, just like a stove.

On that strike I was carrying two 500-pound cluster bombs (CBUs) to lay across the site. To show how controlled the war was at this point, and it was before September because Jim Stockdale had not yet been shot down, I took a route to the target that took me nearly to the Chinese border by way of a railroad. I came south down the railroad tracks to the target and passed two trains sitting on the rails. I could have chewed both of them up with the CBUs, but you just didn't touch anything unless it had been cleared, and only the SAM site was cleared.

Another example of control occurred when this photo bird accidentally went within the Hanoi sanctuary area. From the message traffic, and the letters and explanations the pilot was writing and giving, you would have thought we lost a carrier. Really, a very serious incident.

Early on we had an advantage over the North Vietnamese of nearly reaching the target before they knew we were coming. For instance, when I crossed over that world's biggest flak site, the gunners were sitting on top of their weapons just shooting the breeze. Later on the defenses became more sophisticated, certainly by the time we started bombing in Hanoi. In fact, construction of the radar sites in the no-go zones that eventually would eat people up was readily visible.

The war in 1965 was very much a tonnage war. As a POW, I lived with an Air Force first lieutenant who'd been based down in Cam Ranh Bay and flew in the backseat of an F-4. He said on many missions there weren't enough bombs to load everybody up, so each aircraft took one bomb just to get the sortie. Now that's a sick war. Pilots were exposed to tremendous losses with very little gain and all because of the sortie competition—let's get more than the Air Force or Navy is getting. An example of the competition was the need for pictures. Air Force planes were built with cameras, but the Navy got away from cameras except for the A-1s. Suddenly, the Air Force is getting all the media coverage because their camera film is on TV so CINCPACFLT (Commander in Chief, Pacific Fleet) sent out a message that we were to send a plane on our missions equipped with a camera pod.

I said there is no way I'm going to send a plane over a combat target just to carry a pod for taking pictures. I refused to do it, saying the Navy has airplanes that take pictures; they're called photo recces. But as a compromise, a camera was devised that would fit on our wing, although we gave up the radar altimeter. For years we'd been arguing to get the altimeter because at night it was very critical sometimes, when landing in bad weather, but that's the mentality which drove the war.

Planning of the air wing strikes was handled by the attack squadron commanding and executive officers. We'd be up a lot of nights planning until three or four in the morning, and maybe at noon start flying. Or plan until 8:00 or 10:00 P.M., and start flying at midnight. It became very tiring, but you don't recognize the fact you're tired. That's the insidious thing. In looking back, my shootdown was just stupidity. We were going home in two weeks with just one hard strike left, and I guess I was just tired. In prison I talked to a number of POWs who said the same thing; they just weren't doing what should have been done and that's why they were there.

I carried a Bible with me on the ship, letting it fall open somewhere to read, and one night the passage said something about "and he shall fall into his enemies," and I wondered if that was a premonition. I also dreamed one night of being a prisoner, a dream I believe brought on by worry. I worried more about losing somebody than getting hit myself. I agonized over planning, of finding the best way to the target.

I'd been hit several times, had the canopy blown out, and hadn't been injured. You begin to think [the enemy] just haven't got it. It's sometimes easy in war to lose a sense of perspective. I can vividly think of a morning where my wingman and I were running the roads, that period of the day light enough to see the ground but still dark enough to see lights from the ground, and just about everybody was shooting at us. In the daytime it's impossible to see how much you're being shot at, but at that time of day, rifles all over the place were winking. I told my wingman, take the right side of the road and I'll take the left. As we pulled off, I came over a rise and this automatic weapon was really pumping it out, and he just kind of ticked me off. So I climbed up, rolled in, and laid a 500-pounder on him, one of the best bombing runs I ever made; there was just a big smoking hole where the gun had been. I felt so damn good, I thought, You smart ass, that'll teach you. It was a gross overuse of ammunition, but it sure felt good. I'll never forget that feeling.

On 13 November I had a brand new guy on my wing—Lt. (jg) Vance Schufeldt—and I believe it was his first trip, or one of his first trips, in North Vietnam. We went on a routine little milk run down to Dong Hoi, a quiet area where nothing much happened, because of reports the river southwest of Dong Hoi was navigable and passing traffic. The two of us went around the river; and there was no way boats were going down that river; it was full of rocks and rapids. On our return, we decided to crater a road junction in case traffic was going through there at night. Our thinking was to slow them down, and possibly come back at night and look for them. On the way to the junction, about ten miles from the coast, I passed a clump of trees where it looked like a lot of traffic had driven, very easily a truck park. Schufeldt orbited, and I went down very low, maybe ten or twelve feet off the ground, looking under the trees. Nothing was around, and I wasn't going particularly fast because it was a quiet area.

Pulling off and heading toward the coast, I heard a gun start firing. I looked back and could see these two streams of tracers from a 37-millimeter, a twin mount, almost dead astern from me. If this had been one of my first flights—and I've thought of this moment a thousand times—I would have turned hard left because the gunner tracking me would have overshot. But there was a little broken overcast at about four thousand feet, and my intent was to just pop up into the overcast, figuring he'd lay off. So I pulled up, but I wasn't going fast enough to really pull up hard; and with the easiest shot in the world, just a dead astern-on shot, he hit me. The first round, I think, must have been directly in what we call the hell hole area, just aft and under the seat where the control junctions, electrical busses, and all are. My controls were immediately disconnected, the stick wouldn't do a thing, just like a noodle, and all my electrical gear in the cockpit went off.

A second explosion followed, much more muffled, but I don't know whether it was an engine explosion or the plane getting hit a second time. By that time, I was climbing right side up and heading toward the water, some six to eight miles away. My thoughts were to keep the plane right side up until I got to the water, punch out, and search and rescue would pick me up. But the aircraft began to slide off on the wing, and although I picked her up with my rudders, which were still functioning, I couldn't hold it, and the plane started rolling very rapidly. I couldn't tell whether I was right side up or not, and then came the sensation of a drop, which meant the aircraft was going down; so I ejected. The seat fired, and in the next instant, I was hanging in the parachute. Pulling down the ejection curtain, I thought, this is going to be rough. But I cleared everything and wasn't hurt a bit.

I ejected somewhere below twenty-five hundred feet. My wingman circled, and below, the Vietnamese were all around howling and yelling. I was afraid of getting shot in the parachute, although as far as I could tell nobody was shooting at me. I landed on a little rise covered with some sort of brush about two to three feet deep, [with] one small tree, and no place to hide. I got out of my chute, tried to pick up the radio and headed up a hill. In those days, the radio came in two parts; the battery was separate in the seat and had to be hooked up. I was trying to get this battery out of my seat when I could see a head pop up just over the bush. I forgot the radio, ran up the hill, and slid under the brush. Why that I don't know, but it seemed like the thing to do.

I was lying on my back and could hear the Vietnamese coming closer and closer. One guy passed ten feet in front of me, carrying a sickle on a stick and slashing down through the brush, and another came right up to my feet poking with a stick. I had a gun, and the thought occurred to me I could kill him, but I felt that might not be the most prudent action to take, so I just put my hands up. At that instant, I don't know who was the most afraid because he jumped back as if he'd uncovered a snake and proceeded to howl something.

Just like that, two guys, militia of some sort, were on me. I'm sure they would have cut me to pieces had I killed the guy. We went and sat in a slit trench while the A-1s flew overhead looking for me. The North Vietnamese were running up and down, everybody had a rifle, and they were all shooting at the A-1s. This guard would turn around and see if I was looking, then squeeze off a round as an airplane went by. What's funny, three out of five shots were misfiring because of their poor ammunition. Before we moved toward this village, the North Vietnamese searched me, taking my watch and all that stuff. I wasn't mistreated, and they were fascinated by the Velcro fasteners, snapping and unsnapping them. I was left with my clothes—a lot of guys were stripped—and bound around the biceps and back, although my hands were free.

Along the way, every time the A-1s came by we'd hide in the bushes. At one point while moving along a rice paddy, an A-1 came down and there was nowhere to hide. We lay down, and I went down full length thinking maybe the pilot would see me. He had his lights on—it was about noon—and went right by. We got up when he passed and started down the road again, and the A-1 came back straight at us. I thought, Geez, I hope he's not going to shoot us; and then it dawned on me that standard operating procedure for the SAR people was not to expend any ordnance until the pilot had been located. The Spads started firing, and I figured if they were firing they saw me; but I couldn't even see where the rounds were landing it was so far away. All the guys were punching off their rockets as they left, and I figured they must have seen me on the ground. We then moved to a little village and sat there the rest of the day.

Nobody was particularly mean to me, really, just curious. The kids were a bit bothered, throwing rocks and smarting off as if to acknowledge their importance. Some guy came up with about two-thirds of a French-English dictionary. He was a policeman, *detective* is what he pointed to, and had pointy-talkie cards [to help him] ask me if I was hurt, hungry, or thirsty. That night we went to a body of water; rocks were unloaded from a boat kept submerged during the day, and we started what came to be about three nights of a circus. We went from village to village; there'd be speeches, and I was put on display. While traveling I was always blindfolded and lying down in the boat, but sometimes I'd recognize a building we'd passed several hours before so I knew we weren't moving very much.

About the third night we went to an old Catholic church; there was nothing in it except a bunch of wooden pews. Groups of different ages came in, and again there were a lot of speeches. At one point, a group of teenagers yelled something and the guard moved me. An old guy had climbed into the rafters with a big bamboo pole, about six inches thick, and was about to bash me in the head. The guard threw him out, but as we left he made another attempt to stab me with a long, pointed stick. The guard again turned him away, and that's the only real threatening event that happened all the way to Hanoi.

There wasn't any kindness, although on the first day I was sitting underneath a tree when an old lady squatted down and just stared. Unless you know Orientals, you can't appreciate the blankness of the Oriental stare. You have no idea what they're thinking, just an absolutely blank stare.

She stared at me for some time, then went off and came back and offered me some bananas and stuff. I think she was genuinely sorry, but that's the only evidence of kindness I saw the whole time.

I was concerned my wife Marge would be worried, but I also thought the war would be over in six months. Really, that belief got to be called the "new guy syndrome." As guy after guy came in, you'd ask him how the war was going—and I'm talking three years later now—and they said it would be over in six months.

For the first few days or so after my capture, I kept calculating a bunch of Marines would be coming for me, and I'd still be able to finish the cruise. A little bit later, I figured to still catch the ship in the Philippines and make it home; and pretty soon it was catch the ship in Hawaii, but still make it home. Finally, the realization came—Harry, you're not going home for a while.

Harry Tarleton Jenkins, Jr., arrived at Hanoi's Hoa Lo Prison in the early morning hours of 23 November. The Maryland native was taken to room 18, grimly nicknamed the "Meathook Room," for a quick interrogation, then transported by three guards to a cell. Still in his flight suit, Jenkins was made to sit on the floor. His ankles were manacled and locked together by a long steel bar topped by a heavy piece of lumber. His wrists were tied behind him, upper arms laced tightly together from elbows to shoulders. Jenkins, the fifty-fifth American POW and the first senior officer to be tortured upon arrival in Hanoi, was left alone to ponder his fate.

Chapter 6
Under the Flares

North Vietnam learned the lessons of modern aerial warfare rapidly. Over the relatively short span of thirty-six months, Ho Chi Minh and his supporters helped North Vietnam make the transition from a country with a technology-poor, ground-oriented military to one boasting one of the world's strongest and most sophisticated air defense networks. The motivation for the dramatic expansion program was quite simple. During the 1965–68 ROLLING THUNDER program, United States aircraft daily dropped an average of eight hundred tons of bombs, rockets, and missiles on the cities, people, and countrysides of North Vietnam.

Vietnamese Communists made their quantum firepower jump with the help of the Soviet Union and China to a lesser degree; the two powers provided surface-to-air missiles, anti-aircraft guns, small arms, and jet aircraft almost as fast as the dock workers at Haiphong, unencumbered by the threat of U.S. intervention, could unload the precious cargoes. They also sprang forth with an array of technical advisors and food products to support their Communist brethren. American intelligence officials reported the Soviets in 1964 allocated North Vietnam the equivalent of $25 million, primarily in military aid. The ante jumped to nearly $240 million in 1965 and a whopping $670 million the following year. By 1967 the number of Russian ships reaching North Vietnamese ports rose to 185, one ship every other day, up from 122 the previous year. China, with a lukewarm attitude towards its bordering neighbor, chipped in less— the equivalent of $35 million of military aid in 1965 and $50 million the following year, most of it in small arms and mortars. The Chinese also provided much needed foodstuffs, including 200,000 tons of rice in 1966 and 500,000 to 600,000 the following year.

As testimony to Soviet and Chinese largesse, North Vietnamese missile sites grew from a round zero in mid-1964 to estimates three years later of two hundred SAM sites nationwide and some thirty missile battalions in the Hanoi area alone. Each battalion contained up to six missile launchers plus accompanying radar, computers, and generators.

Surface-to-air missiles, however, were just one element for U.S. pilots to reckon with. By September 1967 the defense system included some eight thousand lethal AAA guns firing twenty-five thousand tons of ammunition each month at American planes, a complex radar system, and computerized control centers. An elaborate warning system was devised, the more sophisticated systems keyed by Soviet observation trawlers on duty near American carriers. These spy ships relayed how many aircraft were leaving the deck, their bomb loads and side numbers, and it wasn't overly difficult for the North Vietnamese to compute where and when the aircraft would arrive, and to prepare a proper welcome. The primitive alarm systems utilized observation towers, whistles, gongs, drums, and triangles to warn of impending attacks.

The North Vietnamese Air Force evolved from nothing more than trainer planes and transports to a fleet of approximately 110 to 115 MiG aircraft by March 1967, a figure excluding the large number of MiGs shot down by U.S. Navy and Air Force aviators throughout the same time period. The quality and ability of the North Vietnamese pilots was certainly questionable, but they did manage to bag forty-eight U.S. aircraft by 1 November 1968, compared to 111 MiGs downed by Americans in the same period. Like their counterparts on the ground manning SAM and AAA sites, many MiG pilots learned their new-found profession in a hurry. Some were trained in Russia, but were called back to Vietnam long before their training program was completed. Some had never before been in a car, much less a jet, prior to venturing skyward.

The MiG pilot held one ace card up his sleeve in the battle of the skies, the ability to count on "enemy" help to aid his cause. Over the early course of the war, the rules of engagement (ROE) kept the U.S. Air Force and Navy pilots from maintaining the upper hand. North Vietnamese aircraft had to be visually identified before American aviators could shoot at them, certainly a tough requirement for planes flying at the speed of sound. Also, North Vietnamese air fields during the early stages of the war could not be attacked if the MiGs below did not rise to challenge the strike group; several important bases, Phuc Yen for example, were not struck until late 1967.

Other rules of engagement pertinent to the air-to-ground and road recce pilots stated that only "military" trucks could be hit—leading to the hundred dollar question of what is a military truck as opposed to the civilian version—and such trucks had to be moving on highways and not parked in villages. This rule was amended to trucks within one hundred meters of the road and later three hundred meters, but trucks were still off-limits within village sanctuaries. The bottom line: President Johnson's interdiction campaign was not designed to bring the full brunt of American air power against the North Vietnamese. The large-scale use of air power would not rain down on North Vietnam until 1972.

"It [ROLLING THUNDER] does not seek to inflict maximum damage on the enemy," said Adm. U. S. Grant Sharp. "Instead, it is a precise application of military pressure for the specific purpose of halting aggression in South Vietnam."

Unfortunately, American aircrews died while fighting under these less than ideal conditions as the North Vietnamese became very efficient at employing their defense network. Between 1965 and 1968, the Navy's Seventh Fleet lost 382 planes over Southeast Asia, of which fifty-eight fell victim to SAMs and the rest to AAA and small arms fire.

What specifically awaited American aircrews over the beach? For starters, rifles and light automatic weapons. These were effective up to an altitude of only fifteen hundred feet; but they could be placed in and fired from any location, and were inexpensive.

Deadly AAA barrage included a range of weapons from .50-caliber heavy machine guns to guns with a 5-inch bore. The .50-caliber was particularly effective against low flying planes up to forty-five hundred feet, while the larger calibers—.85 and .100—had a ceiling over twenty thousand feet. AAA was also radar-guided for better accuracy and night-time use.

The SAMs (Soviet-supplied SA-2 Guideline missiles) consisted of a thirty-five-foot-high, two-stage, radar-guided rocket topped by a 350-pound explosive warhead. The missile, with a ceiling of sixty thousand feet, was fused to go off on contact; by proximity or altitude; or on command from below. SAMs were typically fired in pairs, and in most cases were lethal if they exploded within three hundred feet of an aircraft. The first SAM site was discovered in April, yet Navy pilots were forbidden from taking immediate defensive action. A second SAM site was uncovered about a month later and by mid-July, several more sites were photographed in the area of Hanoi and Haiphong. Defensive strikes were not approved for any of the sites, primarily because Washington leadership feared killing Soviet personnel involved in training the North Vietnamese crews.

Writing in the 8 April 1971 issue of the *New York Times,* former CTF-77 commander, Rear Adm. Edward C. Outlaw, proclaimed, "It was feasible to have destroyed this site [the April site] and all others still under construction which were ultimately completed. It was not until the North Vietnamese had shot down some numbers of our aircraft that our combined air forces were permitted to strike back at these now well-established, defensive sites. Since then, approximately 115 of our planes [Air Force and Navy] have been destroyed by surface-to-air missiles launched from pads which I believe could have been destroyed at a minimum risk before they became operational."

On the night of 11–12 August the first Navy planes fell victim to SAMs. Lieutenant Commander Francis D. Roberge and Lt. (jg) Donald H. Brown of VA-23, flying A-4Es from the deck of the carrier USS *Midway,* were struck by SAMs while on a road recce some sixty miles south of Hanoi. Brown's plane was lost and the other limped back to the ship.

Navy reaction was immediate, but ill-conceived and quite costly. On Black Friday—13 August 1965—seventy-six low-level "Iron Hand" missions were launched to seek out and destroy SAM sites. Five planes and two pilots were lost to enemy guns, and seven other planes damaged, but no SAMs were discovered.

One of the pilots killed in the futile SAM search was Cmdr. Harry Thomas, skipper of VA-153, an attack squadron flying off the carrier *Coral Sea.* His loss placed Cmdr. David Leue in charge of the "Blue Tails," so named for the splash of blue on the tails of their A-4C Skyhawks.

A product of the Great Depression, Leue "lived a few summers on the beach in tents but so did thousands of others. My Dad died when I was twelve, and for a time I went to live with my aunt and uncle in Illinois, who were on the other end of the economic spectrum. Eventually my family moved to Buffalo [New York], where my mother worked building P-39s while I was in high school."

In high school Leue joined the Navy's Flying Midshipmen program designed for prospective aviators. "I wasn't going to be able to go to college, but along came the Midshipmen program, like a gift from heaven," said Leue. "I was crazy about airplanes as a teenager and later, while flying the Corsair, I used to look out and say, I can't believe I'm doing this. It's the greatest thing that has ever happened to me."

Too young for World War II, Leue's first taste of combat came several years later in Korea; he took part in over one hundred missions. "I completed three cruises with VF-54 in Korea, two in [F4U] Corsairs and one in the F9F2. At that time, naval aviation was straight deck and paddles, but to the aviator it had a lot of the same elements of the Vietnam war."

An event occurred in Korea which caused me to think about and concentrate on the Far East long after the war. After [General of the Army Douglas] MacArthur went ashore at Inchon, we outflanked the North Koreans and our carrier, the [USS] *Boxer,* was sent home. But when the Chinese came over the hill, the squadron and Air Group 2 was immediately sent back to Korea aboard the [USS] *Valley Forge.* We went back into combat on the 23d of December 1952 as the Marines were fighting their way out of the Chosin Reservoir. On this first strike, our load was napalm, and we'd been briefed to expect many Chinese troops at this certain road crossing. We came to this intersection, this mass of humanity, and hit them with napalm. The division pulled up—and I'm flying wing on a gent named Charlie Melville—and cut down a road reportedly jammed 'with many troops.' We headed down the route and didn't see any troops on the road, and in fact never did.

I was behind Melville, and as a wingman, you shoot when he shoots. The Corsair carried six 50-millimeter guns and twenty-four hundred rounds of ammunition, and the two of us were right down in the rice paddies blasting away. In fact, I was going by telephone poles, looking up. On the second run, I noticed people were climbing these telephone poles and waving. These were people, not troops, and they were trying to escape from the Communists and get on our ships, and we were just killing them by the thousands. And this mass of humanity on the road just stood there—the stoic Asians didn't run—and we blew a hole right through them.

For the only time in my life, I pulled up, secured my guns, and orbited; and there was a big conflict in that act.

Between wars, I thought and thought about that day and those people, who feared the Communists so much they stood up and were annihilated by us. That's how much they wanted to get away from the Communists. Well, when I got back into it the second time, I knew this was the same fight; it was orchestrated by the same people, supplied by the same people, and to say the least, I was highly motivated.

Air Wing 15 deployed to Southeast Asia in November 1964 aboard the carrier *Coral Sea,* participating in FLAMING DART's two raids and the initial ROLLING THUNDER strikes. Leue joined VA-153 in May 1965 as executive officer, taking part in his first Vietnam combat hop on 17 May. Prior to Leue's arrival, Cmdr. Peter Mongilardi, then skipper of the Blue Tails, assumed duties as air wing commander, and Harry Thomas took over the squadron as skipper. Before the long cruise would end in December 1965, both Mongilardi and Thomas were dead. Leue spent a relatively few short months working with the duo, but the period was intense and memorable, as would be both the combat deployments he completed. The 1966 deployment came aboard the carrier *Constellation,* accompanied by attack squadrons VA-155 and VA-65, the first unit to actually fly a fully operational A-6 in combat.

Harry Thomas and I were the only guys in the air wing with Korean experience, plus he had night experience. Tremendous work was done at night in Korea, and I used to lie in the bunkroom at night and pray for those guys. By using flares they tore up trucks and stopped trains at night, and we killed what was left in the daytime. Frankly, I was petrified of night work when first introduced to it while flying A-4s in the Mediterranean. I mean I've never been that scared in my life, praying each night that I was going to live through it. But my experiences of life show many of my greatest fears, when overcome, become my great joys.

When I got to VA-153, Harry had already started the business of an A-4 squadron bombing trucks at night, and I took this thread he started and built the tactic up. We taught young, first-tour aviators to hit trucks at night underneath a flare, and these young guys were so blasé about the danger of it. They embraced the tactic, gutsed their way through, and became very good at it. We were the boss at night—like the guy with two guns on his hip, standing at the doorway, and nothing moves. And when we caught the enemy, we killed him.

Our efforts weren't a gigantic strike the JCS said to go hit—something that had been hit forty-four times before—because I knew that every night down Route 1 and Route 15 there would be masses of trucks. The North Vietnamese had a very good warning system, and you needed to be smart enough and have the discipline and training to catch them. Most A-4 squadrons had that ability but didn't realize it. We took a simple tactic and made it highly successful even though our A-4Cs were severely limited fuelwise.

We carried flares and bombs, all low-level, lay-down ordnance. You could not see a truck from ten thousand feet, or dive-bomb it; you had to get down underneath the flare and look at it. The rules were don't go low in the daytime; it sounded crazy to go low at night. But it was absolutely safer to go low at night than in the daytime, if you could overcome your fear of the hills and the dark.

Typically, I'd put my wingman at four thousand feet, lights out, and we'd always tank just before coasting in. I'd get on Route 1, [at] about five hundred feet, and rocket down the road with my wing down a little bit, and just like that I could see trucks. They'd throw a little lead, so I would jink, but the North Vietnamese were lousy shots at night.

To find a specific spot, the two of us would coast in using strictly visual navigation, judging flying time and distance from a specific point by DR [dead reckoning]. We stayed at an altitude to clear all terrain, like instrument flight rules [IFR] clearance. Once the flares were released, then underneath it was VFR [visual flight rules]. We'd operate at 100, 200 feet, dropping all lay-down ordnance—snakeyes, cluster bombs, gun pods—eating up a lot of trucks.

One night in 1966 I found what I believed to be a missile battery convoy. I coasted in and strafed the lead truck while my wingman hit the back one, got it burning, and trapped the convoy. We ate 'em up. There was exploding ordnance, fuel running down a hill and exploding, and the scene was visible for hundreds of miles. The two of us eventually ran out of ammo and called in the A-6s to finish it up. Most of the time the missions weren't that spectacular; normally two, three, four, up to ten trucks. But while I was out there, nothing moved—and all of the supplies and weapons were going down to kill my buddies, my brothers, in the South.

Our night tactics complemented the A-6, yet still did things they weren't capable of doing. The A-6s were better against hard targets, radar significant targets. We were better truck hunters because of our experience.

Another interesting mission came again on the second cruise in July of 1966 and involved [Cmdr. Edmund] Bud Ingley, the CO of VA-155. Ingley's squadron flew A-4Es and became very enthused about night missions, doing some good work. On this particular hop—a very black night—Bud and I were scheduled to operate in the same area. Normally we were kept apart by forty or fifty miles; rather than reschedule flight times, the two of us worked the problem out. We stayed on the same radio frequency and because the A-4E didn't have to refuel on a typical mission while the A-4C did, Bud and his wingman were going to be ahead of my wingman and me.

I was about to coast in when Ingley called up and said, "I've got some trucks on Route 116," which was between Routes 1 and 15. But he made a mistake and was actually over Thanh Hoa, a very heavily defended area. The idea of operating underneath the flares was to look for relatively undefended places. Ingley made a mistake, got over Thanh Hoa, and all at one instant, there were tracers zipping through the air, flak bursting, and stuff cartwheeling. Combined with clouds over the city, the whole scene was just like a surrealistic Salvador Dali painting, and I could hear Ingley over the radio, pulling Gs and yelling, "It was Thanh Hoa."

About that time, I'm coasting in on my target area and find two miles of trucks—and I measured it on a map—nose to tail with their lights on. When I taught people to find trucks, I'd tell them, don't expect to see a truck with its lights on like he's driving down the freeway; these guys aren't crazy. You've got to go where you think they are, get the flares out, and find them at low altitude. This night was the exception. I surmised later on, the driver's early warning system—firing a shotgun—must have broken down because of all of this noise over Thanh Hoa.

I dropped on them with a gun pod, and the gun pod wouldn't fire. One of the deficiencies of the A-4—a wonderful airplane—was the internal gun system. I had better guns in Korea flying the F9F2. But I did get some rounds off, started trucks burning, and my wingman Riley Harrell, although relatively inexperienced, jumped in there and had some good hits. Ingley and his wingman also arrived, and he got his gun pods going, and between the four aircraft it was IFR from all the smoke and burning trucks. Two miles of trucks we burned that night, and there was still a lot so we called in the next cycle.

Our squadron successfully attacked trucks in two cruises, and I'm convinced that's the most good we did. The strength of naval aviation is the tremendous leeway to develop individual tactics, and we had great flexibility. Plus, I never cancelled a night mission for weather in Vietnam, period; and I'm talking about thunderbumpers end to end. I've never been one to say who is right and who is wrong, but I found a formula to keep the North Vietnamese from delivering goods that were going to kill my buddies. I could do it with almost total freedom, I was the boss, I was super enthused with it, and it was a great frustration to me not to be able to translate this enthusiasm in general terms to other squadrons. Very few squadrons ever embraced the night tactics like I did from Harry Thomas; in fact, they thought Dave Leue and 153 were a bit crazy.

Coming back from cruise I was all pumped up on the night mission and ready to spread the gospel. Jude Larr, my neighbor, received the okay from his skipper, Gene Sizemore (who later became an admiral), for me to brief their squadron. I gave them the pitch, going through the tactics and trying to emphasize the mission was a simple but effective means to make the A-4 productive at night. I gave them the whole show, Sizemore thanked me, and I left. Years later Jude told me Sizemore got up and said, "What you heard here, forget it." And he walked out, wanting no part of it. Jim Morin, the commander of our sister squadron, would not touch it. Who's to say who's right? These guys were all successful in the United States Navy, they all went on to make admiral, and they felt it was a foolhardy mission. They really did, although we lost more dearly in the daytime than we did at night, and I feel I did more at night than during the daytime.

It also doesn't make a hill of beans, but no person in the squadron ever received any kind of reward or recognition for going well above and beyond at night. The A-6 types received accolades, they covered themselves with glory for what my guys did night after night in a dumb A-4. Night work was the A-6 mission, so we were doing something out of the ordinary. But the people that did it know they did it, and are proud of it. I'll say this, the junior officers, the JOs, never blinked. They were wholeheartedly for the mission, and watching the young fellas, I marveled they handled it so well.

Harry Thomas was killed on Friday, 13 August, a day after a SAM shot down an A-4. We all went on a mass, low-level strike, and the North Vietnamese shot down five CTF-77 airplanes. We were looking for SAMs at low level and exposing ourselves. It was a dumb tactic, a mistake, and was never done again.

The Navy did give us great tactical flexibility, and that incident is the only one I know in which we were directed in a certain tactic. Because of the missiles, our orders were [to] stay low, and both Harry and I knew going low in that environment was very, very dumb. Harry was worried, and at the time he had more combat experience than anybody I knew. Harry just flew into a volley of flak on the deck. We found out that, even at high speed, you just can't beat massed automatic weapons. It'll hurt you bad, a lesson Harry and I already knew.

I really got mad when Harry was killed because we had a piece of equipment that could find SAMs. I had been in VA-81, the fleet introduction squadron for a device called the APR-23 Redhead. They were in 153's airplanes, but nobody knew anything about them. So I said to Harry, "Do you realize we're getting SAMs and we have equipment

to find them?'' Harry said, ''I'm interested, let's go try and sell it.''
Well, nobody was interested, but I got with the maintenance people
and started to tweak them up. Then came this big strike and I said,
''Harry, we ought to tell them this is a bad way to do it. Let's try to
use our equipment and our heads rather than launch a lot of people,
and lose a lot of people.''

Well, my worst dreams came true. Then I really got mad, went over
people's heads, got the attention of the CARGRU [Carrier Group Com-
mander] staff, and we developed a tactic based on the material and
information available at the time.

Pete Mongilardi, CAG, was shot down on a day recce, rather ironic
because our squadron and the ship were supposed to have been going
home. We were in Japan for one last liberty and had already offloaded
all our ordnance and airplanes. In fact, Thomas, Mongilardi and I went
on liberty together, ran into the admiral, and found out we were going
back to Vietnam.

On the first day back, CAG flew on an armed recce. We briefed
together in case one of our wingmen went down, and as luck would
have it, my wingman couldn't transfer his drop tank. I sent him back
to the ship and joined up with Pete. Armed recce is usually two people
flying down a route, really target practice for the local AAA batteries
as you come down the pike. I always said if I made it to admiral, I
would not have done traditional armed recce. Too many people are
lost.

We were in the area of Thanh Hoa, and I was flying an airplane
with instrument problems. Normally on the deck, the pressure instruments
jump as everyone is catapulted. Mine stood dead still, but it was a
bluebird day and there was no way I was going down the first time
back. Plus, I'm with CAG. I launched and there was no air speed altimeter,
pressurization, any of that. It was no problem except that when we ran
into trouble I wasn't exactly sure how high we were. There were some
broken clouds, and maybe three or four thousand feet below, I saw
this little power plant. We carried 1,000-pound bombs and I said, ''I'm
breaking off and rolling in on it.'' Mongilardi replied, ''No, it's against
the rules of engagement.'' At that time you couldn't hit a power plant.
Our exchange pulled me away from Mongilardi and his wingman Paul
Reyes, and as I turned to rejoin them, Mongilardi said, ''I'm rolling in
on a little bridge.'' A call came up, ''Flak,'' and I heard him get hit.
He actually keyed the mike, I heard a couple of deep breaths, and I

called Reyes to ask "Where are you?" Paul said "We're by this rain storm and I've lost CAG. I don't know where he is." Well, he'd been shot and killed; a real tough loss.

Mongilardi was a superior air wing commander, naval officer, and warrior, as was Harry Thomas. But to survive, you couldn't let death get to you. There was great respect [for them], but the next day you got up and went; that's all there was to it. You could not let emotion break through.

People don't realize there's a steady rate of attrition with naval aviators. I had three combat cruises in Korea, five total in my naval career, and I'd been on a peacetime cruise in the Mediterranean where some twelve aviators died.

My philosophy was, if I've got to go, I'm ready to go today. I put everything else out of my mind and tried to concentrate on what I was doing to the best of my ability and exclude everything else.

The way we fought the war was not militarily sound. We were super proud of being able to kill trucks at night, but in one single day I could have done more than I did in two cruises, and maybe more than the whole fleet [did] in a year. One simple answer: say this is a war zone—Russia, Poland, Czechoslovakia, China, or whatever ships are in Haiphong harbor. If you sail in here, we'll sink you. With impunity and a Bullpup missile, which I was an expert in, I could have sunk more trucks with one simple flip of the wrist and with no danger to myself. There wouldn't have been thousands of sorties, killing guys against the side of a hill—with red balls of fire going by. We were a naval force supposedly able to control the seas; but politically our leaders said anyone could sail into Haiphong and offload, and we couldn't touch them. But then, when the trucks were up in the hills at night, when the North Vietnamese guns were ready—now it's fair [to attack]. In the history of the world, nobody will understand that.

The real tragedy of Vietnam isn't that I fought and lost buddies. I was a professional; as I've said to my wife, and I'm embarrassed [to be saying this], I *enjoyed* Vietnam as a professional aviator. The real tragedy is the South Vietnamese who were uprooted. I always said there would be a bloodbath [in South Vietnam] unless we won. Well, it's been a holocaust [since we left].

There is a great sadness that people I knew very well died over there. I dearly loved Homer Smith; he was captured alive; and I'm sure tortured to death. He was the skipper of VA-212—the first Walleye bomb squadron—and went back in 1967 to get his two hundredth mission (he'd already been relieved of command) and was shot down. But see, that was his spirit—Let me at 'em. I understood that completely.

Homer was a Naval Academy graduate, and the guy was so hard-nosed I said to myself, I hope he's never captured. He was and never returned. To me, it's wrong that he suffered and died. Every guy that came back compromised himself; he had to or he would have been dead. I don't take anything away from them; becoming a POW was my greatest fear, and I just have the greatest respect for those individuals. But I have more respect for Homer Smith and guys like him, the JOs who died. They shouldn't be forgotten.

Chapter 7
CAG

Survival in the skies over Vietnam required a mixture of aviation skill, the capacity to follow established combat tactics, the support of good leadership, and sheer luck.

Leadership was extremely important, particularly at the air wing level. Each carrier acted as an independent war-making machine, and the combat tactics employed by one air wing on-line in the Gulf of Tonkin might be far removed from another carrier's air wing on-line at the same time. As in any profession, not all air wings were equal in the task of air combat—putting bombs on target, and survival—and the differences more often than not could be traced to leadership.

Air wing command was usually placed in the hands of an individual who'd completed a tour as squadron commander of an attack or fighter unit. The CAG was typically a better than average pilot with a solid record of performance, and more than likely he was a pretty fair politician. By another definition, he'd survived in a profession unforgiving of error.

Supported by the staff of the ship's captain (and the admiral's, if the admiral was embarked aboard the carrier), CAG directed the tactics of his air wing. Targets may have been preselected, but the approach to the day-to-day grind of combat fell squarely in CAG's lap.

The position was dangerous in the wartime environment of Vietnam. As lead in many of the major strikes, the CAG was an ideal target for the North Vietnamese guns, and many an air wing commander, along with senior squadron personnel in leadership roles, didn't return home. A "Catch-22" of sorts also existed, if one believes survival in combat is enhanced by experience. Very few of the early CAGs had combat experience—the war just wasn't old enough—and later the squadron commanders with experience weren't allowed to return to Vietnam.

"I felt like I was an expert in keeping guys alive in combat," remarked Cmdr. Dave Leue, who completed 235 combat missions with VA-153 in 1965–66. "I had a Ph.D. in how to get into tough places without getting killed, without getting equipment hurt, and that's why I wanted to go back to Vietnam as an air wing commander."

Leue did not receive a Vietnam command, but instead went to an East Coast carrier destined for deployment in the Mediterranean. The problem was simple: he'd compiled too much combat time. Under the rules sent down from on high, the experienced and proficient did not return to practice their trade until much later in the war when bodies were at a premium.

Wes McDonald brought limited combat experience to Carrier Air Wing 15 in July 1965. He'd led VA-56 in the Gulf of Tonkin retaliatory raid, joining Cmdr. James Stockdale and his squadron in destroying oil tanks at Vinh. Stockdale, CAG of Air Wing 16, was already serving in the gulf when McDonald arrived. But by September, Stockdale's new address was the Hanoi Hilton.

It was another CAG shootdown, that of Pete Mongilardi, that brought McDonald to the unanticipated command of Air Wing 15. "I was scheduled to get CAG-5, but that wasn't going to take place until about August or September," remembers McDonald. "Pete Mongilardi was then killed in the first part of June, and I was the CAG who was in workup, so they immediately changed my orders and sent me out in relief."

I got over there and the morale was really low. The *Coral Sea* air wing had gone over in November of 1964 and started coming back in June; then [the carrier] got the word to steam south, "You're going to be on the line for an indefinite period of time."

Pete Mongilardi, the CAG, had been bagged the first day back, which didn't go down well. Here comes the new CAG out. They didn't know who the hell I was, or how well I would do in combat. It was a testing period.

The skipper of the ship—[Capt.] George Cassell—was very understanding. He called me to the bridge and said he was glad to see me there. He wanted me to get out and lead. And, oh by the way, he said, "I know there is some drinking going on on this boat, and I'm not going to be walking around the ship at night trying to find and catch guys who've been flying combat hops and find whether they're drinking or not. But I want you around; I don't want to see anybody drinking on this ship, and I don't want anybody drunk on this ship. You understand that, CAG?" "Yes sir, I do," was my reply.

The drinking was never really condoned, nor ever officially recognized, but the skipper's welcome to Yankee Station was we know there are things being done that we don't generally do in peacetime, and it better not get out of hand or it's going to be your ass.

At that time in the gulf, there generally was a day and [a] night carrier. We worked twelve hour splits, usually about 6:00 to 6:00. The day carrier handled the road recces and the alpha strikes as the case might be. If a couple of alphas were scheduled and enough planning took place, we would slide off the twenty-four-hour routine. For example, I was on the strike in which Jim Stockdale, CAG-16, was shot down. My group had the first strike, but went to our alternative because the weather closed us out. On the way back to the ship I called Jim—and told him he ought to go to the alternates because we couldn't get to the target. Jim did, and that's when he got shot down.

We didn't run air wing strikes simultaneously, maybe about ten minutes apart. One wing would go in and hit the target and about the time the North Vietnamese were beginning to dust themselves off, the second group would hit them. The last guys would get the BDA [bomb damage assessment photos] and that was always an interesting hop, particularly in 1966 when we were using the RA-5C. The F-4s were trying to fly escort for the RA-5C, and this hummer would go burner, faster than the speed of heat, and they couldn't stay with the plane. The consensus as to who flew the BDA was "Hey, not me boss, I went the other day."

The workdays for the plane captains, ordnance people, and the guys maintaining the airplanes was at least eighteen hours. For the pilots the hours were a good fourteen to sixteen considering the time before launch and the time to shut down afterwards. But every pilot didn't work that long, and there was a limit of two hops per day at the max, although every once in a while down South you might get three. But we tried not to extend guys.

As CAG, I always wanted to lead the alpha strikes. If we weren't launching alphas, I'd just take my turn in the barrel. Basically, I needed a little time to plan, and if there wasn't anything big going, my ops officer and I would alternate.

Nighttime recce was pretty much left to the guys to do their thing. They knew to work Route Package 1 or 3, or an assigned area. Targets were fair game at nighttime, but you couldn't go into a town. Night work was awfully hard, looking for truck headlights, dropping flares, and bombing off the light from the flares, which in itself was a dangerous thing. Guys were good at the night work, and they tried awfully hard; but the results were sometimes less than what we would have liked. Yet we made it tough for the North Vietnamese; they couldn't just run the roads at nighttime without having to at least put up with harassment and some damage. Nighttime was more individual effort than anything else and there were guys who really liked it. To be candid, I didn't fly that many night recce missions because nighttime was planning time. CAG, fortunately, was involved in all the planning.

At the planning sessions, the ship's weapons officer and strike planner were always there with the assigned targets. After working out the targeting parameters, types of weapons to be used, probability of damage, and so forth, those two would always brief the captain of the ship. If the CARGRU was on board, his planner would also be there and the admiral [would] later [be] briefed.

I'd say the wing used the capabilities of the airplanes as well as we could. I don't think we were constrained in that sense, except we weren't target rich; let's put it that way. If we needed to get bombs on target, we'd have the F-4s go air-to-mud, as dumb as that was, although the F-4 guys got pretty damn good at it. Later with the A-6s, we really began to get some things started with the laser-guided weapons, exploiting that capability as a bridge buster.

I flew three to four months on the 1965 deployment aboard *Coral Sea* and two months, May and June of 1966, on the *Constellation*. CAG was basically a twelve month tour, and combat exposure played into the equation.

The second cruise—which started down in South Vietnam—we may have had competition sorties, but I don't remember competition sorties up North. It was pretty well recognized [that] targets were there in the North; you had to get them, and you tried to effectively attack them. Seriously, I can remember down South if *Coral Sea* were running against Connie, and Connie flew 125 sorties one day, then *Coral Sea* was trying to fly 130 the next day. The South had the easy targets, the easy missions to load and turn around and go and do. I don't remember that competition up North, I really don't. When I came back as CARGRU in 1972, we definitely were not playing those games.

Working South was a picnic and up North a pain in the ass. But what really used to kill us were the absolutely stupid bombing halts the president ordered in trying to negotiate some kind of settlement. We knew damn well that after a bombing halt, the North Vietnamese would be back twice as strong as they were before, redefending all the God damn targets of importance.

In 1965 two other CAGs and myself, all out there at the same time, got together and decided one way to end the war in 1965 was to cut the rail lines coming out of China from the west and the north, to mine the harbor at Haiphong, to cut as many bridges as we could, and then keep flying until we had attrited all the missiles the North Vietnamese had in-country.

We brought the plan back and discussed it with COMNAVAIRPAC [Commander, Naval Air Forces Pacific] and tried to take it to Washington. It never sold [then] although it sold seven years later. In 1972 we finally mined the harbor, and by that time the government really got serious, bringing in B-52s and bombing the rail lines. We did in fact cut all lines of supply, and the North Vietnamese fired all their missiles with no way of getting more.

Certainly the perceived threat from China existed in 1965. We were definitely constrained from flying anywhere close to the damn border, and, of course, there was a concern over any kind of bombing or hitting Third World ships—that was a very touchy situation in Washington. I can better understand it now, but I didn't appreciate it at the time.

I really thought there was too much micro-managing of targets. We had a list of targets, and even on the list of approved targets we couldn't go against some of them. Hell, Washington wouldn't approve them. We'd submit a target list to CINCPACFLT [Commander in Chief, Pacific Fleet] of what we wanted to strike, and we'd get back an approved list that many times didn't reflect what we felt were the better targets, and in some cases targets were listed that we knew damn well had no value. But that was the God damn target and we had to get it.

There were other things, really trying to a lot of guys hanging it out. You couldn't drop bombs in North Vietnam anywhere except on approved targets, and in the early stages of the war, a pilot had to bring back his bombs and drop them on Tiger Island. The restraints early in the war occurred because the Johnson administration was really trying to settle the war; I'm convinced that's the reason. But to a guy out there fighting, the situation was just ludicrous.

In the early stages while bombing up in Laos, we were hitting little dirt trails and bridges. Christ, if you bombed off the trail or were off target by a significant miss distance, and if that fact ever got reported to the ambassador to Laos, my guys were afraid they were going to get a green table [court martial] although we tried to assuage them. There were a lot of concerns about what we were doing from both the younger and older guys, and I think the people who ran the war have to take the heat. I, for one, was running the war, but was, I thought, at the operator end, pissing and moaning like the rest. We were trying to fix the problem, the younger guys were trying to carry it out, and they honestly did a damn good job. There were a few who went away feeling like the war was all screwed up, that it wasn't worth fighting for. I, and others like me, felt there were reasons for fighting, but felt the war was being run stupidly by the politicians. I think we dumped most of the blame on the politicians.

An incident took place after the 1965 cruise, when I was in Washington, D.C.; a rear admiral, an aviator (who'll remain unnamed) called me over.

"We got a letter from one of your lieutenants about what was happening with the war. It can't be like that."

"Yes, it is kind of like that."

"Well, the lieutenant said this, that, and the next thing, and dammit, that's not the way it is."

"Yeah, that's kind of the way they see it, admiral. You can't blame the guy for criticizing because he's frustrated as I'm sure you are. But he's there, and he's the guy on the sticking end of the frustration. You're just back here in Washington, and you really don't know what the kids are going through."

The JOs, despite all the problems, did a good job. I had a wingman. I guess it was the last day on the line, and the target was a truck park. This young jg was scared, scared that he was going to buy it on that last hop. The kid was about the color of my briefing paper, which was white that morning. The consensus that day from the young guys was forget it. "Hey CAG, we're going home tomorrow; we're leaving the station tomorrow." My reply was "Hey gang, we can't forget it, we're going to go out and get that truck park." As it turned out, there was rain, low visibility over the target area, and we got partway there and the weather plane said scrub it, go to your alternates. There was almost a cheer over the radio.

Adrenaline ran awfully heavy every combat hop, so much so that carrier landings really became a piece of cake. They became easy—the landing was no longer the focus of the flight you'd been on.

On a training flight, you were banged off the front end with a rubber band and from that point on, able to do damn near anything as long as the airplane stayed in the air. In that situation, landing aboard the carrier became the test of your skills. Everything built toward getting back aboard.

During the war, going off the front end with the bombs still was a little dicey and did get the adrenaline running a bit. But then, you were pumping, trying to remember everything about the target while going in—the location of the defenses, threats to be aware of, what the target looked like, how to deliver the ordnance, and what the skipper said. Finally, the weapons were dropped, you zig-zagged away from the target, hoping not to get hit, got over the beach, breathed a big sigh of relief. Coming back aboard the boat became a big ''I could care less.''

Sometimes we got a little overtired. Guys came back terribly fatigued, and sometimes guys did dumb things because they were getting a little bit comfortable in the war. Individuals violated the cardinal rule: don't ever make two runs on the same God damn bridge. Get in, get out, and don't give them a second shot. A lot of guys got hit on the second run because the enemy had enough time to focus on them, track them around. Maybe that was from mental tiredness, maybe not.

In 1965–66 SAM evasion tactics were still being devised. Originally, we stayed low, below the SAM horizon or control area. By [us] staying below two thousand feet, the North Vietnamese couldn't get the radar guidance working. But that also put a pilot right down into the standpoint of all the small arms; people throwing rocks in the air, duck shit, or something the plane could ingest and go down from. We were down low when Harry Thomas got bagged on Black Friday. Obviously, that wasn't a very good tactic.

Next came the business of going in at medium altitude and breaking down whenever there was anything coming up. A warning airplane would give a quadrant, say the northeast quadrant, and everybody flying in the northeast quadrant would break for the ground.

We then found out that [flying] at 3,000 to 5,000 feet kept you away from the guys shooting with rifles, but put you into the automatic weapons fire phase. [But] by going fast enough, there was a chance of beating them, and if you knew where the SAM sites were (and we generally had relatively good information), you could then pop up to 8,000–10,000 feet and roll back in on the target. Of course, [by] popping up and slowing down—and the A-4 slowed down as soon as you pulled up with a load of bombs—the plane just hung there.

Tactics after I left were to run in high, get the speed up, and hit the target. By that time, the airplanes all had ECM equipment, the locations of the threats were known, and generally, the pilots were a lot smarter. When I returned as CARGRU, we ran in high, pushed over into a steep dive, dropped our ordnance, and got the hell out as fast as possible, jinking and climbing at a relatively high mach. Basically, that's the way I remember the war finishing out.

In late 1965 a basic electronic device called the Shoehorn was placed in the airplanes, which sensed when a certain band [of] radar was emanating. The Navy technicians did a marvelous job in getting that equipment out to Cubi Point [Philippines] and retrofitting the airplanes. Admittedly it was very rudimentary compared to the equipment that's in the airplanes today, but anything in those days would have been a help for the guys.

Chapter 8
Firsts

Summer of 1965 brought two new arrivals to the rapidly escalating Southeast Asian conflict: the first East Coast aircraft carrier and the initial deployment of the Grumman A-6 Intruder.

Although the war in Vietnam was a Pacific Fleet "engagement," there weren't enough pilots, planes, ordnance, and carriers in the Pacific Fleet to meet the requirements of President Lyndon B. Johnson, Secretary of Defense Robert McNamara, and other members of the Washington brain trust. The USS *Independence* was the first Atlantic Fleet carrier deployed to Vietnam, returning by year's end to a hero's welcome in Norfolk, Virginia. Five other Atlantic Fleet carriers—the *Franklin D. Roosevelt, America, Forrestal, Saratoga,* and *Shangri-La*—completed a total of seven WestPac deployments, while the nuclear-powered USS *Enterprise* became a permanent contribution from the Atlantic to the Pacific Fleet, leaving its Norfolk home in October 1965 for residency on the West Coast. A final carrier, the USS *Intrepid,* was shifted from an antisubmarine to an attack role, making three Vietnam deployments in 1966–68.

By design the twin-engine Grumman A-6A Intruder provided the Navy with the world's first truly all-weather, day or night tactical attack aircraft—capable of carrying nine tons of ordnance and operated by a pilot and bombardier-navigator sitting side by side. Yet all was not well with this multi-million dollar airplane.

"The A-6 had some interesting missions," remembered then lieutenant Donald D. [D. D.] Smith, who arrived on the *Independence* in late summer 1965, assigned to VA-72, an A-4E squadron that in October would earn the distinction of being the first Navy squadron to knock out an enemy SAM site. "I envied them and the idea of taking a lone plane in at night, properly equipped, doing deep interdiction work, and then coming out. That had a lot of appeal.

"But the A-6 back then wasn't equipped for the mission, and was really very lucky to pull something off. CINCPAC read their mission and sent the A-6s in, but they couldn't do the job. The mission was there, and supposedly the capability was there, but the squadron really had problems. Their gear wouldn't work; it wasn't reliable."

Because of equipment failure, the A-6 Intruder in many respects proved to be nothing more than a double-breasted A-4 until it was deployed for the third time with VA-65 off the *Constellation* in 1966. By then, experience and constant maintenance had made it an effective airplane.

Summer of 1965 also witnessed several other notable events. Nguyen Cao Ky became president of South Vietnam; Lyndon B. Johnson increased draft calls to allow a personnel build-up that would increase the U.S. forces from 75,000 to 125,000; and the North Vietnamese formed their largest road repair organization to date, the "Youth Shock Brigade Against the Americans for National Salvation."

To thwart the American bombing campaign and keep supplies flowing to the South, immense numbers of North Vietnamese citizens were organized to spend all or part of their time repairing roads, bridges, and railroads. By 1967, reports indicated 97,000 North Vietnamese worked day and night at this endeavor while another 370,000 to 500,000 were said to be working on it several days a month.

Youth Brigade members were males and females between the ages of fifteen and thirty, with the females obviously dominating the workforce because most males were already in the army. The tasks were repair work and new road construction, the recruits receiving five dong ($1.50) per month plus clothes, sandals, cigarettes, soap, and room and board.

Because bridges were a primary target in 1965, the Youth Brigade and other groups like it, aided by North Korean advisors, devised more than a half-dozen ways to move trucks across a river after the bridge had been destroyed. Alternatives ranged from finding a simple ford to making temporary bridges of thick bundles of bamboo or of flat-bottomed, wooden canal-boats tied together. Another way was to build a structure underwater. Under ideal conditions, sunken spans could be placed in the water so that a truck could drive across them, but a recce plane would not spot them.

North Vietnam claimed in 1965 to have built or repaired twenty-six thousand miles of roads bombed by U.S. pilots, a figure equaling at least one-fifth of all the North Vietnamese roads.

The task of bombing the thousands of miles of roads and numerous bridges in North Vietnam went to pilots like D. D. Smith. A Minnesota native and father of three, Smith was a gifted stick and throttle talent. He completed two test pilot tours, including one as the Navy's top test pilot, and he served two combat cruises with VA-72, totaling 138 missions off the carriers *Independence* and *Roosevelt*. (The *Independence* would

arrive home in December of 1965 while the *FDR*'s deployment in the
Gulf of Tonkin extended through the latter half of 1966.)

Smith was quite content to become part of the combat action. "I had
come from the Postgraduate School at Monterey, and this was to be
my second fleet tour, so I was a fairly senior lieutenant. I very much
wanted to go out to the war and was really disappointed when I received
orders to the East Coast RAG [Replacement Air Group] at Cecil Field
[Florida]. But I had a lot of time in the A-4, and because of this I think I
got orders to VA-72 which had just arrived on the line in Vietnam."

Bang, I was out there, spending three or four days, eight hours a day,
going over squadron procedures with the standardization officer, an Air
Force captain on an exchange tour. The two of us just sat in his room
and discussed rules of engagement, standard operating procedure, and
on and on.

My first combat flights came in September on a couple of the easier
strikes. Over the beach for the first time, Vietnam looked like any other
piece of air I'd flown into, just peaceful down below and quiet. Except
pretty soon puffs and tracers started drifting up. I remember being very
confused as to why they were so mad at me, why people were shooting.
I hadn't done anything, and obviously I didn't feel carting a load of
bombs to drop on them constituted any problem.

There was light fire almost everywhere you went, and stumbling into
the wrong spot would draw heavy fire. Of course, we carefully picked
our way into the light areas, but you always ran into some shooting. I
don't think I flew a single hop where some fire didn't occur.

In both the North and South we flew road recces, and the alpha strikes
were up North. On some of the recces, the assignment might be [to]
proceed to coordinates in North Vietnam, set up an orbit, go to a frequency,
wait for a call. The event might be an Air Force rescue over the ridge,
and afterwards we'd go back out and expend on targets of opportunity.

Most of the northern road recces produced something pretty useful
to shoot at, and you'd get to know the routes real well. I considered
road graders a great target, as were little highway bridges, maybe some
one hundred feet long. It'd be wonderful to cut a bridge and come
back the next day, and the North Vietnamese would have graded the
dirt right over the cut. There'd be lots of tire tracks, so you'd open it
again, and the next day, [the] same story. Trucks parked in open revet-

ments—say an eight-foot revetment—just daring you to hit them, were a lot of fun too.

The stupid targets were in South Vietnam and Laos, and the latter involved nothing but making toothpicks [bombing trees]. In South Vietnam, I once strafed and bombed water buffalo, that was the target. We called them WBs so it wouldn't sound silly over the radio. These poor water buffalo would be out in the field and [would be] popped with anything available—20-millimeter, MK-82 bombs. Really a joke, embarrassing, and I certainly didn't think much of the mission. The logic was [that] the water buffalo belonged to Viet Cong villagers and provided a source of food. Personally, I can remember only one mission with WBs as the target, but it could have been more, and the mission was not unusual.

We really did a lot of night road recce, but never point [hard target] strikes as that mission went to the A-6. If the night was fairly light, with a lot of moon and easy to fly, then it was tough to see anything because the truck drivers could get along without lights. The better hunting was on nights just blacker than hell; you'd just about kill yourself to fly at all. There was no sense in turning on the A-4 radar; it was nothing and we'd go visual, total VFR, and boy, I tell you it was really hairy.

No matter how black the night, I could always tell where the beach was by that white ribbon of sand. I don't care how dark it was, the white ribbon was always visible. We knew the target areas, and the only game in town was dropping flares to illuminate an area. The leader carried six parachute flares and rockets, and the wingman all rockets. We'd look for headlights, and really not headlights but [what looked like] cat-eyes.

One particular dark evening, the sky was a typical Vietnam milk bowl with no definitive horizon. We had just crossed over the beach, and I saw this long caterpillar of green cat-eyes. Setting my wingman on a perch to roll in, I dropped to the flare altitude of thirty-five hundred feet and pickled off two flares. They burst and drifted down, and I switched to rockets, dropped the centerline tank off, brought the wings up, and pulled on up and around. Between the two of us, we carried 104 rockets, and my wingman fired a whole group, causing a bunch of explosions. I whipped around and came in low firing rockets; I could see the flares starting to trickle out, so I went back up and came around down the flare line, pickling bombs off—one every few one-potatoes [seconds]. I pulled up, started banking, and saw what I thought was a flare and rolled in again. Unfortunately, I'd rolled in on the moon and was going straight up.

I reached about fourteen thousand feet, and all of a sudden the A-4 started shaking. I managed to get the plane under control; but was now going straight down, approaching the flares, and trying to decide whether to pull out or eject; reaching for the ejection curtain, saying yes, no, yes, no. I stayed with it, heading down below the flares and right on across the trucks. Everybody in the world was shooting and really, it was just awful, the closest to death I've ever come.

Finally I staggered back into the air, saying to myself never again. So I came around—and the night was so black, with the next set of flares, I did exactly the same thing. I went up and rolled into the moon. My heart was right back in my mouth, and I came back down between two karst [irregular limestone] ridges. I should have either flown into the karst, been shot down, or hit the ground; but I never got touched, and the two of us came back to the ship with these wild stories about how many trucks we bagged. Somebody came out the next day, and I think the count was twelve trucks. We received a medal for it.

On another occasion, a flare was popped over a lone truck, and obviously as soon as the flare popped, the driver abandoned the truck. I dropped a daisy cutter on it, just one bomb that must have hit dead square center, and when the dust cleared, there was no sign the truck had been there. I'll never forget it. There was a flare right over the truck, a mushroom cloud, and then nothing.

Sometimes in marginal conditions at night, the first sortie fired off would check the weather. One night that task fell to my wingman and me. As the flight leader, I had the flares, and both of us carried rockets. I went up toward Haiphong, spotting the lights of the city, the tankers lit up in the harbor, and the lighters offloading oil.

The weather was bad, really an ugly night, and I called back to the ship and scrubbed the mission. In the meantime, my wingman and I are out there with a load of flares and rockets. I just told him to stand clear. Normally flares are pickled off at about 3,500 feet, light and float for 2,500 feet, and usually extinguish by about 1,000 feet. I lined up, picked up speed, and flew down a row of eight to ten ships offloading petroleum in the harbor—pickling off six magnesium flares around two thousand feet and wanting those hummers to be burning as they hit the ground. I never looked back, didn't see any explosions, nor did

I want any because it would have been too easy to figure out who dropped them. I just wanted to raise the blood pressure of a few people and have a little fun.

Night work was not for everyone, but there was only one guy in the squadron who used to regularly down his airplane at night. We could never get him out. He finally owned up to it, stepped off, and got back to the States. Somebody like that, they'd get him off the ship as soon as possible.

Most of our daytime alpha strikes came on the second cruise, when the war was really heating up. That first tour, we'd strike power plants, the Vinh barracks, ferry boats and ferry boat landings, but never up to Hanoi. The second cruise, we certainly did go into Hanoi and Haiphong, other big towns like Nam Dinh and air fields such as Kep. The targets up North like Haiphong, oh, those were the meanest guns of the war.

Our initial tactic for putting bombs on target, which of course later had to be abandoned, was a sixty-degree dive angle because the only worry was ground fire. A sixty-degree dive rolling in at sixteen thousand feet is straight down the chute, just hanging in the straps. Of course it's not an accurate run—it's hard to correct for winds and Vietnam is a fairly windy place—but we got pretty darn good at it. We'd come in at 16,000 to 22,000 feet, pull down to a roll-in at 16,000 and head in at sixty degrees on the target, pull out high and never, never get low.

For recces, if you really wanted to hit a damn little bridge out in the countryside, the roll-in was at thirty degrees pressed down to fifteen hundred feet even though we weren't supposed to be that low. Multiple runs weren't real smart, but even in North Vietnam if I had something cornered, I went low enough and made whatever runs necessary to make sure the target was hit. Now you'd vary directions or try to get the sun behind you, but it still wasn't smart to make over two runs.

That first cruise, despite the fact that one guy was killed and another shot down, there was no great pall over being in combat. We'd complain about the rules of engagement, about needing a law degree to fly and follow all the stupid rules. There was a constant reaffirmation of the rules, and a very serious concern [about them]. Rules of engagement were a constant briefing item, and changing all the time. The rules were confusing, illogical, and so forth, but most of the guys were professional enough to follow them.

One of the real frustrations was the decision not to allow attacking [of North Vietnamese] SAM sites unless hostile intent was proved, and that's no exaggeration! I flew over missile sites every day and watched their development until finally somebody got shot down, and then we'd go in. Now that was ridiculous. A similar feeling came with [not being allowed to] attack the MiG airfields. As long as the MiGs didn't rise to meet us, we overflew them.

We wanted to hit meaningful targets, and we could see there was a real opportunity to flood a great part of [North] Vietnam by bombing dams and dikes. And what made us real angry was not hitting Hanoi, and Haiphong with the Russian ships just sitting there.

I can also vividly remember reading the paper, and Defense Secretary McNamara saying there "is no bomb shortage, there are plenty of bombs." At the time, I literally had been catapulted off the front end with a single World War II 500-pounder on the centerline. In all honesty, that didn't happen very often, but we did drop a lot of the World War II inventory until it ran out.

Certainly, I feel strongly the Vietnam War could have been over in 1967, totally over, if the air war had been completely loosed from the start. Maybe earlier, but probably some time in mid-1967, if we had done whatever was necessary to flatten Hanoi and make the North Vietnamese say uncle.

Militarily, the SAMs put the hate in the game, not necessarily for what they specifically did, but for driving us into the flak. Initially, we were flying right over the flak. Mind you, it wasn't straight and level flying; we'd jink when the 85- and 100-millimeter guns were pounding and just fly above the small caliber fire. But the SAMs brought us down and changed the game.

I ended up with a lot of Iron Hand missions on alpha strikes and the smaller charlie strikes, which were just tougher than hell. On our strikes we had the flak suppression folks: people who accelerated out ahead of the strike group and suppressed the flak sites. The Iron Hands were missile suppression, and many times we opened the show, firing the first round of the battle. I did not like the Iron Hand mission—it was a tough, sweaty mission. The trouble was they'd get somebody who was not necessarily good at it, but had completed a couple of Iron Hand missions, and he became the Iron Hand expert.

I was in an Iron Hand mode for a long time, dropping the Shrike [anti-radiation] missile, and rockets. At times the mission became real sweaty because you knew the whole world was going to come apart as soon as the SAMs fired off. Around Hanoi or Haiphong, I mean everything would just turn into hell right away. The Iron Hand would accelerate ahead of the strike group, and at that point everything would be calm, not a round in the air, nothing. Yet the missile sensors showed the North Vietnamese radars were all on, and ready to fire. There were pre-briefed sites known to be active, plus others that would come up. You'd pick the hottest one, the biggest threat to the strike group, roll in, get the proper parameters, and fire one or two of the Shrikes off.

From an outsider's point of view, I'm sure the whole alpha strike scene was really unbelievable, indescribable, like a cheap comic book. There'd be the SAMs going up, and smoke pillars climbing all over the sky; Shrikes and rockets coming down, flak bursting all over, and streams of tracers threaded throughout; planes screaming down, all kinds of transmissions over the radio, warbles on the ECM gear picking up the SAMs, planes crossing, and all highlighted by thirty aircraft in and off the target in one minute.

The ability to perform your mission throughout this whole scene was the result of intensity, especially for the bombers. The strike went to hell if the bombs couldn't get to the target. So the flak suppression was left to the flak suppressors; missile suppression to those guys; and while you watched for SAMs, the job was to bore in and simply find that damn target. What unnerved me a bit was all the SAM warbles on the radio. For years afterward when I heard a high pitched warble, sweat would come to my palms. It really was a high intensity situation.

Physically [for me], the alpha strikes brought on a level of anticipation far different from a recce. Recces could be fun when there was the opportunity to really recce a road, shoot at trucks and such. [But] shooting at jungle, bamboo bridges, and footpaths—I did a few of those and it was terrible. A normal North Vietnam recce, I knew the route and what to look for. I'd check a revetment where I normally could find a truck, and if nobody was home, I'd go someplace else. There was plenty to do.

An alpha strike was different, and the level of apprehension varied. Overall, I'd say alpha strikes brought out a level of apprehension not characteristic of aviators. On only one occasion did I sweat a strike—I mean seriously sweat a strike—because at the brief the night before, the planners were very glum. The target was heavily defended, a no shitter, and the consensus was, "We're not real happy to be going in there." I don't recall if I was a bomber or Iron Hand, but I did sweat it out that night, dreading the next morning. As it turned out, the mission wasn't that bad. In fact, I never really had a strike which lived up to its billing, one the briefers said would be tough and actually was. I did, though, have a few where it didn't look too bad but turned out bad.

Certainly, no one could talk about how bad a strike would be or betray fear, especially the briefer. But what might be done is brief a little longer on safe areas and rescue procedures, or [on] what steps to take if hit, or refueling procedures if hit, or constantly emphasize the importance of flight integrity. This reemphasis was the only open manifestation of a tough flight.

A constant safety point was [to] head 120 degrees if the mission went to hell. I always said, When the gear goes in the well, my IQ drops by a third, and when I got shot at, by another third; and heading 120 degrees got you to water from just about anyplace in Vietnam.

As for death, any psychiatrist will tell you denial is a necessary trait for survival in the business, and I realized that fact more after I retired. When somebody close got bagged, a guy you knew well and respected, a cool head who played by the book and was really a good stick, that might get to you a bit. There weren't many ways to rationalize the guy's death because he was at least as good as you in the air, or approaching as good. With others, if there was some personality failure or other problems, or certainly if you knew he was doing something stupid, rationalizing and denying his death or shootdown was easy. And that's not just [in] war, that's [for] any military pilot yesterday or today. It's a requirement for the game.

The difference between going home, becoming a POW, and getting killed was primarily bad luck. There were a few guys with just death wishes, doing crazy things like trolling for SAMs. They'd go slow, high, straight and level, and watch their gears for SAMs. If a SAM lit up, they'd attack the God damn site with one airplane. That kind of stuff is a death wish, and I personally know of a couple of guys who did this. One, in fact, was very sober, religious, a real nice guy who never participated in the parties and always had a Bible in his hand. But he trolled for SAMs.

Besides my night flare fiasco, there were two other frightening incidents in North Vietnam. The first was a flak trap. The North Vietnamese baited us; they set up a rail site, put a bunch of box cars and such out, and filled the hillside with flak guns. Some recce guy saw [the cars], radioed back, and we mustered a special strike, a hurriedly planned endeavor involving about ten to twelve airplanes.

I carried rockets; and there were elements in before me, among them the F-4 Phantoms, shooting rockets and absolutely no good at that. As we rolled in, the whole God damn place went up. It was like I couldn't get my nose down because I'm fighting the streams of fire. Everybody was screaming get the hell out, and I just yawed my airplane so it was pointing roughly at the ground and squeezed off all my God damn rockets, which probably impacted a mile from the target.

Inexperience certainly got us involved in the trap; we didn't come within a mile of those box cars, and while nobody was lost, there were a lot of hits. If nothing else, the North Vietnamese succeeded in terrorizing *me*. I developed a respect for the industriousness of the North Vietnamese—I never really thought of them as a bunch of stupid slopes.

The second frightening incident—a three-hundred-foot SAM miss right over Hanoi—came on December 2, 1966, twenty-three days before my last combat flight. I was the Iron Hand carrying three Shrikes and a load of Zuni rockets. I had fired a Shrike or two and my wingman and I, flying at fifteen thousand feet, were looking for other targets, when I rolled over and for the first time saw this God damn SAM coming level. The SAM had a perfect lead angle, absolutely perfect, and was so close there wasn't time to do anything except tighten my turn into the missile. I thought the only thing that's going to save me is if the missile doesn't go off. The SAM went right by me, the perfect time to detonate, and boom it went off and the airplane just shook. The explosion was so violent I was sure the airplane was gone, and my wingman thought I was down also, saying the plane was obliterated in the explosion. But the SAM frag pattern is fan shaped, a very directional fan, and while the explosion may have looked optimum, [the SAM] must have cut right ahead of me. The explosion just wasn't quite right, but boy it sure looked like a winner to me.

The A-4E was a fine, fine airplane for combat, a great machine except for the guns. The 20-millimeter wasn't much good to start with and after the Shoehorn system was put in, its capacity was reduced from 150 rounds, which was bad, to seventy-five—which was ridiculous. I used the 20-millimeter to check out buildings, see if there was anything in the building explosive in nature. I'd roll in, squirt a few rounds with the gun, and see what happened. If there was some reaction, the plan was to come around and hit the structure with a bomb or rocket. That was about the only use for a 20-millimeter.

On board the ship, much of my time was spent in the ready room, briefing, watching movies, [doing] paperwork. I spent as little time in my room as possible. A lot of people worked a lot in [their rooms], but that's kind of alone, and I didn't care for it too much. I would go down to the ready room, pull up a seat, and do paperwork. I liked to see people. A problem of spending time in your room was that your roomie, on a different flight schedule, might be sleeping. The flight schedule officer would have to schedule eight hours sleep and he didn't care what time of day it was. You were to sleep from ten in the morning until three or four in the afternoon, with a six o'clock brief and an eight o'clock launch.

Independence was very new at the time, one of the best ships to be on. The FDR was a gut bucket, hot and muggy, [with] poor air conditioning and so forth. Generally, it's a pretty good way to fight a war to come back from a flight, put on your blues, and have a totally white-tablecloth dinner at the second sitting. First sitting, where we usually went, was called alligator chow, using Wardroom One. You could eat in your flight suit or whatever. We'd call it alligator chow because it pertains to the junior officers just showing up and doing what alligators do.

There was a lot of drinking, a lot of parties. While combat was going on, you'd have a quiet drink with somebody. My roommate and I had a policy. When I had a night flight, he would always have scotch and a little bit of ice sitting on the writing table when I came in at 2:00, 3:00 A.M., or whatever it was. Your heart would still be pumping from the landing if nothing else, you'd strip off and just sip that. I did the same for him, and we always did it without fail. A real nice, and important, consideration for each other.

Despite the war, there was still competition among the squadrons; say, landing excellence, for example. It's surprising: Why the hell worry about outstanding landings when your ass has been shot at, but the competition was still there and the landings and the inter-squadron competition went unabated. There wasn't a way to compete for excellence around the target because comparable results were rarely seen. Once in a while, recce photos would be available if it were the right type of target—a nice fenced-in power plant—and you were assigned two or three buildings off in the northeast corner. We would anxiously await those recce photos.

I'm not a flag-waving dogmatist as far as Vietnam is concerned, but the most noble wars are not fought for material or territorial gain. We had no designs on ever occupying Vietnam; it was simply the place we drew the line on Communism. We said, This is it, this is where it stops, and we're going to go in as the nation's police force. You can argue whether that was good or bad, but I don't think you can argue whether it was noble or not.

Chapter 9
Frustration

A Task Force 77 pilot hit by enemy fire over North Vietnam was driven by one all-encompassing desire—to get his damaged aircraft to the Gulf of Tonkin. The gulf meant water—and water meant safety and the real possibility of rescue by Navy search and rescue (SAR) teams. In the first two years of the war, a pilot bailing out over water had better than a 90 percent chance of rescue.

Aviators shot down over the North, especially in the area of the "Iron Triangle"—Haiphong, Hanoi, and Thanh Hoa—faced a very small chance of rescue: only one out of six pilots known to be alive and down in North Vietnam or nearby waters was rescued during the war. In most shootdowns, the pilot could at best expect a long stay at the Hanoi Hilton. At worst, death might come at the hands of angry and frenzied villagers, sometimes in a macabre fashion. Stories of decapitation and other brutality—dead pilots were spotted staked down on their parachutes—were not uncommon in remote areas of North Vietnam and "neutral" countries such as Laos.

The Navy's SAR effort relied on a combination of A-1 Spads and jet aircraft providing protective cover, helicopters to pick up the downed pilots, and sheer bravery on the part of helo drivers. Considered the dregs of naval aviation by the vaunted "jet jocks" prior to the war, the helo drivers, in the quest to pull their downed counterparts from the soil of North Vietnam or from the gulf, many times went above and beyond the call of duty. Lieutenant Clyde E. Lassen received the nation's highest combat award, the Medal of Honor, for the helicopter rescue of an F-4B aircrew in June 1968, while other helo drivers certainly performed acts equal to Lassen's.

The first in-country rescue from North Vietnam occurred 20 September 1965, when Lt. (jg) John R. Harris of VA-72 was recovered by a UH-1B helo some twenty miles east of Hanoi. By April 1966 two combat SAR stations, North and South, were formally established at Yankee Station.

Each included a guided missile destroyer with a TACAN and a combat SAR UH-2, and another destroyer to provide protection.

A typical alpha strike SAR scenario would find teams of rescue helicopters and armed escorts flying near the egress routes of the strike. If a pilot went down, his wingman or the strike leader would act as the on-scene coordinator and direct the rescue attempt. Aboard either the North or South SAR station, a destroyer squadron commander served as the SAR coordinator. This individual, with help from the on-scene commander, would decide whether or not to attempt the rescue, normally carried out if the pilot used the rescue radio or was visually sighted. Speed was a necessary consideration of any rescue, with the first thirty minutes after shootdown considered the most crucial. After that point, odds of rescue dropped considerably.

Commander Wynn Foster deployed twice to Vietnam aboard the *Oriskany* in 1965–66, cruises that provided the Iowa native firsthand experience of SAR efforts. Foster watched Medal of Honor winner Jim Stockdale shot down, assumed command of VA-163 after Harry Jenkins fell victim to an AAA battery, and was himself pulled from the gulf after an enemy shell blew off the canopy of his Skyhawk.

Foster joined Vietnam-bound Attack Squadron 163 (VA-163) in 1965 after completing a shore duty assignment at the Naval Air Technical Training Center in Memphis, Tennessee. "I left Memphis in 1964 just about the time Alvarez [Lt. (jg) Everett] was shot down," said Foster, arriving at Lemoore in September 1964. He went through the RAG and deployed the following May aboard the *Oriskany* with VA-163, as executive officer.

Leaving Memphis, I suspected I was going to get involved for no other reason than I always seemed to get orders to the fleet with the war going on, the crisis taking place. I was with AIRPAC [Air Force Pacific Fleet] in Korea; AIRLANT [Air Force Atlantic Fleet] for the Cuban missile crisis, the Bay of Pigs and the Lebanon crisis; and AIRPAC for Vietnam. For carrier purposes, my timing was perfect.

Very early on, the war was laughable, a lot of things were laughable. The lack of preparation, for example. We were going to war, yet throughout our entire training cycle, a lot of pressure came from AIRPAC to fill-in-the-boxes on the big chart, meet the shore-based training requirements.

It was even more laughable between 1965 and 1966. The wing came back and had five months—count 'em—five months from the day we set foot back in Lemoore until going out for the second time. Yet the requirements were still such that everybody had to fill in all the boxes for nuclear weapons training, and here we're going to the world's biggest conventional war.

Near the end of the 1965 cruise, I'd lost my CAG, my skipper, my operations officer. I was really down in the dumps for about two weeks and trying to act like a new, fresh caught, recently promoted CO. I sat down to read the message traffic, and there's a message exhorting the hell out of everybody for not having made their contributions to Navy Relief. To have gone through two combat missions that day and then read that sort of thing—it was hard to imagine people whose mental set was still that way. In many respects, it took the military a long time to catch up with the war. When I came back in August of 1966 to the hospital at Oakland, they weren't really geared up for combat casualties. Why? The administration was still thinking peacetime.

On that first deployment, I was the only guy in [VA-] 163 with combat experience. Yet I could only tell ready room sea stories, and we really went into the Vietnam War literally replaying our experiences of the Korean War. No one ever thought for a minute that we might use nukes on Vietnam. That never crossed my mind. As a matter of fact, the squadron put all that nuclear stuff in the back of the storeroom, as well as at the back of our minds, and really concentrated on conventional weapon proficiency while getting ready to deploy.

The weapons we took to war were basic. The bombing techniques were the old pilot-computed lead with the gun-sight. We had no radar; there was the ground clearance radar, but nothing to give us any help on moving targets, night work rendezvous or anything like that.

Plenty of dumb bombs were available, but no smart weapons except the new Bullpup—the big Bullpup B. Harry [Jenkins] and I, CAG [Jim Stockdale], and a young fellow named Art Avore, who was later killed, went out and shot the new Bullpup before deploying in 1965. The B was a lot more sophisticated than the old Bullpup, but we learned after getting out to Vietnam there was little extensive application for the bomb because the pilot had to stay on a long, steady, descending path to control it to the target. In an AAA environment, that wasn't exactly the thing you wanted to do.

As the first people out there in 1965, we had no one to tell us what to expect. The turnover procedures hadn't really been developed, the rules of engagement were literally incomplete, and we'd get ROE message changes every day. It was really quite chaotic. There were beaucoup international orange flight suits, which are great for spotting people on the ground and exactly what we didn't want. If anything stands out in that early period, it's how well we did for being [so] ill-prepared, and by ill-prepared I don't mean in the training, but in the knowledge of what kind of training we should have.

Oriskany started off at Dixie Station just like conducting training operations. Coinciding with our arrival was an explosion at some Air Force base. We happened to be on Dixie Station and inherited the lion's share of the tactical missions the Air Force would have flown. The squadron flew seven days a week, really logging the time. It looked good in the log book, but nobody was shooting at us. Up North was a shooting war, the South was not.

As a squadron we went out ready to win the war and came back quite a different crew of people, a lot more mature and maybe with a little bit of cynicism. Out went a bunch of Jack Armstrong, All-American Boys going to win this war. By December of 1965 all of us realized it was not a winnable war. It was obvious to us, and obvious to everybody flying over there, we couldn't hit the North Vietnamese where it hurt. We couldn't get the dams, dikes, or damage the rice economy. We couldn't hit villages for fear of hurting people, so before you know it, every village is a transshipment point. We couldn't bomb within a mile of any building with a Red Cross on it, a new rule of engagement, and inside a week the North Vietnamese had red crosses at the end of every bridge in North Vietnam. They weren't dumb; we weren't fighting a rag tag bunch of dingalings in black pajamas. The North Vietnamese were pretty smart.

Our political posturing was also ridiculous in regard to Laos, and that sort of thing. We were flying missions over Laos every day, but at the time the flights were top secret and couldn't be mentioned because Laos is neutral. The same syndrome was used when Nixon got around to [bombing] Cambodia.

Tactically, we telegraphed our punches at least twenty-four hours in advance. The day before an alpha strike, all our rescue assets were moved up North. Say we're hitting X bridge, scheduling the carriers to go after the bridge three days running. Now from the Gulf of Tonkin to North Vietnam, there aren't many unique or innovative ways to get to the target except going from here to there. The routes became stereotyped after a while, and it was frustrating, going after the same target three days running. Holy smoke, the North Vietnamese weren't dumb dogs—they knew our route to the target. We might as well have sent them a copy of the air plan and told them our time over the target.

Hard targets in the early days included bridges and SAM sites. SAM sites, in many cases, were non-existent. When we got to suspected sites, the North Vietnamese shot the beejeebers out of us, and all we found was earth-moving equipment. There might have been some sort of site preparation, but no SAM site. Intelligence was very poor, maybe a couple of blank photos of what was supposed to be a SAM site, and some 1950s French charts. We'd fly through uncharted areas, really very primitive.

The Navy was ill-prepared for night recce, and while the kind of mission we ended up fighting was carrying and dropping flares, the proper equipment for that mission wasn't available. MERs [multiple ejector bomb racks] which eject bombs real well were available, but they punched holes in the flares. So in 1965 the squadron ended up modifying the PMBRs [practice non-ejector multiple bomb racks], which for some reason we took with us.

Off Vietnam, the ordnanceman jury-rigged the PMBRs, and we illegally carried the flares. At the time, it was the only way to meet requirements, unless the CO of the ship said "I won't do it." Then he'd be relieved the next day, and somebody else would have had the job. I think back on the night recce, the two-plane recces we flew into North Vietnam, and shudder. If one guy, for whatever reason, had to part company with his aircraft, the only hope he had to go on for rescue was maybe his wingman knew approximately where he was. That was the best to hope for because nobody knew where you were, nobody was tracking you. There was also no intelligence available to us at night as to whether anybody, other than Navy aircraft, was flying. We didn't know whether there were any Air Force people flying that night, if they were going to be in the same area, and if so, what altitude. That information was nonexistent. Fortunately, the problems weren't there, but the only way to maintain a degree of safety on a black night was to physically say, This is my area, everybody else stay out of it.

Jim Stockdale went down in September of 1965, and I was flying with him. A major strike had been scheduled against the Thanh Hoa bridge, and the weather was so critical there was a question, Should we launch? Finally the word was yes, launch, and sometimes those decisions were made more to clear the deck to get ready for the next launch. Halfway through, the weather recce reported the weather in the target area was zero, and CAG [Stockdale] didn't have any recourse but to go ahead and finish the launch, sending everybody on their secondary missions. He and I went off and just orbited over the gulf, waiting as Harry Jenkins took his strike element to look for a SAM site at their secondary target. Had anything been found, Jim and I were going to join up. After fifteen minutes or so, that group came up empty. We were at our go, no-go point on fuel and headed to the secondary target up by Thanh Hoa. The target was railroad equipment of some kind.

Jim got hit by flak, ejected, and landed in a village. I saw the parachute go down, but didn't realize he was practically beaten to a pulp right there in the village. I made a pass, a low pass over the village, and I was furious, full of unbridled fury and ready to strafe the village—really the only time I came close to hitting the trigger on an unauthorized target. But I looked around and saw all the attention I was getting and decided it wouldn't do any good for me to get shot down too.

The loss of CAG shook the air wing emotionally; it just shattered us all. The man was dearly loved. I couldn't envision the war without a Jim Stockdale. I had nightmares, reliving Jim Stockdale getting shot down time, time, and time again. I carried a guilt complex all the way to 1973 until he came home. I wasn't sure, he might have thought I was somehow responsible for the shootdown and might have blamed me.

Harry [Jenkins] was shot down in November, two weeks before going home. I was in the ready room, briefing for a mission, and strike ops called down and said the missions for the people on the catapults had been changed. The duty officer routinely asked, "Why? What's the nature of the mission?" and the answer was, to fly cover for your boss, he's down. God, I came out of my chair like a bolt of lightning. I told the duty officer to find somebody else to fly my mission and went down to strike ops to listen on the SAR radio circuit. It was quite obvious he wasn't going to get picked up. We knew anybody shot down, there wasn't much chance, a very limited chance, he'd get out. That was proven time and again in Vietnam. We did get people out of North Vietnam, but not near the number we left there.

One of the real sad elements of that story came just two nights before Harry was shot down. The two of us sat in the ready room until the late hours discussing and planning the squadron change of command ceremony back in Lemoore. I remember Harry saying "We're all very tired, not only physically tired but emotionally tired as well.'' He also talked of losing only Art Avore, adding ''Let's hope our good luck holds out.''

Five days after losing Harry, we went out after the Hai Duong Bridge, which is halfway between Hanoi and Haiphong, and lost the squadron ops officer, [Roy] ''Hap'' Bowling. Eric Shade and Jesse Taylor, the wing ops officer, tried to recce the area in Spads and see if there was a possibility of getting Bowling out in a helicopter. They were both hit: Shade made it out and Taylor crashed.

We paid a heavy price, but nothing comes to mind exemplifying recklessness, or treating the war with a degree of casualness. We all understood what was going on, that we were getting shot at, and the chances were we might not come back. My psychological quirk—I was always nervous as hell, just combat stomach, all the way to the point where the catapult let me loose, and then everything calmed down. I was never puckery over the beach, mine was always the anticipation. I think the tension of the anticipation probably made more holes in guys' stomachs than anything else did.

Death couldn't help but get to you, but naval aviation is a pretty close club. We're not outsiders looking at the specter of death—crashing, burning, and so forth. We don't look at it that way because we're all in the same club. It could be me, it could be the next guy. Nobody expects it's going to happen, nobody broods when it happens. Yes, it's very emotional, a traumatic situation. But the next morning, you just shut it out and continue to do the job at hand. We'd prefer to remember people as they were, not brood over the fact they're not here anymore. You learn that way back and recognize the risks involved, and if you don't want to accept those risks, you're in the wrong business.

Chapter 10
Ensign Pulver

Lieutenant (jg) William Leonard Shankel found Christmas Day 1965 a bit different from the previous twenty-five he'd experienced. The Christmas tree, brightly wrapped packages, and delicious dinner were but a faded memory, replaced by a cramped, dirty cell at the Hoa Lo Prison in downtown Hanoi. Shankel, then a twenty-six-year-old aviator—nicknamed "Ensign Pulver" by his squadron mates—had been shot down 23 December while attacking a bridge between Hanoi and Haiphong. He had joined Attack Squadron 94 in the spring of 1963 and had completed one Vietnam tour—taking part in the initial FLAMING DART raids and the opening of ROLLING THUNDER, thus qualifying as a charter member of the "Tonkin Gulf Yacht Club"—and had just begun a second combat deployment.

On 2 December VA-94 and fellow A-4 squadrons VA-93, -36, and -76 arrived in the gulf embarked aboard the nuclear-powered aircraft carrier USS *Enterprise*. The largest warship built until the mid-1970s, the *Enterprise*'s Air Wing 9 (CAG-9) consisted of more than ninety aircraft. On 17 December the first nuclear vessel in combat launched her opening strike against targets in the North and by the end of one week of operations, the Navy's glamour boat set a McNamara-pleasing record of 165 combat sorties in one day. The previous high had been 131. On 22 December the *Enterprise* teamed with the carriers *Kitty Hawk* and *Ticonderoga* in one of the war's biggest strikes to date, with one hundred aircraft hitting the thermal power plant at Uong Bi located fifteen miles north-northeast of Haiphong, the first industrial target authorized by the Johnson administration. The *Enterprise*'s aircraft approached from the north and the *Kitty Hawk-Ticonderoga* force from the south, leaving the plant in shambles. The day's casualties were two A-4s from the *Enterprise*.

The following day—and twenty-four hours before President Johnson's thirty-seven-day bombing halt took effect—Bill Shankel exchanged his flight suit for pajamas and sandals.

About twenty planes were going after a bridge over the Red River, halfway between Hanoi and Haiphong, and I was in the second section. My A-4 was a real dog, and I had to cut corners to keep everybody else from running off and leaving me. I reached the target by myself, pulled up, and rolled in to dive-bomb the bridge. The plane was hit as soon as the bombs left, at the bottom of the dive, and my immediate thought was get out of there and get to water. But the stick went limp, just flopping around the cockpit, and I couldn't control the airplane or fly it, and finally the plane rolled over and aimed itself at the ground. When I went out, the plane was inverted and almost supersonic, and the ejection really thrashed my right knee.

I drifted over this village—all the people were shooting at me with damn bolt-action rifles—and landed in a harvested rice field right next to the village. I couldn't get up and even try to run away because the knee was trashed, and the gooks kept me in the village until dark, when a couple of guys in uniforms arrived, put me in a jeep, and took me to Hanoi.

Mentally there was a strong sense of, Why me? This isn't supposed to happen to me. Mostly I was scared, not knowing what the gooks were going to do, especially with an injury. I was concerned whether they'd take care of the knee.

I was tied up on the way to Hanoi and although nobody ever did escape, later you always think, Well, if I could have gotten loose, I could have wiped out those two little guys, taken the jeep and driven away.

We weren't far from Hanoi, but at some point the jeep stopped and I was placed blindfolded in what I could tell was a dusty, dirty little room. I was only there for a couple of minutes, then put in the back seat of a little sedan, about the size of a post-war Austin. The car was really tiny, and I could barely get situated. Of course I couldn't stretch my knee out, and my elbows were tied together, touching in back. Every time I tried to move, get in a more comfortable position, a guard would whack me on the shin with a pistol. I was miserable, but it beat getting smacked again.

We arrived at the Hanoi Hilton about 4:00 A.M.—really, really late—and I was taken to the part of the Hilton called New Guy Village for a quiz. I was asked my name, rank, service, and date of birth, followed by something like, Where are you from. I wouldn't tell them anything else, so these guys left and went down the hallway, where I could hear Ray Alcorn getting worked over.

Ray was in VA-36, shot down on the power plant raid near Haiphong the day before. I heard him say he was from the carrier *Boxer,* an idea which sounded pretty good. Back come these interrogators, and I still wouldn't tell them anything. Now, I'm sitting on this short little stool, with my bad leg out in front of me, and by this time the knee is about twice its normal size, all black and blue and really looking bad. My arms are also still tied behind my back.

One guy walked around in front of me, grabbed the bad leg, and turned it upside down. My heel was now on top, and I decided very quickly to make something up. "Yes, I'm from the *Boxer*"; but they're not buying it. Finally I told them I'm from the *Enterprise* and they turned my hands loose and brought in a guy in civilian clothes and one in uniform. These two start asking all kinds of questions.

"Where is the officer's pool on the *Enterprise?*"

I didn't know what the hell to tell them, so my story is the officer's pool is one deck below the hangar deck, and one deck below that is the enlisted pool.

"Where are the cattle kept on board ship?"

"The cattle are on the hangar deck, way back aft. If an airplane crashes, cattle are killed and the ship has a big barbecue."

There were more stupid questions before they left me alone, and I was able to get a few hours sleep on the floor. Next day I'm stuck in Heartbreak Hotel, and that's where I met [Cmdr. James] Stockdale. I got in there and heard the regular "shave and a haircut" tap on the wall and knew that could only be an American.

I answered but didn't know they were tapping in code. I tried Morse Code and all this other kind of stuff, and finally a voice from across the hall said get up on the bunk and remove the small transom over the door. I got up there—and it's hard because of the knee, plus my shoulder was also dislocated from the ejection—and looking right across from me is Stockdale. "Hi, I'm Jim Stockdale. Do you smoke?"

"Yeah, but I haven't taken any."

"Go ahead and take them. I just thought if you didn't smoke, you could give the cigarettes to me."

Christmas Eve, they took me over to some hospital, stuck a needle in my knee, X-rayed it, and placed it in a cast. Because my leg was swollen, the plaster from the cast stuck to the leg hairs and when the swelling went down, God that was miserable.

Bill Shankel was returned to "Heartbreak Hotel," a cell block at Hoa Lo, and spent Christmas Day and the following weeks in isolation from all but Col. Robinson Risner of the U.S. Air Force. President Johnson's bombing halt had brought the flow of prisoners to Hanoi to a sudden stop.

Part Three
1966

The war is a dirty business like all wars. We need to get hardheaded about it. This is the only kind of action that these tough Communists will respect.

Admiral U. S. Grant Sharp, in message to Gen. Earle G. Wheeler, Chairman, Joint Chiefs of Staff, December 1966.

Introduction

Peace in Southeast Asia was the primary topic of discussion in America as 1966 unfolded, yet one important party, the government of North Vietnam, was not inclined toward peace. Despite offers of more than ample U.S. restitution—including a one billion dollar Southeast Asian reconstruction package—Hanoi rejected American overtures while at the same time taking advantage of a thirty-seven-day bombing halt to bolster their defense network.

The halt had been conceived by Secretary of Defense Robert McNamara. "It is my belief that there should be a three or four week pause in the program of bombing the North before we greatly increase our troop deployments to Vietnam or intensify our strikes against the North," he stated in a November 1965 message to President Johnson. "The reasons for this belief are, first, that we must lay a foundation in the mind of the American public and in world opinion for such an enlarged phase of the war and, second, we should give North Vietnam a face-saving chance to stop the aggression."

But in a 1972 essay for the Naval Institute *Proceedings,* Rear Adm. Malcolm Cagle reported North Vietnamese "face-saving" attempts never occurred. Quite the contrary, photographic reconnaissance during the pause showed the enemy reconstructing and improving roads and bridges; improving and increasing the air defense of important areas; placing the country's petroleum-oil-lubricants (POL) system underground and into caves; dispersing the military support base; and pushing large numbers of trucks toward the DMZ and the infiltration routes feeding the Ho Chi Minh trail. The North Vietnamese, Cagle related, also used the slowdown to add some twenty early warning and fire control radars, numerous SAM sites, and four hundred AAA emplacements to a defense network that had generated an ample share of grief for the United States during the previous year.

In the eleven months of 1965 combat, North Vietnamese defenses had accounted for the destruction of eighty-eight naval aircraft: A total of thirty-six A-4s were downed by the enemy, one to a SAM and the remainder to AAA and small arms fire; nineteen A-1s were lost; and fifteen F-8s. Thirty-eight Marine and Navy pilots were killed in action, nine joined the missing-in-action list, and eighteen were either confirmed or possible POWs. Another forty pilots were rescued after falling victim to enemy fire.

On the other hand, Navy pilots and their Air Force counterparts compiled enough "facts and figures" to make the Johnson administration bean counters and the members of the Air Force and Navy brass with a fondness for tallying numbers jump for joy. End of the year bombing figures boasted the destruction or damage of 1,200 boats, 800 trucks, 850 railroad cars, 30 highway and 6 railroad bridges, 3 railroad yards (about 10 percent of North Vietnam's capacity), 1 lock out of 91, 6 small power plants, and 2 manufacturing facilities. The number of combat sorties gradually increased from 900 a week during July 1965 to 1,500 by December.

Studies conducted by the CIA and the DIA (Defense Intelligence Agency) estimated damage to North Vietnam in 1965 totaled the equivalent of $63 million, divided between $36 million in damage to economic targets and $27 million to military targets. At the time, the total gross national product of North Vietnam was "guesstimated" at $1.6 billion.

Despite the imposing statistics, the bottom line remained: the North Vietnamese, although paying dearly in terms of a disrupted economy and loss of life, had no desire to discuss peace. Few could also dispute that American air attacks during 1965 had been primarily concentrated on targets of questionable importance. This hesitancy by President Johnson and his advisors to hit significant tactical targets and important economic targets, such as the docks at Haiphong, allowed the North Vietnamese to continue building a superb defense system, a network that would take the lives of hundreds of aviators in the years to come. Likewise, the noteworthy North Vietnamese ability to keep supplies moving from north to south would account for the deaths of thousands of American servicemen throughout the remainder of the war.

When bombing began anew on 31 January 1966, American efforts intensified to the extent the weather allowed. In February about one hundred planes flew over North Vietnam every day and by March the daily average of flights was 50 percent higher. As the monsoon season ended, April sorties increased even further, and more significant targets were attacked. Areas in the northeast quadrant received special attention, including downtown Nam Dinh, the Uong Bi Power Plant, and the Hanoi-Haiphong highway area. The power plant was leveled by twenty-six 1,000-pound bombs dropped from just two A-6As, and the strike so terrorized the North Vietnamese they accused the U.S. of attacking with Air Force B-52s.

Service responsibilities for strikes on Route Packages set five months earlier were altered in April. The shift had two primary purposes, to give pilots more familiarity with their operating area and to reduce inter-service confusion. Originally, six geographical areas or "Route Packages" had been established in which the Navy and the Air Force alternated strikes each week. The revisions gave the Air Force responsibility for Route Packages 5 and 6A (which included Hanoi), covering areas close to bases in Thailand. Route Package 1 went to the MACV Command; and the Navy was given control of operations in the populated, militarily-vital coastal Route Packages 2, 3, 4, and 6B (which included Haiphong).

As the bombing activity increased, the casualties likewise climbed. Eleven aircraft were lost and ten crewmen were either lost or missing in March; a month later, the count totaled twenty-one aircraft lost and fifteen crewmembers either lost or missing.

May 1966 saw four CTF-77 carriers on the line: the *Ranger, Hancock* and *Enterprise* at Yankee Station and the *Intrepid* at Dixie Station. The *Intrepid,* the bastard child of attack carrier aviation, had relieved the *Hancock* in May, bringing thirty-two A-4 Skyhawks and twenty-four A-1s of Air Wing 10 into the war.

Chapter 11
The *Intrepid*

The *Intrepid* ("Fighting I"), by invitation, was going to war.

In 1965 Gen. William C. Westmoreland, commander of U.S. ground forces in South Vietnam, requested from the Navy an aircraft carrier to support combat operations in the South. What he received, much to the chagrin and dismay of crews who would man her for three deployments in Vietnam, was a World War II veteran vividly described by one aviator as "a fate worse than the misery" suffered by escaped prisoner of war Dieter Dengler (see Chapter 14). The *Intrepid,* previously utilized as an antisubmarine warfare support carrier, had few of the amenities needed for warm weather operations—air conditioning was non-existent. Also, her air wing took on "poor cousin" status when compared to the air wings of other carriers on station, because her role was limited to attack-only missions in South Vietnam.

The *Intrepid*'s shift from submarine warfare to attack aviation required several modifications; most notably she had to be supplied with new aircraft. Her S-2 Trackers, SH-3 helicopters, and E-1 Tracers were replaced by the attack planes of Air Wing 10. This hodgepodge air wing, initially directed by Cmdr. Thomas B. Hayward, a future admiral and CNO, included VA-95 and VA-15 (A-4B Skyhawk squadrons from NAS Lemoore and NAS Cecil Field) and VA-165 out of NAS Alameda and VA-176 of NAS Jacksonville, Florida (two A-1H Skyraider units). Three helicopters from Composite Squadron 2 (VC-2) based at NAS Lakehurst, New Jersey, rounded out the air wing. Fighter protection was considered unnecessary because of the limited mission.

The wing began joint training exercises in November 1965 while the *Intrepid* underwent modifications to handle her newly assigned responsibilities.

Lieutenant Commander Don "Linn" Felt, son of four-star Adm. Harry Felt, had hoped to attend test pilot school after completing a tour with

VA-34 at Cecil Field. Instead, he received orders to the *Intrepid* as strike-operations officer.

Felt moved his family from Jacksonville to Norfolk, then attended weaponeering school, which presented a curriculum that detailed both nuclear and conventional tactics. "After one week, which covered the entire conventional portion of the program, I received a call from the ship's operations officer," noted Felt. "He said, 'Forget the rest of the school, report aboard ship.' So I did. On a Saturday morning in January 1966, I came aboard the *Intrepid* docked in Norfolk."

I went down to the wardroom, found the command duty officer, and he had a stateroom assigned [for me]. I said, "Since I'm here, I'd like to see the strike center." He said, "The what?" and I knew there was a problem. They had a full complement of officers with ASW [antisubmarine warfare] experience on board, filling in with two exceptions, and I was the third. The commanding officer, Gus Macri, had carrier attack-fighter experience, and the other was the operations officer, Al Thompson, who had just come aboard. Everybody else was ASW oriented, and the ship was configured that way. I got started with virtually nothing but a notebook under my arm, and a desk in the air intelligence office.

The mission was to be the Dixie Station carrier, so all of our training and thinking was basically FAC, close-air-support type of work. None of the East Coast carrier group staffs were knowledgeable enough to know exactly how to work us up as an air wing. There were to be no alpha strikes as such, so we concentrated on division tactics, long-range strikes, individual bombing, and close-air support. Our sole concern was air to mud.

I acted as the assistant to the ops officer, and my first chore was just to develop the workup package. Just before we deployed, I finally got some work spaces, but had to go out and scrounge communication and put-up boards. I was allowed to design my own strike ops, although again there wasn't much to go on. East Coast carrier strike ops was totally oriented to nuclear war, and configured as such.

The ship deployed April 4, 1966, and myself, the CAG ops officer, and the CAG intelligence officer left early as an advance party. We went to Hawaii for a briefing by CINCPACFLT, [then] on to Subic Bay for briefings, and finally went aboard the *Ranger* and visited with the ship, [where I] received my first immediate observations of how operations were run. The *Ranger* was on Dixie Station at the time, so I not only got to observe, I also was able to fly a few missions with them.

In the meantime, *Intrepid* went through the Mediterranean, Suez Canal, Indian Ocean, and on to the Philippines. Upon arrival at Subic Bay, the decision was made at some level to take all the first rate Mark 80 series bombs off and put on board all the World War II bombs, which really pissed off AIRLANT when he heard about it, because he'd gone to great pains to load us up with the best of bombs. We ended up with fat bombs, and that caused a great deal of consternation with the flight crews and particularly the ordnance handlers, who had to do this double duty of unloading the bombs on board and loading new ones. Frankly we discovered the fat bombs were really effective in the South, particularly with the A-1s cranking off the ship carrying four 2,000-pounders.

Replenishment with the AEs [ammunition ships] because of our large ordnance expenditure rate—and because the old fat bombs were so cumbersome—was slow and difficult throughout the cruise. We didn't have much mechanized equipment like forklifts, and many of the bombs would come over unpalletized, particularly the fat 2,000-pound bombs. The only way to get the bombs to the elevators, or off the aircraft elevators and back to storage, was to roll them down the flight and hangar decks. We were sitting on a time bomb and didn't know it until the accidents [fires] on the *Oriskany* and *Forrestal* occurred. This situation was true on all carriers. Ordnance was hauled off the AEs and built up on the hangar deck rather than taken to the spaces. Wherever a shortcut could be taken to expedite the process, it was done—until a review of the accidents.

Because of our tailored air wing—really a novelty that hasn't been seen since—the guys ashore, the FACs and troops, were happy to get this kind of support. There was really nothing to judge our performance against. Everybody was happy, getting good flight time, doing what they were trained to do, and the results weren't bad. We kind of generated our own sortie race, telling people what we could do. On a typical carrier, the attack planes have varied missions, such as tankers [refueling], flak suppression, or Iron Hand. We did maintain tankers with the A-4, but didn't use them other than for emergency tanking. Everybody was flying air-to-ground.

Particular credit has to go to the A-1 squadrons and their ability to put a lot of ordnance over the beach at any given time. In truth, however, we had a hard time keeping enough ammunition to do that. This was at the time of ordnance rationing, and while there was a lot of controversy over that statement in those days, it was true. We had an aircraft, the A-1, capable of really being loaded up and staying on-station three hours; loaded with ordnance and waiting for targets to come up; yet we were only half arming them. Certainly there were some physical restraints on the loading crews, but when the Navy officials and publicity would come out that, Oh no, we don't have an ordnance shortage; I knew we had an ordnance shortage.

The aircraft of the Fighting I launched their first strikes against enemy targets on 15 May. Flying ninety-seven sorties, the A-1 and A-4 pilots provided close-air support for ground operations within fifty miles of Saigon. The targets included Viet Cong concentrations: primarily supply, storage, and training areas. During the first line period and most of the second, a total of fifty-nine days, the air wing operated in the II, III and IV Corps areas of the South, completing 4,738 sorties without losing an airplane. Fifty-five hundred tons of ordnance reached target, destroying some fourteen hundred structures and damaging fifteen hundred more, according to a rather interesting if not downright imaginative public affairs recap of the air wing's efforts. Some 145 junks were also sunk and 164 damaged, and 500 bunkers destroyed, plus another 100 damaged. The numbers war—sadly becoming the basis for the entire conflict—raged on.

Basically we flew in the daytime, on cyclic ops with the A-1s launched every three hours and the A-4s on a ninety-minute cycle. Everybody was hot to trot, and the only danger was small arms fire. We pretty much stayed above it, although minimums [altitude] came down at times and we dropped napalm. The minimums were based on staying out of the bomb frag patterns, especially with the 2,000-pound bombs.

My job, as it turned out, was to write the flight schedule. There really wasn't anybody else that had the working knowledge except the ops officer. We would transmit a skeleton flight schedule—number of sorties we'd launch in the cycle—to the Seventh Fleet liaison officer in Saigon and get back a notice with time on targets, locations, who to check in with, and preferred ordnance. We would then match up the ordnance loads according to what was on board. I was in constant contact with the weapons department, so they could keep a good count on what was available. Having worked with the CAG and squadron ops officers, I kept the continuity of knowing what the wing wanted, their preferred ordnance loads, and we dealt and negotiated different loads if possible. I think it worked out pretty well.

On most carriers, the air plan is written by the air-ops officer. I pretty much wrote the *Intrepid*'s air plan as strike-ops officer because that was the whole game; all we did was strike ops. The air-ops officer was more of a CATCO [carrier air traffic control officer]; he'd drift in and out but he didn't know too much and deferred to me. Both he and the CATCO officer were ASW types, and they were worried about general CATCO business pretty much. He was a nice guy and tried to get involved, but there wasn't that much for him to do.

CAG Hayward was an F-8 driver, and in fact, wasn't all that happy about taking this rinky-dink air wing. In late June he was relieved by Ken Burrows who stayed for the rest of the cruise and into the next one. Ken had an A-4 background.

In the middle of our second line period, a couple of staff guys headed up by the chief of staff, or the ops officer of the CARGRU staff that was Yankee [Station] team commander at the time, came out to visit. They made a great point to ask me, in some detail, how I needed to modify my strike routine and spaces if *Intrepid* was asked to come up North.

"We're going north?"

"No, we didn't say that. This is just a 'what if' drill."

"Well, I'll have to think about it."

I decided we needed room to put up maps of all the Navy Route Packages up North because there'd be responsibility for targeting, providing photography, and that sort of thing. So I told them, We'll need more space, maybe knock out a hatch or something on this bulkhead. Now, do you want me to start doing that?

"No, no, no, don't do that. We were just wondering."

Well, about five days later I'm told to do it. I said, "Wait a minute, don't tell *me* to do it." We got hold of the CO of the ship, and he was told don't spread the word, but we're going north. Sure enough, north we went. Our operations area, so we were told, was Route Packages 2 and 3; we were not going into 4 and 6 because the air threat was too high. The strike center was reconfigured and up North we went.

In forty-one days of operations in North Vietnam, Air Wing 10 flew 2,595 attack sorties and dropped 3,704 tons of ordnance. Transportation centers and waterborne traffic were of particular interest, and the *Intrepid*'s pilots joined other Yankee team carriers in September and October strikes at Ninh Binh and Thanh Hoa.

Most of the work was armed recce, and the Spads were still going inland a ways, particularly down in Route Package 2, south of Vinh and that area. The A-4s were operating up further North. We hadn't been up there very long when the word came down: Well, uh, we want you to go hit a few targets in the southern part of Route Package 6B.

These strikes involved A-4s only, and the Yankee team commander arranged the timing of the strikes such that the carrier *Ranger,* for example, would send in her strike, come out feet wet, then the [*Ranger*'s] fighters would turn around, and pick up and take in our strike group. This double jeopardy wasn't appreciated by those fighter pilots, and there was some question as to whether they should receive four points rather than two [toward getting an] air medal.

But that's how we worked around the fighter issue, which created a lot of problems at the planning level. It didn't create much of a problem with our pilots; they were just doing their jobs in pretty credible fashion.

During this time period—on October 9—the Spad drivers from VA-176 shot down a MiG. They were on a RESCAP [rescue patrol] mission in the southern part of Route Package 3. Two got jumped, two came steaming to join them, and the four MiGs were slowing down and trying to manuever with the Spads to get a shot, when the high speed Spads roared in. There was a speed advantage and the Spads came right up behind the MiGs and had a couple of shots at them. One MiG blew up and another went smoking over the horizon.

An interesting [follow-up] anecdote to that incident occurred as we returned from the cruise through the Suez Canal, heading to the Mediterranean. During the northern transit of the Suez, I had some Egyptian Air Force people come aboard who flew MiG-17s and -19s. As the pilots were being taken on a tour of the ship, a couple of them stopped at the VA-176 ready room door which had a big MiG kill sign on it.

"Oh, this squadron shot down a North Vietnamese MiG. What kind of planes do they fly?"

"A-1H Skyraiders."

The squadron commander refused to believe a Spad could shoot down a MiG. He would not believe it, yelling it was all propaganda.

Intrepid was gone for seven months, returning to Norfolk in late November and regrouping for a fast turnaround as all the West Coast carriers were doing. But now having been North, we needed a few things. The primary need was photo capability, that's what we requested, receiving three RF-8s from VFP-63 and a fighter detachment, three F-8s from VF-111 as escorts for the photo guys. To make room, one of the A-1 squadrons went away. We picked up VSF-3, an A-4B unit from Alameda. The VSF squadron provided A-4s as fighters to ASW contingents, giving them air-to-air capability in the area of a possible threat. It was decided to put a VSF together as an attack squadron and send them aboard *Intrepid*. We also had my old squadrons, VA-34 and VA-145 from Alameda, as the A-1 squadron.

The ship left Norfolk in May 1967, but was held up in the area of the Suez Canal in early June. Animosities were stirring up between Israel and Egypt, and the Sixth Fleet was gearing up to become a force. I think NAVEUR [Naval Force Europe] said, "We've got *Intrepid*, a combat ready carrier in the Med, can we keep her?" Our group finally went through the canal, the last ships before the war started.

The *Intrepid* arrived at Yankee Station on 21 June. Hitting targets between the Chinese border and the DMZ, Air Wing 10 pilots bombed several major bridges, warehouses, industrial complexes, railroad lines, highways, and military installations.

We were in the same mode of having to rely on fighter cover from other carriers, but now, with our own photo detachment to bring back bomb damage assessment and get targeting of places we were interested in. The Navy was flying three alpha strikes a day into all areas, and I thought we had pretty good targets—railroads, power plants, and such. The losses were significant, but the targets were good.

As the guys operated into the AAA and SAM threats, they'd sometimes come back shaking their heads. There was a concern in the A-4 community, particularly with the A-4Bs going up North. Not that the A-4B was any less capable than the A-4C; the aircraft were about the same

as far as thrust-to-weight—maybe the C was even heavier. But the grind was tough for the guys, to keep going up North; and there were pressures that, I think, reflected pressures for the sortie count.

One of the guys who had been in VA-34 with me quit, [he was] one of these early protesters of fighting the war. None of us understood his decision, and I suppose he was a bit before his time. He wasn't on the *Intrepid*, but I got a letter from him or heard somehow that he was having problems. He liked to fly, but not in this war. But that wasn't his choice. His wings were yanked, and off he went never to be heard from again.

Operating aboard the *Intrepid* was miserable. It was hot, and there were long hours particularly up North. I had a room not too far from the strike center, under the flight deck, which is a hot place to be anyway. As was done on so many of the old "27 Charlies" [older Hancock-class carriers], we got hold of window unit air-conditioners and stuck them where they'd exhaust into the passageways and keep the rooms cool. I didn't have one in my room, but we did get one in strike ops.

On average I was putting in an eighteen-hour day. By the time the frag orders would arrive from the carrier group as to the next day's schedule and everything placed together, it was fairly late, and I had to get up early. I'd try to grab a nap somewhere along midday, but it was so damn hot. I'd take off all my clothes, have some force-draft blowers going onto the bunk, and just lie there. It wasn't hard to wake up either because there was a catapult just over my head. When the first airplane launched on the next cycle, I'd wake and go back to work. Yes, it was tough.

The *Intrepid* arrived home in late 1967, and went on to complete her final Vietnam deployment in 1968. Linn Felt was promoted to commander, screened for command, and sent to VA-122, the training squadron at NAS Lemoore for the new A-7 Corsair, with orders assigning him as the first executive officer of VA-27. Two more deployments in Vietnam awaited him.

Chapter 12
Intruder

On Wednesday 29 June 1966, the first POL storage strikes of the war were carried out against Hanoi and Haiphong sites by the U.S. Air Force and by U.S. Navy aircraft from the carriers *Ranger* and *Constellation.*

Within an eight-minute time span, A-4Cs of VA-146 and VA-55, flying off the *Ranger,* dropped nineteen tons of ordnance and fired 5-inch Zuni rockets on the Haiphong POL site, the country's largest, while A-4 and A-6 aircraft from the *Constellation* went against the Do Son POL on the tip of the peninsula that forms the southeast arm of Haiphong harbor. A day later, planes from the USS *Hancock* and *Constellation* struck Bac Giang's POL, and on 1 July the two ships were at Dong Nham, thirteen miles northwest of Haiphong, destroying seven POL tanks and four support buildings.

The attacks, long discussed and long delayed, brought to fruition a debate that had raged for over a year between government and military leaders.

"A strike against these POL facilities had been recommended by CINC-PAC and the JCS numerous times, and the idea had been studied by almost every agency in Washington," revealed Adm. U. S. Grant Sharp in *Strategy for Defeat.* "In the meantime, however, there had been enough publicity in the press about hitting the POL facilities that the communists were sparing no effort to disperse their fuel supplies.

"The Hanoi and Haiphong POL storage complexes were still lucrative targets, but by now the North Vietnamese were storing fuel in barrels in caves and along the streets of villages in order to make supplies immune from air attack (they knew we would not strike a populated area)."

Since 1965 North Vietnamese officials had been building underground facilities while the U.S. debated whether POL strikes would raise the ire of Russia or China, or possibly endanger the civilian population of highly populated areas. Only after months of discussions was the first strike okayed, with the provisos that bombers could hit only specific areas and that no third country ships or personnel would be harmed.

The strike was originally scheduled for 23 June, but word of the strike was publicly leaked in U.S. newspapers, and the mission scrubbed until 29 June. The campaign to destroy POL sites continued throughout the year and into 1967, although proponents became convinced the results would not be significant. Or at least they became convinced in hindsight. Said Sharp, "It was clear as the summer wore on, that although we had destroyed a goodly portion of the North Vietnamese major fuel-storage capacity, they could still meet requirements through their residual dispersed capacity, supplemented by continued imports that we were not permitted to stop."

The initial strikes destroyed 80 percent of the Haiphong POL capacity, and by the end of July, the Defense Intelligence Agency categorized 70 percent of North Vietnam's known bulk storage capacity as destroyed along with 7 percent of the dispersed sites. What POL sites remained, however, were significant, including 26,000 metric tons storage capacity in the large sites, about 30–40,000 tons capacity in medium-sized, dispersed sites, and another 28,000 tons in smaller, tank and drum sites. More importantly, the North only needed 32,000 metric tons to meet its annual minimum needs, and CIA analysts stressed the North Vietnamese would have no trouble importing sufficient fuel supplies to keep their significant military and economic traffic moving.

Taking part in the first POL strikes was the *Constellation*'s Air Wing 15, bolstered by the presence of VA-65, an A-6A Intruder squadron. Led by future rear admiral Bob Mandeville, the first pilot to log over one thousand hours in the Intruder, Mandeville's A-6 unit was the third to reach Southeast Asia. But in contrast to predecessors VA-75 and -85, the A-6's of VA-65 were capable of fully carrying out the Intruder's most notable all-weather, night mission.

"VA-75 and -85 lost a bunch of aircraft," recalled Mandeville. In the 1965–66 combat deployments VA-75 and -85 lost a combined total of ten, while Mandeville's squadron had only one airplane shot down and the crew taken prisoner, and a bombardier-navigator from another crew killed and the plane lost. "I attribute our success to the fact we were putting our major effort into night work, and they were putting their major effort into day work. I don't want to say that very authoritatively, but I know 75's case was very much that way. They just didn't do very much night work at all. Now 85, a little more, a little better. But it was just timing, nothing to do with the character of the squadron, who was there or anything else. It was just the knowledge and equipment. Our systems worked as designed."

VA-65's 1966 deployment—12 May to 3 December—totaled one hundred days of combat operations, attacking and destroying four bridges at night, destroying the Haiphong-Hanoi main thermal power network at night, and demolishing countless POL sites, trucks, PT boats and barges. All totaled, VA-65 dropped half the bombs—10.6 million pounds of ordnance—delivered by an air wing that included twenty-eight A-4 and twenty-four F-4 aircraft. Most notably, Lt. Cmdr. Bernie Deibert and his bombardier-navigator [BN], Lt. Cmdr. Dale Purdy, dropped five 2,000-pound bombs on the Hai Duong Bridge, knocking down the center span.

The squadron went over the beach when the rest of the air wing could not. Because inclement weather kept the A-4s and F-4s on the deck during the Connie's last line period, VA-65 aircraft flew 73 percent of all strike sorties into North Vietnam within a nine-day period, and on four of those days accounted for all the strikes flown from Yankee Station.

The night work, Mandeville emphasized in his end-of-cruise debrief, "would have been effective from a morale point of view had we never hit a target. Many of our targets were within the sanctuary circles of Hanoi and Haiphong, and I know it must have been frustrating to them to have airplanes driving around over the countryside at night with impunity." As evidence of their frustration, the North Vietnamese attempted almost unheard of night intercepts by MiGs, and barrage-fired SAMs in their quest to bag an A-6.

The heart and soul of the A-6 was, and is, the DIANE—digital integrated attack and navigational equipment. This piece of hardware combines three radars, a navigation unit, and a small computer, which gave Vietnam-era pilots a visual image of terrain contours and buildings on a cockpit TV screen. The system allowed a pilot to fly through overcast, find the target, automatically release the bombs, and bring the aircraft back to the carrier.

Mandeville was pleased with the squadron's Vietnam showing, more so because he felt the continued future of the A-6 program necessitated an outstanding performance by VA-65 in 1966.

VA-75 and -85 had good talented people, but the airplane [A-6] at that time was a bear. We [VA-65] were super compared to them, and it had nothing to do with the people, just [our] knowledge [of the A-6] and its equipment. Seventy-five and 85 didn't do well with the systems, and the aircraft had to be worked on after every flight. The fact was accepted that the plane would be down. Really a lot of heartburn.

Those two squadrons didn't have the support we did, and I can understand why. The bottom line was if the A-6 didn't work this cruise, there wouldn't be any more A-6s. It was a fish or cut bait situation, and the ship overflowed with technicians. We'd done the mission on the beach, and knew if the support was there, the plane would perform the way it was intended.

On the way out to Vietnam, the air wing had a super turnover with the *Kitty Hawk* air wing in Yokosuka. They updated us on how the war was going, the limited targets, and the fact the floor had been raised to three thousand feet. The turnover was very intense, and we sort of picked up their tactics, all the rules of engagement and rules of the road to make sure we didn't do something dumb. In essence, Air Wing 15 ran the initial portion of the first line period [on the *Constellation*] according to the way they'd done it on the *Kitty Hawk*.

Some of the wing's aircraft (our squadron [VA-65], the [RA-5] "Viggies," and VA-155) were camouflaged—painted at North Island during workups. At home [from above] we'd try to find those planes down in the weeds and couldn't. Boy, we thought, this is really super, but [we were] not yet smart enough to really think what happens when mud is [seen from below] at three thousand feet.

We got over to Vietnam, started losing airplanes, and discovered every one of them had been camouflaged. I finally came to the conclusion that when the wing rendezvoused, the Viggies were visible, so were the A-6s and some A-4s, but not Dave Leue's A-4s because they weren't painted. The camouflage was good looking down, but not so good looking up. The paint was off in three days.

About the time we went up North, the POL campaign started. My first alpha strike was on the Haiphong POL, just north of town, knocking down every site around of any size at all. We then started in on the underground POLs, plowing up all kinds of ground. We'd come in, drop a bunch of bombs at some point near the coordinate offset from some radar-significant thing and, boom, the whole earth would erupt.

Our A-6s were treated like A-6s, saving them primarily for the night mission. Working noon to midnight, we'd do whatever needed to be done in the afternoon but didn't go out to just road recce—find a footbridge, or whatever. Those were stupid missions, but no less stupid for anybody else. In an A-6 you think they're stupid, but they're also stupid in an A-4.

For day alpha strikes, or places where we needed to just carry bombs, the systems weren't important. We could go ahead and let the airplane fly with a downed radar or computer because at that point we'd be just big, double-breasted A-4s. But the night work, we saved ourselves to the max for that. So if operations started at midnight, we'd hit it hard hoping to finish up before dawn.

The squadron had twelve airplanes and we used nine. Of the other three, one was in check, one [was] a parts locker, and one [had] some kind of battle damage. Our day schedule was sixteen sorties on a twelve-hour session, or eight flights of two [planes]. At night, it was usually a twelve-plane launch, in fours or threes depending on the target. The flight officer did the scheduling, and he had my philosophy worked out. Some pilots just didn't go on certain missions because there was no sense in sending the aircrew and airframe to a target unless it was going to do some good. I wasn't involved in personally saying, this guy can go, that guy can't—the flight schedule took care of it. The real aggressive pilots would bitch about not getting tough targets, and the other guys didn't complain much. They did their thing.

One of our bigger strikes was a four-plane coordinated night strike on the Haiphong power plant. Just leveled it. Four planes hit the power plant from four different directions, dropping 1,000-pounders on the basic power plant itself and 500-pounders on the transformer yard, which was spread out. Just fantastic. Whenever we really got a target, and got it down—a bridge or a span in the water—it would really keep you going, pump you up.

Bridges or hard targets, we'd go with five 2,000-pound bombs. For a power plant or heavy reinforced building, we'd carry thirteen Mk-83s, the 1,000-pounders, unless of course the need wasn't that great. Spread-out targets, the load was 500-pounders, twenty-eight of them.

The ordnance situation was tight in June, July; and much better toward the end of the cruise. Initially the squadron took whatever came up from the spaces that was khaki. If it looked like a bomb, we'd hang it and drop it.

Going to the target, we turned everything off in the A-6 after the rendezvous—instruments, radar, whatever—and went right down to two hundred feet. Maybe I was still playing "Cowboys and Indians," but I was bound and determined to do it this way and talked CAG into it even for the alpha strikes. The A-6s always led; in fact, I went down to fifty feet because everybody stacked up. We'd accelerate about fifteen miles off the beach, trying to get the speed up. The A-4s loaded up were the problem, so I had a deal with the A-4 skippers. I wanted their slowest guy at 100 percent and at that point, the strike group was at top speed.

Our climb would begin at five miles off the beach, looking to hit the beach at three thousand feet. Depending on how far in the target was, we'd start a pop-up to target altitude, although we'd try to stay at three thousand feet. Our normal entry into Haiphong or the Red River Valley was go out way to the east, follow the karst north, and then come down. We'd stay in the valleys to have some semblance of surprise, and usually did. Rarely was there a whole bunch of stuff coming at us. We'd get it, but not waiting [for us].

At night our initial tactic involved trying to come in together. Two airplanes went in at one hundred feet over the water, hit the beach at 400 or 500 feet, and split up with the idea of splitting the flak and their [the North Vietnamese's] attention. We decided the hell with that, let's just meet at the target at a certain time. The computer could read out when and where, set out a course, and be within five or six seconds of simultaneous drops. Both planes would always break left to avoid each other—that was a big worry—and yet the planes were probably a mile apart.

Coming to the target, the idea was stay at 300, 400 or 500 feet, depending on the pilot's level of courage, and as fast as possible. With a load of 500-pound bombs, tops is 530 knots in an A-6, which is pretty comfortable. A full load of 28,000 pounds, tops is probably 430, 450 knots, and that's hauling a lot of stuff.

We'd try to work our way in as undetected as possible, and the pilot's last task was to establish a run, allowing the BN time to find the target and get smoothed up. Eight to ten miles was good for the run, coming in at one thousand feet. A certain angle might be necessary for specific targets, and ideally, the aircraft would be running toward the beach when the bombs dropped, so the inertia and momentum was heading toward the water.

In that eight-, ten-mile run, the airplane was most vulnerable, and while [the run] went by fast, it seemed like years. The pilot's responsibility involved trying to make the entry as smooth as possible and get the steering corrected if need be. Every correction the BN made on the radar cursor, there'd be a steering error to correct, just like a gun-sight change. The pilot also needed to make sure nothing was coming at the plane. SAMs were the main threat. With AAA, the flash was visible, and it either hit the aircraft or didn't. SAMs were worrisome—they had to be avoided. Daytime was bad enough, but night was horrible, and horrible because there's no place to go but down, and down is only one thousand feet. It was scary because to push the nose down and drive toward the ground is against basic human nature. Yet you had to correct fast, trying to get the missile into the ground, and not you. That made it very, very difficult. A number of A-6s were lost, driven into the ground by a SAM. I didn't want them to kill me, but flying into the ground was sure no way to escape getting hit.

I felt comfortable at night for several reasons. Nighttime took away the MiGs—only a couple had radars—took away all those people out there issued standard guns to try and kill you, and even the AAA is kind of different at night. Primarily, the freebies were gone, that low-level garbage keeping us at three thousand feet in the first place. We were able to go down on the way in at night, and those gutsy enough could have flown at ten feet. However, the ground clearance mode in the A-6 was not developed well enough at that time [for us] to have confidence in it. You'd take it in at 300, 400 feet, and if it was a bit karsty or a little rough, pop up to 500 or 600 feet, whatever felt comfortable.

Mentally, flying at night was very tough. I remember going into Nam Dinh. Of all the damn places we never did figure out what was there, but it must have been something because the North Vietnamese had all kinds of radar-guided 85-millimeter and SAMs. I remember going in and watching those damn 85s just pop up at ten miles out, watching that stuff come up and thinking, One of these nights. They just can't keep going right here, right there—one of these nights it's going to be the right place.

Working independently at night was a whole different ballgame. I would say about half the targets were individual, one aircraft going after one target. Even if we never dropped, damaged, or destroyed anything, we had to be doing something with the night flying. All that noise, and the North Vietnamese would shoot, shoot, and shoot, and there's nothing there in the morning. That was the beauty of it.

We were never allowed to get into the airfields, which we wanted to do so desperately. But overall we hit bridges, power plants. We waited for the good targets like we waited for the Mk-84, 2,000-pound bombs. Sometimes they came, sometimes they didn't. It was cause for real joy when a new target list came out, and there were some good targets, say, a power plant or a real significant target.

CTF-77 and the *Constellation*'s captain, Bill Howser, gave the squadron a tremendous amount of latitude as to which targets we wanted, which could be hit. We tried to be objective and take the ones in the high threat areas, and good radar targets. Let us give it a shot—save an alpha strike and maybe save losing somebody. Give us three shots, and we'd get a span down at night, which is pretty good because there were alpha strikes—thirty airplanes—that'd go in and never get anything.

The Thanh Hoa Bridge was different, but that's another matter. Seven times we went to Thanh Hoa, and nothing. I had a guy in the squadron named Pete Garber, a real warrior. If wars had gone on forever, Pete would have been CNO. He flew with VA-75; they came back, and he volunteered to go back over with us. Garber wanted the Thanh Hoa Bridge so badly. He had an emotional thing with it and personally made eleven strikes at the bridge. On coordinated strikes, our password after we released bombs—Pete and I started this thing and the other guys probably decided it sounded good—was ''Ho Chi Minh is a son-of-a-bitch.'' I don't know if anybody ever heard it, but that's just the way Pete operated. He couldn't back off and be the trainer unless there was going to be some war.

We lost one guy on the whole cruise, which is fairly unusual, and it was stupid, stupid, stupid. A pilot went back and reattacked a target in the daytime, right off the beach, and got hit. The BN, a young guy, Chuck Merritt, was killed. I never forgave the pilot. You had the rules. Why do you have them? Because people get killed who don't pay attention to them. We also had the infamous George Coker and Jack Fellowes shot down by 85-millimeter. They came back in 1973.

I guess the most impressive feature of Vietnam was the performance of all the people, not just the aircrews but the entire squadron. And not just our squadron, I'd like to feel it was everybody. Just the pride you feel of being in the Navy with a bunch of people like that. It kind of tugs at you. That's the strongest emotion I have about it all. The absolute pride.

Chapter 13
The Parade

The POL campaign, despite its long-term ineffectiveness, stunned the people and government of North Vietnam. Terrified at this new expansion of the air war but certainly not at a loss for action, Ho Chi Minh and his cohorts struck back at their favorite whipping boys, the American prisoners of war.

On 6 July, just a week after the POL campaign began, fifty-two POWs—or "criminals" as the North Vietnamese repeatedly asserted—were marched through the streets of Hanoi, while thousands of residents of the capital city verbally assaulted and physically abused the grounded pilots. Sixteen prisoners were brought in that day from Briarpatch, a camp 35 miles northwest of Hanoi on the Red River, and the remaining thirty-six from the Zoo facility in Hanoi. Included among the POWs were Everett Alvarez, the first aviator taken prisoner, and a somewhat recent shootdown, William Shankel.

The POWs gathered in downtown Hanoi were lectured to, and in the early evening were paraded in pairs, approximately ten feet apart, in front of thousands of Vietnamese sitting in bleachers and standing on sidewalks. Initially under control, the crowd's emotions slowly heated up, boiling over into anger as the POWs marched to Worker's Stadium. Eventually becoming frenzied, the crowd attacked the prisoners with rocks, bottles, fists and feet—Cmdr. Jeremiah Denton, who'd been the executive officer of VA-75, the first A-6 Intruder squadron in combat, suffered a partial hernia from a fist to the groin—and the uncontrolled crowd frightened even the North Vietnamese prison guards. One guard, recalled a POW, was white with terror and almost in tears as he tried to keep the mob from the prisoners. The Americans eventually reached their destination, the stadium doors were locked, a speech given, and the excursion deemed officially over.

Radio Hanoi's colorful and imaginative report on the parade reached the prisoners by way of the camp's radio systems; it was monitored in

Tokyo and relayed throughout the world. "American prisoners were being marched through the streets of Hanoi," stated the broadcast, "when tens of thousands of people poured into the streets shouting 'Death to the American air pirates!' and 'Down with U.S. imperialism!' The Hanoians, though seething with anger at the crimes committed by the U.S. air pirates, showed themselves to be highly disciplined, otherwise the sheer thought of these crimes might have prompted them to tear Johnson's skywarriors to pieces."

Soviet Union reports following up the parade announced the North Vietnamese were deluged with demands that the U.S. pilots be tried and sentenced to death as war criminals.

For one of the few times in their well-devised propaganda war, the North Vietnamese misjudged American reaction to the parade. Even anti-war activists denounced any attempts at trying the prisoners as war criminals or subjecting them to further harassment. Said a *Washington Post* editorial on 14 July: "North Vietnam will invite terrible retaliation if it proceeds to try and punish captured American pilots. The measured restraint of the air attacks so far would melt in the popular passion likely to be generated in the United States by reprisals against the airmen."

Bill Shankel, like his fellow POWs, was never tried.

After my brief stay at Heartbreak Hotel, they moved me to the Zoo. I first started out in the area called the Pigsty and then went to other places like the Barn, Garage, Pool Hall, and the Stable, just all over. Nobody knows why all the moves, but after every move communications became better. You knew that last area, the places to drop messages, and how to flash code back and forth.

I was quizzed a couple of times back at Heartbreak, but apparently the gooks didn't want to know much. I was just kind of ignored, not treated too badly, although the food was soupy green stuff and there was never enough to eat. Eventually, I figured we'd have a compound situation, a Stalag 17 or "Hogan's Heroes" kind of thing where everybody is together. Of course, that didn't happen. They treated us like we were in jail, never called us prisoners, always "criminals," and we couldn't refer to ourselves using rank, or refer to others using rank.

Our major communications dealt mainly with who was where, and what was the chain of command. Chain of command was automatic—find out the guy's date of rank and that's it.

I stayed at the Zoo until July, when I was shipped to Briarpatch after the parade in Hanoi. Initially, the parade was a neat idea, the first real chance to talk to each other. We were placed in little groups before taking off for the park and told not to talk, but did it anyway. I talked to Bob Shumaker [Lt. Robert H.] and Larry Spencer, a guy in VF-92 on the *Enterprise*. I'd known Larry a cruise or two before on the *Ranger*.

They handcuffed us in pairs, and I was with Dick Ratzlaff. A few days before the parade, I'd been moved in with Dick, my first roommate. Ratzlaff was from the *Enterprise* and it's funny, but we had a change of command before leaving on cruise and I'd borrowed Dick's sword. It was still in my stateroom when I was shot down, but he got it back. So at least I was relieved Dick got his sword.

Dick and I were handcuffed together and paraded through Hanoi with all the other cons. Starting out, guys with hand-held bullhorns were in the crowd trying to whip them up, get them going, and the crowd was pretty apathetic. They were really just content to just watch all these dumb white guys walk through. But the further we went, the crowd got meaner. They were throwing stuff, and pretty soon for every one of us, there was at least one guard walking along trying to look like a little soldier with his rifle bayoneted, held at high port and all that.

No one was slugging me, just taunting. We finally made it through to Worker's Stadium; and this was a long way, maybe a couple of miles. By the end, we're actually walking over people, and there was a bottleneck at the entrance to the stadium. These big green doors would open a little bit and pull us through, then slam closed until somebody else got up there. The gooks created a monster with this crowd, and luckily none of us were really hurt.

The story told to us, or at least the story which came over the radio from Hanoi Hannah, said we were being paraded on the way to war crimes trials. Interestingly enough, somebody—Japanese, Czechoslovakian, whatever—was taking movies of the parade. Some time later, these films were aired on American TV, and Mary Ann [his future wife] just happened to be watching TV that night. She saw me and called my parents. That was the first time anybody knew that I was alive, before that I was just listed as missing in action.

When we got back to the Zoo, the gooks started really pounding on people, trying to get war crimes confessions out of us and all that crap. They came to me, asking what I thought about the parade. I told them I thought they were a bunch of animals. Frankly, I was still on a real guilt trip because I'd given away more than my name, rank, service number, and date of birth. You're not supposed to do that. Of course, I didn't give them any information they could use, everything I told them was just pure bullshit. But it didn't seem to matter.

Long before the parade, I was asked to write an autobiography. That was a big thing; you're supposed to write an autobiography, and I refused. I just told the camp commander, a guy we called Dog, "I'm not going to do that." I sat in the Dog's office one afternoon, then was taken out back, tied up, put in leg irons, and thrown in a little outdoor cell.

Someone came around every day and asked if I was ready to write my autobiography, and every day I said, "No." Problem was, I didn't get any food or water out there, and I was out there nearly a week. After close to a week of no water, you get pretty dry, especially in a dusty room with a dirt floor. Finally, the gooks said, "Here, see what your fellow POWs have written." The name of this one story was "How I was procured into the Air Force," and the penmanship was that of a four-year-old. No capitalized letters, no punctuation marks, really a dumb story. This guy was a farm boy in Oklahoma, saw an airplane fly over, and went and got himself procured into the Air Force.

Dog showed me a couple of other stories like that, and I thought, If that's what they'll buy, I'll just put them off as long as I can and see if they'll forget. But eventually, I couldn't stand being without water, and the guards were getting impatient. They started getting physically brutal, coming around and kicking me. The knee was hurting, and we all know happiness is the absence of pain. I wrote some dumb thing and got them off my back.

After the Hanoi parade, I started in again on myself—that one of these times I'm going to last through all this torture and not have to give them anything. When the gooks asked about the parade, I told them what a bunch of animals they were, how they behaved very badly throughout the parade. I really expected them to come down hard on me, but it didn't happen. They just packed me up with some other guys and out we went to Briarpatch, in the mountains not far from Laos.

Fifty-some guys were out there, and Howie Dunn, a Marine Corps major, was the senior officer. All the cons lived in a block of nine separated buildings, and I started in the first building and graduated from there into number two. Because the buildings were separated, we'd communicate by code while chopping weeds, or washing clothes. You'd shake out the wet clothes and snap code, giving the lineup of your entire hut, room by room. Everybody was known by initials, and we knew where everyone was in the camp.

From the time I arrived in July until late in the year, the gooks were getting war crimes confessions from everybody in camp, using the end room right next to me as a torture chamber. I constantly talked to the guys being tortured, and we never got caught, which is incredible considering the bad shape they were in. Tight cuffs, maybe even leg irons, and hands swollen so bad that tapping on the walls was impossible. We talked out the window, our voices bouncing off a wall.

My turn finally came. Each morning I was paraded, arms cuffed in back. Initially, they cuffed my arms in front to carry the *bo*—my bucket. But as my hands began to swell, the bucket became hard to hold, started to spill, and rather than spill it on me, I threw it all over the guard. So my hands were cuffed in back. Bomb shelters were located in each room, really just a hole about four feet deep under this hardwood bed, and you'd be in the hole, arms and wrists sticking out, and the guards would stand on the cuffs to get them as tight as possible. Needless to say, after a few hours there'd be absolutely no feeling at all in your hands.

I was paraded around with a rope around my neck, carrying the *bo* behind my back, and led out of the compound to these ditches. Despite a blindfold, I could tell I was outside because while white guys have a bridge on their nose, gooks don't. Put a blindfold on them and they go IFR, but I could still see out the bottom of the blindfold. They'd make me run in these damn ditches—losing my sandals and cutting up my feet—to this one trench maybe twelve feet deep, with a concrete opening and wooden door on the side of it. There was nothing inside, just a muddy floor, and not enough room to sit down or stand up. I'd be there all day, hands in cuffs behind my back; then at dark they'd run me down the hill, give me something to eat and a few minutes to eat it, and stick me in the bomb shelter. I had to stay in the bomb shelter all night, which meant mosquitoes, spiders, and all the rest down there with me. The *bo* couldn't be dumped—they wouldn't allow it—so all the urine and stuff in the bucket spilled over into the shelter. After a week or so of this fun the Vietnamese became impatient and started beating me and rattling cuffs, which is just excruciating because the cuffs go through the skin and dig into your hide. I decided, okay, I'll write a war crimes confession, another real masterpiece.

On another occasion, for violating some camp regulation, the Vietnamese sat me on a concrete block and refused to let me sleep. I wasn't tied up, so during the guard's siesta each day I emptied out this little coal oil lamp nearby. At night it'd burn for only an hour or two, and while the guards were scurrying around trying to find coal oil, I'd try and sleep. I can't even remember how long I was out there, or what ever became of it. They may have finally even given up on me, but you didn't want to push them too far during the real brutal torture. To do that meant irons and solitary confinement. Fortunately they stopped the practice of withholding food and water. Even if the gooks were really doing it to you, they allowed water and maybe a little thin, watery soup. I don't know what made them do that, although we had the idea the gooks really wanted to keep us alive.

Summer was always the worst time, whether at Briarpatch or Hanoi. The guards got meaner, there were more quizzes, more tortures, more signed statements. Really abysmal. Most of the guards were dumbshits walking around with a gun, really the worst of the North Vietnamese Army. Some of them were prone to being mean, but for the most part the guards didn't get involved in the tortures and other kind of stuff. Turnkeys were the assholes. They'd come and open the door every morning. You'd come out, set down the *bo,* and one or two guys from another room would come by, pick up the *bo,* empty it, and bring it back. The food then came, and the turnkey would open the door and bring it in. You had to bow to the turnkey, really a big issue. Sometimes they'd slap you while bowing, so I always looked at them, really just kind of sticking my ass out. We always tried to play mind games with the gooks, trying to beat them. Most of the time we didn't.

Hairlip was the guy in charge of torture at Briarpatch. He spoke French and engineered all the torture, helped out by Rabbit. Both spoke English. Rabbit lost a bunch of numbers one time when Ross Terry and Nels Tanner were being hammered for names of everybody in their squadron, the captain of the ship and all that kind of stuff. (They asked me for those in Heartbreak and I just gave them names of people I went to high school with. Where I grew up, there was a lot of people of Slavonian and Italian descent, so there were some great names. It took me a half hour to get them to spell Bacigalupi right.) Tanner and Terry gave names like Clark Kent, Ken Maynard, and Tom Mix. Rabbit was the guy who tortured them and got all the bullshit names. The information apparently left Hanoi and I think went to Sweden, one of the Bertrand Russell War Crimes Tribunals. Somebody brought up the fact that Americans are cooperating, they're not under duress, they're a bunch of weaklings. In fact, here we have these two guys who gave all the names of the senior officers on their ship—out popped Tom Mix, Ken Maynard, and Clark Kent, and the whole place went up for grabs. The gooks came down hard on Terry and Tanner, but also on Rabbit and he lost some rank.

Briarpatch had no electricity, and we always knew when a recorded message or talk over the PA was coming because the engine for the generator was started. Hanoi Hannah bombarded us, although I don't think there was a real concerted effort to win us over. But I feel the anti-war movement fueled the fire and precipitated a whole lot of our bad treatment. I really thought word of our treatment would get back to the United States, to Lyndon Johnson, and the anti-war people. They'd all realize the gooks were a bunch of schmucks and there'd be a massive protest. Of course that never happened.

Chapter 14
Spad

Norman Lessard's decision to become a naval aviator was based on one factor, he wanted to pilot the A-1 Skyraider. "I joined the Navy to fly single engine, single prop," claims Lessard. "I'd seen movies and read some books, and, boy, that big engine—eighteen cylinders and three thousand horsepower and big prop, fourteen feet in diameter—to me that was the way to go."

The intensity of the Vietnam air war rendered the Spad all but useless in high-threat areas, and the Navy A-1s found their primary mission in supporting search and rescue efforts to locate downed enemy pilots. Considered well suited for SAR purposes, the Spad could fly slowly enough to stay with the rescue helos and carry enough ordnance to suppress ground fire.

By 1968 the combat Spad, in all but a minor role, departed the fleet and pilots such as Lt. Norm Lessard had made the transition to jet aircraft.

I had a choice between Spads and jets at flight training, and Harvey Melvin Browne and I chose Spads. There were about twenty-five of us that came over from Pensacola to Corpus Christi, graded by our primary flight training. I had my choice and nobody could believe I wanted Spads. Harvey went the same way as did a Vietnamese guy—but they always flew Spads. We stayed in Corpus with VT-30, the A-1 training squadron, and the rest of the guys went to Beeville and Kingsville [Texas] for jets.

Each training class had three people, and my group included Harvey and this Vietnamese named Thanh. Thanh was just all over the sky, coming close to clipping us, overrunning us a number of times while learning to rendezvous. Boy, he'd make you nervous because we were learning too. I met Dieter Dengler at VT-30—his class was a little behind me—and when I came out to VA-122 in September of 1964, Dieter followed a month or two later. The two of us went to Fallon together for training, then to VA-145 at Alameda. I got to the squadron in January of 1965, and about a month-and-a-half later Dieter arrived.

Harvey, the best man at my wedding, went to VA-52, also at Alameda. As a jg, he received the Silver Star. He and another pilot on the *Ticonderoga,* Paul Giberson, tried to save a jet pilot downed in a field. They kept on shooting and using rockets and bombs over this field where the pilot was located, waiting for the helicopter to arrive. Harvey and Giberson were flying low enough to the ground they came back with all kinds of holes in their airplanes and blood and dirt on the prop. But the helicopter never got there and the two of them finally ran out of ammunition.

After joining VA-145, I was in a hurry to get to Vietnam. I joined the Navy as a NavCad (Naval Aviation Cadet), enlisted for a year-and-a-half or two years, then received my wings. I'd become an officer with the exact plane I wanted to fly. Boy I fought for it, wanted it, and now I had it, but was stuck in Alameda because the squadron had just come back from a deployment on the *Constellation* and wouldn't go on cruise again until December.

VA-145 took part in the Gulf of Tonkin retaliatory strike, and one of their own, Dick Sather, had been shot down, the first guy to get killed. A lot of mid-grade lieutenants were in the outfit and very few young guys. I was an ensign six months in the squadron before making jg, and Dieter and I were the two young guys. I looked up to the lieutenants, like boy, they made this combat cruise—one mission—and, boy, when are we going—I'm ready to go and help out in this war.

The squadron deployed in December on the *Ranger,* with two major roles. One was bombing, strafing, and firing rockets over North and South Vietnam; and the other role, RESCAP (rescue patrol), which I felt became more important. We'd fly with the helos going in over the beach to pick up downed pilots, help them look for the pilot, and fly cover for the helicopters on the way out. On the *Intrepid* cruise in 1967, our job was primarily all rescue.

We never went into the high threat areas like Haiphong and Hanoi, but did fly in southern North Vietnam quite a bit. AAA was our primary concern; while the SAMs could lock on to us, they weren't a threat.

There was a lot of competition in 1966, an esprit de corps between the Spad drivers and the A-4 pilots from Lemoore. The jet guys, my contemporaries, always gave us a hard time—that we were slow and didn't have much to do. When we flew cover for them, they appreciated it, but there was no doubt the Spad was heading downhill because of the speed aspect. The Spad cruised around 160, 170 knots, and going over the beach we'd get it up to 200. Straight down, max was 400, 410, and red line was 420.

On RESCAP missions, the A-1 carried four 20mm guns, two hundred rounds per gun. Every once in a while one would jam, but the guns worked pretty decent. We'd also carry rockets, eighteen per pod, and could shoot them individually or as a volley, and one or two 500-pound bombs. In most cases we relied on the rockets and the 20-millimeters.

Our standard rescue procedure was to try and make contact with the pilot on the ground and give the helo a general direction where we thought the guy might be. If contact had been made, we'd hang off just to stay away from the pilot to keep the attention from him until a helicopter could get in. If we were fortunate enough to have a couple of extra Spads airborne, those two guys might fall in with the helicopter and the other two cover the pilot. With only two, one guy would go back out to fly in with the helo and one stay overhead.

In the event of ground fire getting close to the pilot, we'd try to slow the advance of the enemy. I'd get down to five hundred or one thousand feet to strafe; while it was possible to get lower, I didn't see the point of it. Five hundred feet was low enough.

Occasionally, there might be a dual mission. Initially we'd bomb, heading out with a couple of 1,000-pounders and some 500s, finish that mission, and stay out another cycle. We'd cover a rescue if needed because there'd still be plenty of rockets and guns left. The A-1 could carry a good load.

There were times we'd take off at midnight, hang off Haiphong at eight hundred feet, four of us, and come back at six-thirty, seven o'clock in the morning to land. It'd get boring, and we'd have the throttle, RPM back, going as slow as possible, just hanging on the prop. The hum, the drone from the engine would really get to you about 2:00, 3:00 A.M. You'd get real sleepy, and while the radio picked up Vietnamese music, that wasn't too much better.

The only time I was given pills to stay awake stemmed out of an incident where I fell asleep in the cockpit. The launch was at 5:00 A.M., flying wing on an Air Force rescue plane. If I remember correctly, we were on an east-west path, turning around and heading back at about two thousand feet. I went to sleep heading for Hainan Island about 6:30 [A.M.], waking up just as I was about to go over the island. The radio was blaring with the guys telling me to turn around, but nobody knew where I was because they'd made the 180 and I hadn't. After that incident, the doc gave me some pills in case I was tired. But that was not on a continuous basis, and I don't believe [taking pills] was common in my outfit.

The Spad could usually hang in the air anywhere from three to six hours, and the seat would really get hard. As a remedy, the doc ordered the squadron a bunch of donuts, a hemorrhoid tire tube with a hole in the middle. You could inflate it, then take the air out as the hop went by, or change it any way needed to make the seat more comfortable.

One night mission, Denny Enstam, myself, and an Air Force pilot spotted a truck. Enstam rolled in first and dropped a 500-pounder, and I followed and also dropped a 500-pounder. I pulled off and boom, there was a sudden bang and crash in the cockpit and all this smoke. God damn, I thought, I've been hit, and I start yelling "I've been hit! I've been hit!" All three of us had all our lights off, of course, and the night was real hazy, very bad visibility. The light from the flares made it very vertigo inducing and I became really disoriented. Denny started yelling, "Where are you? Where are you?" as did the Air Force guy, and I had no clue at all.

Eventually I got straight and level and settled down, realizing the engine was still running and the plane still flying. Checking this smoke-filled cockpit, I found the donut had burst—what I thought was smoke was actually talcum powder from the donut!

We got back to the ship about seven that morning, and I don't know how they got the word but the ship knew. I hopped out of the airplane—the Spads were always the last ones to land so it was real quiet—and the captain of the ship makes a remark about Norm Lessard and his donut. To this day, I don't know how they found out that quickly about the problem.

Except for RESCAP, only on rare occasions did I feel our objectives were constructive. Any time we were helping somebody, that was time well spent. But as far as trying to win the war, trying to hurt the North Vietnamese materially, to get rid of their guns, food, or whatever they were shipping south, that was really frustrating. For example, there was a bridge on Highway 1 along the coast, and really not a bridge, just a bunch of mud built up at night. To bomb it, we carried a 2,000-

pound bomb in the center, and 1,000-pounders on the outside wings. During the day we'd blow it up, and at night the North Vietnamese would build it up and get across it, and on and on it went.

Sorties were always a big deal, the sorties and how they handed out the medals really upset me. Our AI [aviation intelligence officer], Frank Schelling, would keep the squadron abreast of the sortie count: How many sorties the ship flew that particular day, how many the ship flew this particular day last year, and how many are projected the following day. The A-1s were always good for sortie and the wing would launch us even if the weather wasn't real good. Really, a sad way to run a war.

Air medals were by the number. Two points per flight, twenty points or ten flights for an air medal, really a crazy way to give out medals. The medals didn't matter to me—what's a medal, that plus a buck gets you a beer—but if the Navy's giving them out, it should be done fair. I'm not saying this happened all the time, but from my experience you could have two guys on the same mission, and if they did something good, the senior guy would get the more important medal. The younger guy, who'd done just as much, who was sticking it out just as much as the senior guy, would get the lesser medal. I don't believe it was fair sometimes, and a couple of times it was absolutely not fair.

As the first cruise ended, I started to see the big picture, to get discouraged and disappointed. I was twenty-four years old and those romantic, flying-in-the-sunset ideas were fading a little bit.

The close of Lessard's first combat cruise also witnessed another revelation, the return of Dieter Dengler, shot down in early February.

Dengler became the focus of a worldwide media blitz in midsummer after escaping from a Laotian prisoner of war camp. The German-born, twenty-eight-year-old had been shot down while piloting an A-1 on 1 February over Laos and captured by the Communist Pathet Lao. "Today was a bad day," read Lessard's 1 February diary entry. "Dieter was on a hop with Ken, Spook, and Denny, and he disappeared. Dieter was the last man to roll in when he was observed by Spook to start a normal recover. Due to limited visibility, the flight lost sight of him. The search continued all day and part of the night with no luck."

A day later Lessard and another VA-145 pilot spotted the wreckage and called in a helo. "We got to the area around 0730 and at 0900, we found the wreckage," he recalled in the diary. "To us from the air, it looked like there was no one in the cockpit. They [the helo crew] went out and took pictures and it looks like his donut was on the ground by the wing. So we hope he is still alive in the woods and jungle."

Dengler, according to his 1979 book *Escape from Laos* and the 1966 newspaper articles, saw Lessard's aircraft, but attempts at radio contact proved fruitless. Within days the former Air Force enlisted man was captured on the Laotian side of the border and marched to a POW camp where he began a five-month odyssey through hell. Among a list of indignities, he was tied upside down to a tree while ants crawled over his face, dragged behind water buffalo, beaten by guards, and forced to supplement an inadequate diet with rodents, vegetation, and, in one instance, a snake which had recently eaten two rats. Dengler's weight dropped from 157 to 98 pounds.

Dengler escaped twice, the first time only eight days after his capture. He was recaptured within a relatively short time. Some five months passed before Dengler and six other prisoners again eluded their captors on 29 June. Twenty-two days later—after traveling in circles and watching Air Force Lt. Duane W. Martin beheaded by a local villager—rescue came by helicopter when an Air Force Skyraider pilot sighted the German native and radioed for assistance.

Dengler, the second and last American prisoner to successfully escape from a Southeast Asian prisoner of war camp, visited the *Ranger* and Lessard prior to going home. His return was shocking, but yet not totally so. "We said it then, and I still say it today. If anybody was to escape, it's Dieter," notes Lessard.

As Lessard could attest, Dengler marched to his own drummer.

On our cruise I roomed with Tom Dixon and next door was Dieter and a guy by the name of Don Farkas. I'm sleeping one morning, we'd flown the night before, and it's about ten or eleven o'clock. All of a sudden there's a thud, thud in the next room. I got up and yelled to Dieter, "What the hell are you doing?"

"Aw, I'm just checking something out over here, come on over."

I went over to the next room, and there's Dieter with his pistol shooting into a block of wood.

"Dieter, what are you doing?"

"Aw, I've got this silencer, I made it down in the machine shop coming across the water. Boy, I'm ready now."

I couldn't believe it, shooting a pistol on the ship. But that's Dieter.

Ken Hassett, our ops officer, was always after Dieter to get a hair cut. Dieter's German accent was very obvious, and he'd play dumb saying, "I don't understand." Dieter could really piss a person off, and he was always getting in trouble for his uniform or lack of military manner.

In the air, Dieter was a good pilot from what he had a chance to show right at the beginning because it ended real quick.

As far as him getting shot down or crash landing, or whatever, he did disappear on us. He said he was shot down, hit by ground fire. If Dieter was just playing around and saying, "I'm going to crash land the plane"—he did have his pistol and German passport with him, but I knew he carried that stuff on other flights—he landed in the worst place possible. The field looked like a forest fire had gone through and there were a lot of tree stumps. He either flew into it because he was very low, messing around, or got hit.

I saw Dieter again on July 21, my birthday. He was skin and bones; his tooth was broke. He stayed on the ship about a week, then went home. At first the Navy stashed him at Balboa Hospital in San Diego because he had a lot of malnutrition. Eventually Dieter ended up flying A-4s before getting out of the Navy.

Chapter 15
Purple Heart

Commander Wynn Foster, VA-163, and the aircraft carrier *Oriskany* returned to Dixie Station in late June 1966. Foster, who had suddenly assumed command of VA-163 following the shootdown of Harry Jenkins in November 1965, would just as suddenly lose that command less than a month later when a 37-millimeter shell tore through the cockpit of his A-4 Skyhawk, severing his arm.

The tragic incident had a definitive effect on the pilots of the *Oriskany*. Wrote VA-164 attack pilot Frank Elkins, in his journal, *The Heart of a Man,* "[Foster's] accident had given everyone a different twist in their bowels, a different fear. It's easier in some ways to see someone blown to bits instantly than to see a man lose his arm. I've always said it's easier to die for an ideal than to live for it. Dying takes only a moment's courage, while life is a battle against day-by-day eroding and grinding forces."

Foster remembers his short-lived reign as VA-163's skipper as far from typical.

The squadron had a one-month stand down after getting home [in late 1965]. Five month turnaround, one month stand down, and essentially four months to get ready to go back to war, and in the middle of all this we were expected to deploy for two weeks to Fallon.

I dug in my heels, telling CAG Bob Spruitt there's no way am I just going to lay back and accept that. We're going to have a morale problem, if nothing else in the squadron. Lemoore is called a master jet station, let them put their money where their mouth is and *be* a master jet station, and support the fleet the way it's supposed to be done. Is there any reason we can't load our planes here, fly the missions up to the targets at Fallon or El Centro [California], come back to Lemoore and be home with our families at night?

AIRPAC condescended to allow it on a trial basis, and I didn't bother to do any research and find out whether anybody else ever followed it up, or whether everybody just got back and did the old standard peacetime cycle.

The turnaround was [also] made somewhat traumatic by a decision to swap pilots with the East Coast, so we could spread the wealth, as it were. Trying to pick three pilots out of nineteen or twenty is a pretty agonizing situation for a CO, realizing a pilot is obviously going to look at leaving as a reward because he just got out of going back to war. Yet from the CO's viewpoint, I wanted to go back with the best possible squadron. Two of the three were transferred because I didn't have confidence in them and didn't want that problem in addition to all the other worries. One was a reward, Lt. Larry DeSha, who'd just gotten married and done a superb job. I thought what a great wedding present.

Heading back to Vietnam, the maturity among the guys who'd been there was a big advantage. The John Wayne-Jack Armstrong type of attitude was gone, except for Bill Smith. He was a hard charger, one I had to try and keep the reins on. I didn't want to inhibit him too much, so [that] he lost the hard charger attitude. Yet I didn't want him to get the impression he could do anything he wanted. Bill was a superior aviator—he could fly that airplane, and do things with the airplane like you couldn't believe. The problem was the junior officer with 400 or 500 hours of cockpit time who came along and said "I can do that too." But he couldn't.

Before getting back to combat, I had one kid who turned in his wings. The situation was very involved emotionally, and it's one of the prouder points, the high point, of my career as a CO. That kid was in the wrong business. He was going to kill himself and maybe somebody else. It was a case of something had to be done, either fire him outright, or try to get him to do the initiating, which is what happened. He finally made the decision after a series of conferences, agreed he was in the wrong business, and turned in his wings. The decision took a hell of a load off and made it a lot easier all the way around. He instantly turned into a different personality. It must have been a humongous burden for all those years, trying to maintain the image, live up to whatever criteria he had set for himself, and he was just living with a constant ulcer. When he finally made up his mind it wasn't for him, I was really pleased. I'd been a small part to saving a life.

Foster's final combat mission came on 23 July while leading a four-plane strike on POL storage near Vinh.

"I'd flown a lot of missions, been in a lot of pucker situations," remembers Foster. "I was always relatively cool, figuring if it happened, it happened. When it did, I couldn't believe it."

My wingman, Tom Spitzer, was flying his first combat mission, and I spent a lot of extra time at the briefing, wanting to make sure he didn't carry any uncertainties in with him.

We split up—Marv Reynolds was leading the second section, and I was going to come in from the north, going south, and Marv was going to follow about thirty seconds later. I never got there. Spitzer and I undertook flak, barrage fire, and all of a sudden there was this large bam. My canopy and the left half of the wind screen were gone, but my mask was on and visor down, so except for a lot of wind noise it wasn't completely uncomfortable.

I'd been doing about 450 knots when the shell hit, and it seemed to me within seconds the plane was going about 240 knots and starting to shudder. Two hundred and forty knots—that's too slow for a fully loaded combat aircraft. When I was hit, my arm must have jerked back instinctively and pulled the throttle back. What I first remember is the aircraft started falling off to the left, and I moved the stick to the right to level the nose and nothing happened. I looked down and the reason nothing happened, I didn't have an arm anymore. Blood was splattered all over the instruments and my right forearm was sitting down in the starboard console.

My initial emotion was utter disbelief, like I'm just hallucinating and I'll look again in a minute and the arm will be there. The next thing that went through my mind was I'm not going to become a POW and—having no idea whether I was even going to be able to survive long enough to make an intelligent choice—I turned and started heading back to the gulf. One of the lessons we learned early on in 1965, and it just became second nature, the Gulf of Tonkin meant safety. The gulf was security. Get out to the gulf where you had a fighting chance.

As soon as I crossed the beach I felt a lot better about it. It had crossed my mind that if I had to punch out over land fertilized with human dung, how long would I have lasted? I'd have been a statistic today. I still was in bad shape, and I realized I was in bad shape, but that bogeyman was off my back. They weren't going to get me.

I started getting tunnel vision, and realized I was close to passing out. So I grabbed the arm, and tucked it behind my vest for no other reason than not wanting to leave part of myself behind, reached up and pulled the curtain. In retrospect, I should have been presented some sort of medal for sport parachute jumping, landing within a quarter of a mile of the south side destroyer, and another medal for canny perception. I picked the only destroyer in the Gulf of Tonkin with a doctor on board. I didn't know that at the time, but he was there.

I jumped out at 200, 215 knots, landing in the water. The doctor said later it was one of the fortunate things that happened, going off and punching in the water—the salt water helped cauterize the blood vessels and slowed down the bleeding. There was a danger of dying, and I damn near killed myself by taking morphine. That's the worst thing for anyone in shock.

From the destroyer I went back to the *Oriskany*. There were all types of messages from brass throughout the fleet, and plenty of newspaper coverage. I was a hero for a couple of days. My change of command was at Cubi Point when the *Oriskany* went into port. I was brought up from sick bay on a gurney, went to sick bay at Cubi, then spent three agonizing days at Clark Air Force Base. The wound was still open, and the doctors stretched the skin, the most agonizing experience I've ever gone through. The doctors didn't feel they could properly treat the injury, and sent me stateside to Oak Knoll Naval Hospital [in Oakland]. I was high on Demerol all the way across the Pacific.

In 1966 there was very little to be found in the way of counseling. I was naturally inquisitive of my position as an officer after eighteen years. The only person I could find with an answer was a first class petty officer: "the best we can tell, you are going to be retired as a commander on 80 percent disability."

"Ah," I said, "the president of the United States no less, Harry S. Truman, signed my commission as an ensign in the U.S. Navy, and I've been around long enough to know the officer structure. You just don't get bumped out at someone's whim. What if I fight this all the way to the president and the president says no?"

"You'll probably retire at 80 percent disability as a commander."

That reply answered my question. There was no reason not to fight, and I did, and I was successful. I was just at the right place at the right time, the first guy since World War II to be retained on active duty with a major loss of limb.

Chapter 16
Oriskany

The morning of 26 October 1966 was unlike any previous morning in the Gulf of Tonkin since the air war in Vietnam had begun over a year-and-one-half earlier. The USS *Oriskany,* home to some three thousand men and Air Wing 16, was engulfed in fire, smoke, and the smell of death.

The *Oriskany's* early-morning flight operations had been cancelled because of bad weather over North Vietnam, and ship's personnel were in the midst of removing ordnance from aircraft for return to the storage areas. Below decks two sailors were transferring nearly seven-foot-long parachute flares from an ammunition cart in the passageway, to a storage locker. A single flare—capable of generating a brilliance of two million candlepower—was mishandled and ignited, setting off another 700 to 800 flares in the locker. The resulting explosion and fire opened a Pandora's Box of mayhem, threatening fuel supplies, the bomb-storage area, and ordnance-laden aircraft parked on the hangar deck.

It took three hours and seven minutes to extinguish the magnesium-fueled fire, a blaze that threatened the entire ship and killed forty-four officers and enlisted personnel, including twenty-five pilots. Many of the dead were asphyxiated—trapped in staterooms, victims of dense smoke and acrid fumes. Included in the toll was the *Oriskany's* air wing leader, Cmdr. Rob Carter.

"The fire on the *Oriskany* was a stupid mistake," related Denis Weichman, then a lieutenant commander assigned to Attack Squadron 164. "The people unloading the flares weren't qualified for the job—one was a cook if I'm not mistaken."

Some 350 bombs, including 1,000- and 2,000-pounders, were thrown overboard from the hangar and flight decks in the desperate effort to save the ship and lives.

"My room was destroyed by the fire," noted Weichman. He called the tragedy "very demoralizing, very sad. It was very tough to come back home with the squadron decimated like that." Four of the dead were pilots from Weichman's unit, Cmdr. Clyde Welch, the Ghostrider's executive officer; Lt. Cmdr. Daniel Strong, and Lts. (jg) William Johnson and James Brewer.

Weichman twice sailed to Southeast Asia with VA-164 and the *Oriskany,* undoubtedly two of the most tragic deployments of the Vietnam conflict. The 1966 cruise took the lives of eight Ghostrider pilots; in addition to the four in the *Oriskany* fire, four more were lost in the operational arena. Ensign George McSwain and Lt. Frank Elkins lost their lives while unsuccessfully maneuvering to avoid SAMs over North Vietnam. Lieutenant (jg) Donovan Ewoldt died as the result of an aerial refueling mishap, and Lt. (jg) Williard Bullard disappeared into the waters of the Gulf of Tonkin one August night after an ill-fated catapult launch.

The 1967 deployment, which began in June and ended on a chilly January morning as the *Oriskany* anchored in San Francisco Bay, earned near legendary status by virtue of extensive losses suffered. Two VA-164 pilots, Lt. Cmdr. Richard Perry and Lt. David Hodges, fell victim to SAMs, while Lt. Cmdr. John Barr and Lt. (jg) Fredric Knapp never left the cockpits as their A-4E's slammed into the soil of North Vietnam. A fifth pilot, Lt. Cmdr. Richard Hartman, fell victim to AAA fire on 18 July. Although captured, and sighted in a POW camp, Hartman never returned home. Five other Ghostrider pilots were shot down and rescued, including Weichman, who was picked up in the Gulf of Tonkin by a search and rescue crew.

For Weichman 1966 had marked the midpoint of five consecutive years in which he had seen combat in Vietnam, and the frustration of an ill-fought war was beginning to well forth.

Coming back from Vietnam in 1965, I had my choice of orders and transitioned to the A-4, then joined VA-164. We deployed to Vietnam in June of 1966 aboard the *Oriskany,* and my incentive at that point was to go out and win the war—I really felt we could. But there was so much frustration, hitting the goofy targets—the bamboo bridges and suspected supply dumps—and driving by the nice big targets, the Haiphong Harbor facility and the air fields. God, there was so much frustration—like the fishing boats. Sailing east to west across the gulf, they were supposedly fishing, so you were not to shoot at them even though they're radioing ahead every time a launch went off, reporting how many airplanes and what direction. But running north to south, then the boats are "bad." Or Haiphong Harbor—watching the damn tankers offload all the supplies. We should have mined that place early on.

There was a lot of ready room talk about the areas we couldn't hit, but one topic rarely discussed was why we were there in the first place. Nobody questioned that. Twenty-some years later I find that strange, but at that point nobody brought it up. The concern was why can't we do the job right. That question came up, sometimes vehemently, as people soon became tired of flying by all the good targets, unable to touch them.

Professionally there was a lot of competition within the squadron for the good flights; there really was. If somebody was left off an alpha strike, boy you'd hear about it. "Why can't I go? He went twice yesterday, now it's my turn to go twice." A lot of that bantering took place, which I thought was good. People weren't afraid to fly, in fact I don't know of any pilot who refused to fly in 164 or any of the squadrons I was with. Personally there was never a mission I was afraid to fly. Combat flying became routine after a while, and, in fact, complacency could set in and that was dangerous. Losing an airplane or a pilot would have the tendency to break the complacency, and we lost our share of pilots and planes.

One time, I became a bit disoriented while flying the Shrike, anti-SAM mission. Escorted by an F-8, I went in and fired a few Shrikes at the known sites. The escort called a SAM coming, telling me to break. I broke down and away, but the missile detonated underneath me and some of the shrapnel hit the nose of the airplane. The navigation system was lost. I became separated from the rest of the flight, and for the life of me, I couldn't remember how to get back to the gulf. My only navigation reference was visual, and I couldn't remember whether the sun came up in the east and set in the west, or vice versa. I made the right choice, but for a while the answer just wouldn't come. On the way back, I took another hit in the belly with an 85-millimeter, and eventually landed with no navigation system, no speed brakes, and 134 holes in the bottom of the airplane.

Experience was the key to confidence and survival. The first combat cruise involved a matter of getting used to combat, seeing and feeling what it's really like. Next time back, you built on that experience, really the big kid on the block instead of the new guy. There were many tricks of the trade that came from experience. No multiple runs especially in a high threat area; always jink to dodge the flak; don't release below standards; don't pull off the target area the same way each time; good aircraft separation—we had one SAM bring down two airplanes because the pilots were too close—and don't hang around the target and take pictures; that was definitely not such a good idea. A study in that time frame revealed most shootdowns were the result of a mistake—flying at the wrong altitude, flying over an area of known enemy concentration, or not watching what was going on outside the cockpit. Then there's fate, like when your number is up, it's up. Luck has a lot to do with it.

About three-quarters of the way through the '66 cruise the *Oriskany* fire occurred. I had just launched on a flight to Japan for a little R & R [rest and relaxation], and got back to the ship as fast as I could, picking it up about a week later, maybe even five or six days, in the Philippines. The squadron lost the XO, maintenance officer, four pilots in all. Really bad for morale. For a short time after the fire I ended up as the squadron XO.

In 1967 the *Oriskany* came back out, with the first combat flights taking place in late June. Dick Hartman was shot down in July, ending up on a little karst hill. We had radio contact and resupplied him for about three days. Eventually, the area became too hot—the North Vietnamese moved in a lot of troops and antiaircraft guns, and a few rescue planes and helicopters were shot down—and the decision was made to leave him. To this day, I can remember his voice pleading, "Please don't leave me." We had to, and it was a heartbreaker. Hartman was captured and later his name appeared on a POW list, but he never came out.

This second cruise was really a high point of the war, and we lost an awful lot of people. Air Wing 16 became known as "Bloody 16." It seems to me the squadron went out with fourteen brand new A-4s and something like twelve were shot down. Of course we picked up replacements, but really only one or two of the original planes were with us when we came home.

Some of the air wing's problems certainly were tactics, but when you go three times a day into Hanoi or Haiphong, three big alpha strikes, you're going to take some hits. CAG-16 was doing what had been done and worked in the past, but it didn't work in 1967. We followed the same tactics so often the North Vietnamese were setting up for it, they knew what to expect. Eventually, CAG picked up on a little diversity, helped by suggestions like "CAG, we're not flying with you anymore." Unfortunately, too many people would say yes, or go along with what

CAG wanted despite the fact it wasn't going to work. Somebody didn't want to make the leader mad.

During my last cruise in 1972, a Russian tanker had anchored near Hon Gai, and at night the little lighters would come out, tie up and take the fuel, then wait for the next evening and run it back. We sat up there with flares and got four of the lighters as they made the run back. When the line period ended, the ship went to Hong Kong, and a couple of us ran into the captain of the tanker at a bar. He was a nice guy, a Soviet, who told us "Hell, I'm just driving the ship and not involved in anything else." But he had a question. "Why do you guys go in at the same place every day, at the same time, and fly over the same gun, and get shot at every time? Why do you do that?" The question was a good one, and we certainly were guilty of real dumb things. Virtually all the alpha strikes had to be at the same time every day. Routinely, day in and day out, same time, same altitude. We'd come in at eighteen thousand feet, and the North Vietnamese knew it, setting all the charges for that altitude. They also knew we released at forty-five hundred feet and pulled out by thirty-five hundred.

Alpha strikes into Hanoi or Haiphong were exciting. You'd get seventy to one hundred SAMs coming up at the flight, just zipping by all over the place. The strikes would consist of thirty, maybe forty airplanes—whatever could get off the deck—and there'd be lots of excitement, lots of chatter on the radio. Sometimes there'd be no way to get a word in edgewise. Targets of opportunity, many times nothing was available to shoot at except a swinging bridge. Those targets were a waste of time—hard to hit and would be back up the next day anyway.

Shooting people didn't bother me a bit. Hell, those bastards were shooting back, and the only way to win a war is when there's not enough of them left to shoot. The only time I recall not shooting was a target of opportunity mission. I found some guy pulling this rickshaw-type thing down the road with hay or whatever in the back. He was looking back at me when I rolled in the first time, and just trying to run faster, and I just got to laughing and didn't shoot. I came back around, lined him up, and there he was again, looking back and wondering, "Is he or is he not going to shoot?" I just couldn't do it. Hell, the poor guy probably had an atomic weapon in the back of his rickshaw.

Chapter 17
Alpha Strike

Late 1966 found the Navy's fighter community in somewhat of a quandary. The basis for their dilemma was a lack of action up North. Two years of air combat had produced a mere fifteen MiG kills, certainly a less than stellar tally when compared to the excitement—and medals—generated by their attack counterparts.

According to retired Navy Captain Len Giuliani, "Some of the most boring missions were the fighter guys'." Giuliani, who totaled 357 Southeast Asian combat missions from an A-4 and A-7 cockpit in 1966–67 and 1971–72, asserts that "by and large, there were a lot of boring times for the fighter guys because only a small percentage of the time were the MiGs attacking."

The primary role of the fighters was TARCAP (target combat air patrol) protection for the strike group coming in and off the target, and BARCAP [barrier combat air patrol], protecting the aircraft carrier by way of a two- or four-plane "barrier" from possible MiG intruders.

"The fighters would get all nervous and cranked up," said Giuliani. "And don't get me wrong, they were over there facing a threat. But it wasn't the same threat. Statistics show 80 to 90 percent of the airplanes were lost within a mile-and-a-half of the target.

"That tells you a message: the fighter pilot was not facing the same threat, but I think he was facing the same adrenaline stimulus, so he was investing that into his day's work, with not much in return. In my mind, that made it a tougher mission mentally."

Within due time, added Giuliani, the fighter jocks "wanted to hang bombs on their airplanes and go drop bombs." Many of the F-4 and F-8 community did just that, taking on flak suppression duties and dropping bombs on targets when the need for aircraft sorties arose.

On his 1966 Gulf of Tonkin arrival, Giuliani was not a complete stranger to operations in Vietnam, having been assigned in the gulf to VA-94 four years earlier. "We were briefed on contingencies," noted the Princeton

graduate in speaking of the 1962 cruise, but the problems "weren't ours."
Four years later, all the problems were American—and growing.

When the war started, I was the weapons training officer [WTO] with
VA-125 [the West Coast A-4 training squadron]. The guys going through
the RAG—by and large they were charged up about the war. Some
didn't want anything to do with it, got out and went to the airlines, but
they were probably going to do that anyhow. I can't really think of a
guy who left because he was afraid to go to war. There were a lot of
fence sitters, most of whom stayed in because they'd been trained to
fight and the time had come to do it.

I made lieutenant commander in April of 1966 and went on cruise in
May aboard the *Constellation* with VA-153. I was the weapons training
officer and the assistant operations officer. The squadron included a lot
of relatively new folks, a half dozen or so nuggets [first tour aviators],
other guys who'd come back from non-flying tours, and three who were
fairly current.

There's a lot of apprehension of going into an unknown [situation],
and what calmed you was the realization it's *not* an unknown. Dropping
bombs is something you've done for a long time. What's unknown is
how you react at the moment of truth. As a nugget, I might have reacted
a little differently. But as a lieutenant commander my apprehensions
were about the combat environment, not could I handle the airplane or
handle myself in a bombing raid. I knew I could fly the airplane, drop
bombs, and hit targets. I had spent two years as a RAG instructor,
getting a lot of flight time. I was about as current as a guy could be
technically—I'd been the WTO and was as up on conventional weapons
and tactics as anybody. That background made it a lot easier to deal
with the other apprehension, the fact I'm dropping live bombs on people,
and they're allowed to shoot back and liable to hit me. Like anything
else, the more confidence you have in the task at hand, the better you
handle the environment.

My first combat mission came June 15 on Dixie Station. We flew
fifteen or twenty missions at Dixie, then went to Yankee Station. There
was a lot of action in 1966, a great deal of flying. Under ROLLING
THUNDER, the Air Force and Navy carriers were each given sectors
of the country to work, with broad guidelines as to the kinds of targets
and what needed to be accomplished in the line period.

As an example, the *Constellation* would roll into Yankee Station and be given Route Packages 2 and 3 to destroy lines of communications, concentrate on bridges, barge crossings, and so forth. That was the guideline, and it was up to the ship to accomplish the task. The way we chose to do it involved forming a group—myself as an attack pilot, two fighter pilots, and a photo guy—and each night we'd go to the combat information center [CIC]. On the wall would be a big chart of North Vietnam, and we'd look at our sectors and schedule photo missions to examine targets. Back would come the reconnaissance photography; and we'd see which targets we wanted to hit, based on our guidelines, and schedule the strikes. Our basic mode of operating was small strikes, launching anywhere from six to twelve airplanes at a time to go bomb a target. It was a good job, very interesting and time consuming. We'd go fly—twelve hours of ops—and then meet after ops, collect all the recon, and meet anywhere from four to eight hours.

These smaller strikes were interspersed with the large air wing alpha strikes, which the flag or someone above was directing. The flag was at least coordinating the alpha strikes, assigning targets to individual ships.

I felt the group of us in our little world were doing a good job, had control, and the chain of command listened to what we had to say. All of us felt pretty good about the way we were conducting business. Not everybody was happy about the way we dropped bombs on people and this kind of stuff—the war philosophy—but given the fact we were there and had to be doing it, we were doing all right.

The age-old problem that ran throughout the war was we weren't cut loose to really do a number on the North Vietnamese, and I agree with that. Yet I don't necessarily disagree with having to do it that way. It wasn't World War II, but [there was] a whole new philosophy of world relations—how countries get along with each other, diplomacy, and the whole nine yards. You can argue forever about the degree, but the theory of just tightening the screw a little at a time to accomplish your diplomatic mission was, I think, a valid one. When the big bomb is what's lying at the end of the road, and at the beginning of the war you're coming off twelve to fifteen years of an entire emphasis on the nuclear option, the theory of slowly tightening the screw is probably a good one.

What I used to tell the guys at Yankee Station—it's time to pay attention to the flight schedule, the target, and do it right. To me, survival was more important than worrying about something I had no control over. If you'd like to philosophize, be pissed off, or worry about this, that, and the other thing, wait until the ship gets back to Alameda, then worry all you want. Worrying over here will just increase your chances of maybe not going back.

That first cruise, in a thirty- or forty-day line period, we might fly ten alpha strikes. Rest of the time it was cyclic operations, midnight to noon, or noon to midnight, and we really concentrated on night, armed reconnaissance over the main lines of communication. Although everybody thought we were kind of crazy—in fact, our sister squadron, VA-155, thought we were—our forte was night, low-level weapons' delivery under the flares to get trucks. We had a pretty fair amount of success, started a lot of fires, got a lot of targets going. It was very effective. We lost one pilot, but in my own mind I can't say that the way we lost him was attributed to low-level tactics.

On the alpha strikes, target assignments were generated in the late afternoon or evening before. That night, strike leaders would be assigned, and they'd usually grab a team of one person from each kind of airplane, and plan the strike. The meeting consisted of gathering in-flight photography and the intelligence information available, planning a route to the target and coordinating with the strike operation people on the ship.

Also looked at was the type of support aircraft needed, electronic countermeasures, fighter cover for the TARCAP and BARCAP, where to put the support aircraft, and so forth. All that was discussed. This planning effort, sometimes simple, sometimes long and complex, usually lasted a couple of hours. During the process, a series of training aids would be made for presentation to the strike group at large. Usually it'd be on a piece of butcher paper, showing pictures of formations, diagrams of tactics to be used, and that sort of thing. A lot of the data—radio frequencies, IFF [identification, friend or foe] squawks, weapons data and so forth—you'd have to carry with you.

The next morning or afternoon, depending on the launch time, there'd be one mass gaggle briefing to discuss everything pertinent to the strike group and let everyone know what everybody else was doing. This would be followed by individual elements, depending on how the strike was going in.

The strike could be any time of the day, although as a general rule you were better off with the sun high. That way, no matter what direction you rolled in, the gunners were looking up into the air. Ideal was a

1:00 or 2:00 P.M. strike. If the sun is low at dawn or dusk, you can always plan your roll-in to come out of the sun, but while traveling to and from the target, gunners who aren't looking into the sun have a real good view of the group.

Depending on how big the strike, and how complex the brief, we allowed two hours, sometimes even two-and-a-half hours before the launch. If the brief started two-and-a-half hours before launch, that actually meant there were two hours, an hour and forty-five minutes, before launch to physically brief—with forty-five minutes to get suited up and on the flight deck, the airplanes turned, and the launch under way. It all depended on the target, where the threat was, how complex the strike, and how many planes were taking part. I participated in strikes which briefed for forty-five minutes, and others which took the full two-and-a-half hours and more.

Normal procedure would be to launch and rendezvous at some location, possibly over the ship or somewhere en route to the target. The fighters always had to tank, and, generally speaking, the tankers would tag along. About halfway to the coast, the admin stuff usually was over, and the strike group would form up into the final over-the-beach configuration. Typically, there'd be three groups of airplanes, one from each bomber squadron—so maybe ten to sixteen bombers. The navigation lead would normally be in one of the bomber elements in front of the group, followed by the three bomber groups and the support aircraft, normally fighters or an ECM guy. The TARCAP would be on either side, or maybe one trailing and one to the side just kind of floating around. The BARCAP would just go on and do their thing, generally leaving the strike group.

A typical mission would be a target say in the triangle between Nam Dinh, Hanoi, and Haiphong, and if the plan called for the medium altitude, SAM-evasion type exercise, the group would drive across the gulf at 10,000 to 14,000 feet and at a few miles off the coast, start descending to 7,000 to 10,000 feet. There'd be a max speed on the airplanes given the bomb load, and the whole gaggle would start a jinking evolution, usually a direct function of how nervous the strike leaders were.

Typically, the strike was maybe twenty, thirty minutes from the beach, at most, and by the time you were finished tanking, setting up all the switches—switches were my big personal task en route to the beach— and testing the ECM gear, it was time to turn the master arm switch on, descend, and go across the beach. So it wasn't really boring, but at times there wasn't a whole lot to do.

Coming across the beach, the tempo really picked up, and there was a lot of flying to do. The formation as often as not moved all the time, jinking, trying to navigate and maintain a position in the strike group, and trying to account for, and look at, SAMs coming here, there, and everywhere. Emotionally, a sense of apprehension is the best way I can describe coming across the beach. I wouldn't call it fear, although I guess it was. Something drove you to pay attention to what was going on because the North Vietnamese were serious. After watching a few guys go down to SAMs, well Jesus Christ, I'd better pay attention to what's happening. And the last thing you wanted to do was park an airplane over enemy real estate because you didn't watch the formation, screwed up, and flew into somebody.

There was a real drive to watch for the threats, looking for the SAM lift-offs, keeping your head on a swivel. As far as I was concerned, the cockpit work was done once the group hit the beach. That was the end of it for good because if the switches weren't set up, you screwed up. The only reason you might want to go into the cockpit is a quick navigation read, or you'd get a SAM track audible in the headset and couldn't find the SAM. The scope would give an indication of where the SAM was coming from, then you'd be right back out of the cockpit, looking.

The target time after hitting the beach depended on what route was taken in. Generally speaking, a coastal route, bam, you're in and out. Some of the high threat places we used to visit, like Thanh Hoa and Nam Dinh, were not that far off the beach, maybe two to eight minutes. There were quite a few deep targets, Phuc Yen, Hanoi, and a couple of places on the northwest railroad, which, depending on what route you'd take, could be as many as twenty or thirty minutes from the beach. The further northeast a group might go, towards Hanoi and the Red River, the coastal areas had to be crossed and the initial ten to twenty miles were well populated and a fairly high threat.

Personally if I wasn't looking and concentrating on threats or other airplanes, I was looking real hard at the ground and making absolutely certain where I was and what I was doing. I worked real hard at navigation, feeling along with the old salts that speed is life, and knowing where you are accounts for a lot too. Nothing would make me madder than to pop up and look down and find I'm not at the target area. People did get lost, and lost is not knowing where you were in relationship to the ground. To hit the target, you had to know exactly where the aircraft was to the ground. Simply, it was a matter of concentration, and I concentrated, looking for threats, other airplanes in the strike group, and navigation.

There were two ways to go after the target. Roll in all at one time, or quite often the group would split up into two groups. Some people liked three, but I felt it violated the KISS [keep it simple, stupid] program. Two groups are good because it splits the defenses. Generally speaking, each group would have a different aim point unless the target was a bridge or something. It wasn't unusual to have two different aim points in the target area and if the objective was an air field, there might be any number of points. For example, a couple of planes would go for the runway cuts at different points and others for aircraft and hangars.

Approaching at altitude, the target could be picked up visually. With a low-altitude strike and popping up, you were navigating like hell, and at the roll-in point, the task was simply following the guy in front and paying attention to interval. Releasing high, interval is not all that critical, but at low altitude the frag pattern from the guy in front of you is a problem. You're either right with him, or thirty seconds behind. Of course, the further behind the less healthy it was because the madder and madder the guy on the ground was getting. The best solution was get up as close as possible, and everybody get in and get out of the target area.

Rolling in, the concentration was finding the aim point. That's the whole purpose of being there, and again navigation played a major role. The more detailed navigation you'd done en route, the better off you were in trying to find the aim point.

Leading the strike group or element to the target, that was an easier problem than following, since your tasks were navigating and watching out for the threats. It got a little more difficult from behind, because you were watching out for airplanes, trying to keep the right interval for the bomb run, watching for threats, and trying to find the aim point. The actual bomb run, you either made your own or flew on some guy's wing and released when he did. From an odds point of view, everyone was better off to make their own bombing line because once the nose was pointed at the ground, you were predictable anywhere from two to eight seconds, and if the ground folks could see your roll-in point, they might put up a barrage, and there was a chance to get hit. No rule prevented you from being hit in the run—probably 80 to 90 percent of our losses were within a mile-and-a-half, two miles of the target—although there was a lot to be done to reduce the chances of getting hit.

A minimum pullout—3,000 to 3,500—kept the aircraft above the small arms fire and reduced the number of bullets available. Above the minimums, the worry was the 37-, 57-, 85-millimeter guns. You really never were out of their range. On a low-level mission, the alternatives were to pop up to 400 or 500 feet for a level delivery, or up to 6,000 or 7,000 feet and complete a twenty-degree dive.

Low level was, and is still, a big point of controversy, and it's dangerous. You can't do it every day, and that's what got people in trouble. When I came back in 1972, we carried out low-level tactics for alpha strikes. I can think of one particular strike where it wasn't the smart thing to do, and another where it worked absolutely perfect. On the day Randy Cunningham shot down three MiGs, we were one of three carriers conducting strikes and our target was the Hai Duong Bridge, kind of in between Hanoi and Haiphong. Sixteen to eighteen planes at one hundred feet right up the valley behind Thud Ridge, which spits out into the delta about ten miles north of Hai Duong. We just turned south, popped up, dropped our bombs and got out of there. We saw guys in parachutes; SAMs were going off all over the place. Yet only at the top of my pop-up did I hear a very brief audio tone indicating a SAM radar and not in a track mode, but a search mode, and that was it. Never a peep out of the ECM gear, never saw a round fired, and while we saw SAMs, they were going at other people. I did take a hit, a small arms shot in the wing, and I have no idea when I got it. But that was it, sixteen or so planes got in and out, while the other wings were going into the jaws of the dragon. For that day, low level was the way to go.

After dropping bombs on a target, the usual tendency is to look back, but only if everybody is in sight. It's absolutely typical to look back at where the bomb went, and I don't think I ever dropped a bomb that I didn't look back.

Once the bombs were gone, you dialed in four or five Gs or whatever to get that nose over the horizon. As soon as the nose was over the horizon, you released the Gs and turned one way or the other. You had to know which way the guy in front was going to turn, and the guy behind had to know what you're going to do. Not predict, but he had to know. The idea was to maintain integrity off the target, and pick a route to get back that was just as safe as the route you came. Hopefully you cleaned all the bombs off your wings, were light on fuel, and now had a high-speed, highly maneuverable airplane. As often as not, we'd just go down about fifty feet and scream across the delta as fast as we could go. A preplanned exit was nowhere near a populated area, and you just didn't haul ass to the beach. It was important to maintain integrity, and the only way to do that was by briefing the exit just as well as you briefed the entry.

The place where the strike usually went to hell in a hand basket was pulling off the target—there was bomb smoke all over the place, and guys were doing this, that, and the other thing. You really had to pay attention to what was going on.

The most dangerous part of the mission was over, once the bombs were off, or at least the odds were much better because en route to the target you were in this big, bulky airplane, carrying a lot of crap on the wings, which is not very maneuverable. Then you had the bomb run to make, which is not the best bet. Now, you're through all that, through the 80–90 percent casualty area, and hopefully the bombs hit the target and you feel just great. Yet you had to be careful and not get carried away, or misnavigate, fly over somebody's downtown, and get popped off with a .45. But no question about it, you did feel a lot better on the way out.

Chapter 18
The Golden Dragons

The "World Famous Golden Dragons" of Attack Squadron 192 returned to the waters off North Vietnam in November 1966, their third combat deployment and a cruise that would prove to be both intense and noteworthy.

By December Cmdr. Ed McKellar had taken command of the highly honored NAS Lemoore–based squadron, relieving Cmdr. Alan "Boot" Hill. At this time the squadron, flying the A-4E Skyhawk off the deck of the carrier *Ticonderoga,* was participating in bombing efforts that inched progressively closer to North Vietnam's two largest cities, Haiphong and Hanoi.

Four months later, as the monsoon season came to a close, the Dragons took part in strikes considered by some to be the most intense of the Vietnam air war, and possibly in the history of air warfare as well. That month, VA-192 lost Lt. Cmdr. Mike Estocin during a strike on the Haiphong thermal power plant. Estocin's actions on that mission and on another earned him the nation's highest military award, the Medal of Honor, the only Navy jet pilot to earn that distinction for a combat role.

McKellar brought to the squadron a vibrant attitude, talent, experience, and confidence. He had completed some 125 combat missions in Korea, he had flown with the elite Blue Angels flight demonstration team, and he was eager for the challenges of command.

"I think it probably helped my image more than my leadership ability," said McKellar of his background. "When you walk into a ready room, it's not the stripes on your sleeves, it's where you've been in the air that another aviator takes [as] the measure of a guy."

"It's nice to be able to come in and have a tour with the Blue Angels under your belt, and a war already under your belt; so when you stand up and say, 'Follow me,' they're apt to do it rather than wonder where in the hell you're taking them."

I flew out from the states, joining the squadron in December of 1965 as the Tico and squadron were just completing their final line period, and spent Christmas in Hong Kong. Why did I do that? Certainly I could have waited for the ship to get back to the States. Two reasons. In those days you never knew when they were going to turn around and extend the ship. It was usually the rule for that to happen, not the exception. Number two, I wanted a chance to meet the personnel in the outfit under an operational environment rather than try and get acquainted with them when they understandably had their mind set on something else after nine or ten months at sea.

I had a good ten days in Hong Kong laughing and scratching with these guys who were going to be flying for me, and with me, and then spent about eighteen days in transit back to the States. By the time we got back, I had a pretty good measure for each one of the guys in the outfit, whereas it would have taken me a good two months to get that knowledge had I waited for the ship to get back to the States, and them to get back from leave.

The CO was Alan ''Boot'' Hill. We'd gone to war college together, and he and I served in VA-125, the A-4 RAG, before he went over to take 192. I had the measure of the man, I liked him personally and professionally, and I found it very desirable to work for him as XO.

At this time there were some eighteen or so A-4 outfits at Lemoore, and the Navy had set up this competitive system for the Battle E [Efficiency] Award and the Safety Award. Whether or not those particular elements accurately measured a squadron is not important, the fact was they were being awarded by the Navy for the best overall battle efficiency, based on numerous measures, and the best safety record. These honors were available to win, and so I figured we've got to be best on the mountain in our community. Once you get to be the best, cram it down the other guy's throat. This way you get all the other squadrons to hate you, and it's a competitive hate, because you're king of the mountain. It's my guys against everybody else.

By getting this syndrome going, and first you had to be the best— you can't be lousy and say you're good because everybody laughs at you—then every time you go to happy hour, you go as a glob. We never went to happy hour unless all of us were there except the duty officer. I felt nothing could be worse than to walk in at happy hour at Lemoore and have people ignore you. We'd walk in, and everybody would say, "Here come the Golden Worms," and that type thing. Super, we fed on it. They noticed us. To be ignored was unacceptable, and the JOs felt it. You against the world, because once you got over there, to Vietnam, and got feet dry, it *was* you against the world. So we just used the other squadrons as training vehicles, and there was one helluva lot of leadership at Lemoore in those days. We were just an element of it.

In combat we were better than everybody else out there. Whether we were or not is immaterial because each one of those guys in the ready room were convinced we were God damn good. We were good at winning Es, we were good at safety awards, we were good at every competitive measure, so we had to be good out there. It's all up in your head, and we, the squadron leaders, kept reinforcing this by saying the other squadrons just can't wait to knock you guys off. Quit screwing around at the ramp, tighten up the landing intervals, pay attention over the beach. It's not the Vietnamese, it's these other squadrons just waiting to knock us off. You couldn't beat the Vietnamese under the frigging rules and guidelines coming down from Washington, D.C.; you couldn't win that war. So let's fight this one, and that was part of the motivation.

With this ready room psychology, all for one and one for all, it came out across the beach when we went feet dry. It was a natural evolution. We were better when we got here, so we've got to be good over the beach. I had those JOs fighting for the Shrike missions, and they were really the most dangerous God damn thing over there. It was wild, no question about it. I never said, "Okay, you've got the Shrike today." Never. That had to be something people volunteered for before we got over there, during the turnaround and training, and we set the stage by saying, "This is going to be a high risk job that somebody is going to have."

The Shrike pilots, these guys more than any other element of the alpha strike program, kept the alpha strike formations in one piece. They were out there ahead of the strike group by five to seven minutes literally chumming for SAMs, literally *chumming* for them. And they did a damn good job. Estocin ate it because of it, and that's regretable, but that was their job and they recognized that fact. The more SAMs we could get to fire at the Shrike missions, the fewer SAMs were being fired at the formations, which had to basically stay together to complete their part of the mission.

Early on we teamed one Shrike pilot up with one of the fighter jocks from VF-191 or -194, and those two flew together all the time. We didn't break that up—it wasn't, "Sam has got the duty so get another F-8 wingman"—those guys flew together every time they had a Shrike mission, and they practiced together on the beach before we even got to Vietnam. They knew each other very well and just carried that across the beach with them.

Those air wings that did not refine the Shrike tactics were getting busted up, broken up by the volleys of SAMs the North Vietnamese were shooting at us. I don't want to comment on other air wings and their tactics, but I do know Air Wing 19 alpha strikes were never busted up by the volley firing of SAMs. I'm not saying we didn't get SAMs fired at us in the alpha gaggle, but never to any number that would break it up and destroy our ability to complete the mission. A lot of the air wings kept the Shrike guys basically on the wings of the formation, which we felt was ludicrous, and in CAG-19 we didn't do it that way. Developing the Shrike tactics was probably our best accomplishment from a combat standpoint.

The number of Shrikes on board the ship depended on the pipeline. Sometimes there would be more than enough; other times we wouldn't have enough, there'd be a shortage. In that case we'd have to hold the Shrikes on the rails until getting a definite indication of a SAM tracking, then we'd fire. When there were plenty of them, then we'd just try to keep Shrikes in the air at all times. We didn't care where in the hell they went; certainly we hoped they'd go against the radar screen. But the fact the North Vietnamese knew that we had an antimissile weapon in the air had to influence them the same way we knew there was a SAM coming at us. That influenced our thinking, and if it didn't, it certainly should have.

Our bottomline: if we got the North Vietnamese to turn off their tracking equipment, it's just as if the damn site was knocked out. All you needed to do was knock the site out for maybe twelve minutes or so, average, and the alpha gaggle was on and off the target. So if they turned off the damn radars for that length of time, the mission was accomplished. That's why if there was no shortage of Shrikes, we'd keep the damn things flying all the time as soon as there was any indication of radar search or radar tracking.

The SAM site operators, some were very proficient, some inefficient as hell. There was an element of training on their part, much the same way some squadrons were a little bit more prepared than others. Some sites were damn good, others weren't worth a damn.

The primary Shrike pilots in the '67 time frame included Gary Scoffield, [Mike] Estocin, Rick Millson, John Parks, and Jay Finney. Mike had really hung it out in late April. It was a concentrated period of time, we were in the Haiphong-Hanoi area on four different occasions just before the end of the line period. He was hit April 20 but got back, and on April 26 he got bagged. I don't know what was going on in Mike Estocin's navel, so far as he was calm, excitable, or what. But outwardly he was ideally suitable for the Shrike missions that he volunteered for. Mike was always the guy who wanted to be out on the point doing something extra. When he wasn't flying, his job on the ground for the squadron was always something interesting. He was just a helluva good, all-around naval officer. Just give him a job and he got it done.

We put Mike in for a Navy Cross, wrote the citation up, and left the line. While in Hong Kong, word was received from Seventh Fleet that if we'd resubmit Estocin's Navy Cross, the climate was very favorable to get a Medal of Honor approved. I think it was about 20 percent political, 80 percent accomplishment.

In those days, by the letter of the law, you weren't able to combine separate missions and say, because of all these things, he deserves this. It was one mission, one award. But in this particular case, we wrote the thing up because it was a very concentrated two-day period, and then submitted it. The second time, we sat in the Hong Kong admin suite trying to write this Medal of Honor citation, which I thought was kind of a little unusual—laughing and scratching in Hong Kong trying to write a Medal of Honor. But we did, submitted it, and he certainly deserved it. I would have written it up as a Medal of Honor to start with except they just weren't giving them out. He certainly richly deserved it.

Our wing commander was Billy Phillips, a born and bred fighter pilot. Billy was good, and he loved to fly; and Billy was frustrated as hell because he couldn't get a MiG, but that's aside from the point. He recognized the fact he had some damn good attack jocks running the show and also understood the name of the game was getting ordnance on the ground, not necessarily getting ordnance in the air. It was important to keep MiGs off you while performing a mission, but the mission was air-to-ground, the mission wasn't air-to-air. He understood that and let us take the lead on those things.

When the weather permitted, alpha strikes were flown twice a day, one in the morning and another in the afternoon. That's really the most you could pull, although on a long summer day you might get off three.

From my own point of view, the toughest element about an alpha strike was waiting to go. We had weather holds in those days. If you went out in September, the carrier got the winter on Yankee Station, a relatively low overcast over Route Packages 4, 5, and 6, the northern part of Vietnam. During the other part of the year, that area would be relatively clear and Laos, Route Packages 1, 2, 3, and South Vietnam would clobber up. We were out there in 1966–67 during the period of time when the northern portion would suffer more overcast, so a lot of times we'd be on these weather holds waiting to go. A target was approved, I'd get strapped in the cockpit, sometimes get the engine started and taxiing towards the cat, and the weather recce would come back and say no.

So the starting and stopping was a big pain in the ass to me because I was generally either leading the whole damn thing as one of the COs, or one of the groups if it was a two-element type of strike. Then having to back it all out and wait and go again in the afternoon, or again tomorrow, that was the tough part.

There was always a weather divert, and most of the time the weather divert would be open. I don't think it happened but once or twice, that by the time we got to the target, after the weather recce said, "Yes it's going to be open," that we actually couldn't get through a hole and get down and hit a target. But we always had a fallback position; if the target was clobbered, everyone had an alternate place to dump ordnance. And you always had the dump X down there in the DMZ, horizontal bombing which I always thought was really a way to piss away ordnance. But we never dumped ordnance in the ocean.

In VA-192, the typical ordnance load was a duty centerline drop tank and usually three 500-pound bombs on each wing. The squadron always had the Shrike missions, a minimum of two sections. If we were going to downtown Hanoi, we'd sometimes have three Shrike sections. Generally, there were twelve to fourteen birds on the ship. Let's say there were a couple back at Cubi for heavy maintenance, so twelve were free, and with the Shrike mission, you're down to ten for strike. The other A-4 outfit might be able to produce all twelve, so generally speaking you might end up with eighteen air-to-ground A-4s, and this is a small deck air wing. Eighteen strike birds, a couple of Shrike sections, and usually a minimum of four sections of CAP escort.

There was tension on an alpha strike; it was nothing like getting in the car and going to church. The longer you stayed on the line, the shorter people got with one another. But again more than anything else, it was the waiting around after getting geared up to go. I was never bothered once we got going, it was just the damn waiting around.

Target selection, that was done for us. You could argue whether hitting a bicycle factory in downtown Hanoi was really worth the trip, but that was the target. We were always pretty much left to our own devices so far as how we were going to perform the mission, how we were going to hit the target, which I was thankful for from an operational standpoint. Whereas, the Air Force philosophy, the damn thing was spelled out from start to finish—the tactics, the approach, the exit, how to hit them, what's the dive angle, what's the release point—all spelled out, which I thought was gross. Too often it was all spelled out the same way day after day, and the North Vietnamese are not stupid; they ate the Air Force alive a lot of times. At least with us, if we wanted to go in at one altitude, and another altitude the next, and vary this and vary that, we could. We concentrated on doing whatever we possibly could; we never showed them the same formation twice. At one time, the squadron experimented with three-plane divisions instead of four in our alpha strikes. There was an element leader, with a guy flying loose on each wing, and it was easier to maneuver against SAMs and that sort of thing than the four-plane division. The idea never caught on but it worked very well for us in a combat situation, which is a traditional deviation.

As the squadron CO, I had two objectives. First was to bring everybody back alive because it's no fun going to some wife or girlfriend and trying to explain what happened. Well, I obviously didn't achieve that, losing the XO [Mel Moore], operations officer [Mike Estocin], and the maintenance officer [Dick Stratton], which lets you know the front office was out there taking the lead on these things. I mean we didn't drop JOs. We could have, but we didn't. It was the department heads and the front office hanging it out the most.

Moore and Estocin were on Shrike missions, and beyond any reasonable doubt that was the highest-threat mission over there. If you look at the F-8 losses, and I'll bow to history, but most of the F-8 combat losses came in support of Shrike missions. Stratton shot himself down. He just woke up and had a bad day. How do you account for that?

Death and losing folks, well it goes with the territory. But when you take a loss, the important thing is you don't sit around and dwell on it. If the morale in the ready room is borderline to start with, the loss of a key guy may be enough to send you off the deep side and things really start going down hill. But if you go out there well trained and with a lot of spirit—and nobody enjoys not having Sam at the dinner table when you had breakfast with him—you can live with it. I think morale and motivation represent the key and essential elements that we're dealing with. If you've got people that have that overused phrase of "esprit de corps," if the unit has morale, then they've got the situation by the balls, and really can do most anything. And that spirit is built on knowing that you're good.

My other objective was to keep CAG off my back. That's it, bring as many people back as possible and get the job done. What else is there? There isn't anything. Everything else is bullshit.

I kept a relaxed atmosphere, and the JOs were pretty damn relaxed. We were the first to get Corfam shoes and everybody wears them now. We'd come to inspection looking better than anybody else, but hadn't spent a helluva lot of time with the Kiwi polish and all that. We didn't want scuffed shoes, but there were other things to do more important. Our brass buttons were anodized, never needed to be polished yet looked like they were chrome plated.

My command change with Boot Hill was in midair. Why? It was ludicrous to take the time in the middle of Yankee Station operations for everybody to get in their duty white suit and go to the focsle and have a change of command in the middle of the frigging war. That was a little much, out of place as hell, whereas having a change of command in the air seemed very appropriate to me. We came back over the ship after a mission, had a little three minute change of command in the air, nobody dropped a stitch, and we didn't waste a whole bunch of time. Made a lot of sense and the JO's loved it; they didn't have to get out of their sweaty flight suits and get into tropical whites to watch a couple of other guys play change of command. In this particular situation, it's how you got the thing out of the way as quickly as possible. We honest to God didn't have time to do it the way it's supposed to be done, and this just made a lot of sense.

To write medal citations, I devised a way to do it as easy as possible.

During our turnaround in 1966, Gary Scoffield, the administrative officer, went down to AIRPAC, or wherever I sent him, and gathered up all the approved medal citations from the Navy Cross on down. I wasn't interested in the citation itself, only the justification, and we created a little medal booklet.

I told Gary, "When you get over to Yankee Station, flying two alpha strikes a day, you're not going to want to stay up all night writing these things. You're as lazy as all the rest of us. Just get the ones that have been approved, and let's build an awards' manual." I wanted Estocin to win an award, and I didn't want to keep the admin officer up any later than the rest of us. All that had to be done was change date, place, and person. The people approving the medals, they have normal tours, so the selection board was never the same, and anyway, they weren't going to say, "Didn't I read this last year?" Kind of ludicrous, isn't it? But I have a philosophy about medals. Number one, we passed too damn many of them out. I think there's a definite purpose when properly applied, but too often we get in medal races the way we got in what are called sortie races. This air wing must be better because they got five Silver Stars and umpteen DFCs [Distinguished Flying Cross] and we didn't earn that many.

Many simply get awards because, okay, you were CO of a squadron. All CO's of squadrons get Bronze Stars at the end of their tour. The Bronze Star I always thought of as a combat award, but this one is for being CO for a period of time and not getting fired. Too often you'd go over the beach and perform a mission, and get a medal for it. What I'm saying is we gave out too many.

When a guy, myself, finishes up his military career with two Silver Stars, two Legions of Merit, three DFCs, two Bronze Stars, thirty-two Air Medals, and so on, it really is a little too much. Nobody could have done all that, and somewhere in there, there has got to be a twinge of bullshit. Probably a great deal of it. Or when I look and see the Joint Chiefs of Staff all sitting in their regal splendor. [Former CNO Adm. Jim] Holloway, I love Admiral Holloway, but he's got so many medals his wings are underneath the shoulderboards. Isn't that a little gauche?

As for the sortie race, hell it was a statistical war. We were into counting everything. We counted bodies on the ground; we counted missiles in the air; we counted number of sorties; just a statistical game. McNamara was a statistical guy; he enjoyed statistics. Everybody enjoyed statistics. Statistics got you the E, statistics got you the Safety Award. So if somebody had been out there before and the air wing had flown X number of sorties, we wanted to beat that. It was this competitiveness again, not necessarily generated from Washington at all, but generated within ourselves. Plus, whether we admitted it or not, we were flying against the Air Force. The Air Force flew this many missions, how many missions can the Navy fly? And after the war is over, all you've got is statistics and losses, and they're statistics within themselves. So when you're going to justify the next military budget before Congress— hey, we did this, they did that. We were helping the Navy compile their stats, plus we all enjoyed flying to start with, and you'd be as bored as hell on the ship, so you might as well fly.

Winnability of the war was not an issue we dwelled on as professional aviators. We were being paid to fly under the ground rules that were specified, and that's what we did. I'm sure each and every one of us sometimes dwelled on the unexplainable ground rules under which we had to operate. It was particularly difficult in a command position explaining it to a junior officer if he asked. Fortunately I didn't get that question too many times.

My guys, with very few exceptions, enjoyed the act of flying off aircraft carriers, and they reveled in the comradery of being with others who enjoyed this profession. Sure we all thought about going over there and getting shot at and laying your ass on the line for an unwinnable purpose, but it's nothing that you dwelled on. You couldn't dwell on it, for God's sake, or it would destroy you.

The all-weather A-6 Intruder began combat operations over North Vietnam in July of 1965. Nearly a year later, Attack Squadron 65, commanded by future admiral Robert C. Mandeville, arrived on Yankee Station aboard the carrier Constellation. Mandeville's Intruders flew almost 1,300 day and night sorties, dropping over 10 million pounds of ordnance during their June to November, 1966, combat operations.

USS Enterprise, *home to A-4 Skyhawk Attack Squadrons 36, 76, 93, and 94, arrives at NAS Alameda on June 21, 1966, following an eight-month combat tour. VA-94 pilot Lt. (jg) Bill Shankel missed the return, shot down on 23 December 1965.*

Lt. Cmdr. Robert Turgeon of Attack Squadron 22 brings his damaged A-7E Corsair aboard the carrier USS Coral Sea for a barricade landing following a 1972 combat mission over North Vietnam. VA-22 pilots—led by Redcock executive officer Len Giuliani, a veteran of three Southeast Asia combat tours—participated in the mining of Haiphong Harbor in early May.

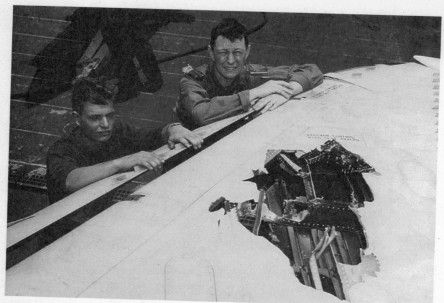

This A-4C flown by Attack Squadron 153 executive officer Cmdr. Dave Leue—photographed with his plane captain—was hit by 37/57 millimeter gunfire during a 17 July 1966 combat mission flown from the Coral Sea. The hole on the underside of the wing was approximately twice the size of the upper hole.

Pilots of Attack Squadron 216, the Black Diamonds, brief an upcoming combat hop in the unit's ready room aboard the carrier Bon Homme Richard.

A-4C of Attack Squadron 153, the Blue Tails, assigned to the carrier Constellation *in 1966. During their May to November combat deployment, VA-153 pilots averaged 99 missions each, a quarter of which occurred at night underneath flares.*

A week after participating in the 5 August 1964 Gulf of Tonkin retaliatory strike, two A-1H Skyraider pilots from Attack Squadron 145 fly over the Constellation. *The lone fatality of the strike, and the first naval aviator killed during the war, was Lt. (jg) Richard C. Sather of VA-145.*

Attack Squadron 147 A-7A in flight over the carrier Ranger *following a combat mission. Lt. (jg) Rusty Scholl and his fellow Argonaut pilots were the first to fly the A-7 in combat during their 1967–68 deployment.*

Rockets are armed prior to launch of an A-1 Skyraider. The intensity of the air war over North Vietnam proved too much for the dependable but slow A-1, and by 1968 her days as a combat aircraft had ended.

A-4 readies for launch off the flight deck of the carrier Intrepid. *Lt. Cmdr. Linn Felt served as* Intrepid's *strike operations officer throughout the carrier's initial Vietnam deployment in 1965, a unique tour because of the ship's all-attack role.*

Bombs fall from the racks of an A-4 Skyhawk over North Vietnam. By war's end, 257 A-4s had been lost in combat flights alone, attesting to the deadly threat facing Navy light attack pilots.

A-4C Skyhawk from Attack Squadron 93 recovers aboard the Ranger *in early February, 1965. VA-93 and sister squadron VA-94, led by Cmdr. Paul Peck, participated in both FLAMING DART raids and the early stages of ROLLING THUNDER.*

Five Mk-83 1,000-pound bombs and seven-shot rocket pods are loaded aboard VA-215 A-1 Skyraider embarked aboard Hancock.

Snakeye bombs, with fins open, stream behind a strike aircraft.

Simultaneous strikes were made on 16 January 1968 by A-7As from Attack Squadron 147 against highway and railroad bridges crossing the river at Hai Duong. In upper left corner, A-7 begins roll-in on a bridge.

"Bomb farm" aboard the Ranger. Ordnance is stacked outside carrier island in preparation for launch.

A-4 Skyhawk from Attack Squadron 164 fires off a Shrike anti-radiation missile. The Shrike mission over the skies of North Vietnam was considered by many to be the most dangerous task of the air war.

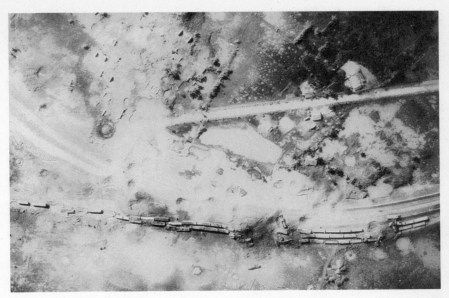

Alpha strike launched on 21 September 1966 from Constellation *destroyed a railroad yard east of Thanh Hoa and south of the Thanh Hoa bridge.*

Smoke billows after A-7 strike against barges hidden along side of North Vietnam river. Timeframe is 1967–68.

Zuni rockets, four to a pod, loaded aboard an A-7 Corsair. Lt. Cmdr. T. R. Swartz, flying an A-4C Skyhawk on 1 May 1967, shot down a MiG-17 with a zuni rocket while on a flak suppression mission.

A-7 Corsair from Attack Squadron 147 seconds away from landing aboard the Ranger. *Noses of an A-6 Intruder and F-4 Phantom are visible at left, and trailing the carrier is the plane guard destroyer.*

Part Four
1967

Some are worried about civilians killed in North Vietnam. I'd rather see them weep a little over some of our aviators who are being killed.

Sen. Sam Ervin, Jr., North Carolina Democrat and member of Senate Armed Services Committee, quoted in *U.S. News & World Report*, 23 January 1967.

Introduction

As the third year of the conflict in Southeast Asia unfolded, U.S. military commanders, most notably U. S. Grant Sharp, commander of American forces in the Pacific, pushed hard for an expanded air campaign in North Vietnam. In no uncertain terms, Sharp told top officials of the Johnson administration the flow of supplies from China and Russia must be stopped and proposed a plan to destroy six basic areas in North Vietnam: electric power, war industries, transportation, military bases, POL, and air defense.

Sharp's requests, and those of the Joint Chiefs of Staff, were heard, debated, and, to some extent, acted upon. President Johnson's "spring air offensive" included attacks on electrical and power plants, as well as the mining of rivers and the relaxation of restrictions on air raids near Hanoi and Haiphong.

The Navy's first "smart" weapon—the Walleye TV-guided air-to-surface glide-bomb—made its combat debut in March with Attack Squadron 212 (VA-212) commanded by Cmdr. Homer Smith, based on the USS *Bon Homme Richard*—nicknamed the "Bonnie Dick." Pilot controlled, the Walleye locked onto its target prior to dropping. After the bomb was released, the TV-eye directed the bomb toward the aim point without further pilot support. The initial launch on 11 March went against a large military barracks at Sam Son, and on Commander Smith's releasing it, the bomb, as promised, hit the intended target, plummeting into a window of the barracks.

In terms of sheer numbers, U.S. aircraft in April flew nine thousand attack sorties, a figure that jumped to eleven thousand sorties during May and June. Increased American military activity in the Hanoi/Haiphong area brought a deadly reaction from the North Vietnamese. Seven U.S. aircraft were shot down during some fifty April air-to-air engagements, and five fell victim to surface-to-air missiles, as a new high of 246 SAMs reportedly were fired. But in May seventy-two air-to-air engagements turned in favor of American aviators as twenty-two MiGs were blown from the sky and just two U.S. aircraft were lost.

Evidence of the expanded bombing campaign saw an estimated 85 percent of the total electrical capacity of North Vietnam inoperative by mid-June, the result of the power plant attacks in the Hanoi/Haiphong area. More telling was the toll on the people of North Vietnam. Continual air strikes over Hanoi, wrote John Colvin, counsel general of the British Mission in Hanoi during 1966–67, "seriously inhibited schooling, repair work, and cultivation. . . . The country and its people were close to collapse which, for the first time, no amount of excited exhortation could correct."

Military pressures for widening the war continued throughout the summer on an unrelenting basis, and President Johnson eventually approved all but about a dozen of the fifty-seven targets the Joint Chiefs of Staff requested. On 20 July sixteen targets were approved including a previously forbidden airfield, a rail yard, two bridges, and twelve barracks and supply areas, all within the restricted circles around Hanoi and Haiphong. Three weeks later—9 August—an additional sixteen fixed targets and an expansion of armed reconnaissance were approved. Efforts were also undertaken to isolate Haiphong with strikes against road, rail, and canal traffic.

The mounting pressure was interrupted, however, when the North Vietnamese put out peace feelers. All bombing in central Hanoi was halted for ten days on 24 August. That hiatus eventually extended through October.

August also witnessed hearings on the air war by the Preparedness Subcommittee of the Senate Armed Services Committee. Chaired by Sen. John C. Stennis, the hearing, as reported in the New York Times–published Pentagon Papers, "gave the public its first real knowledge of the policy division between Secretary McNamara and the Joint Chiefs over bombing." McNamara, as noted in Sharp's Strategy for Defeat, "took issue with the military view of the air war, and defended the bombing campaign to date as being carefully tailored to our limited purposes in Southeast Asia, aimed at selected targets of strictly military significance." The bombing of North Vietnam, he emphasized, "had always been considered a supplement to, not a substitute for, an effective counterinsurgency land and air campaign in South Vietnam." By year's end, McNamara resigned from the post he had held for Presidents Johnson and Kennedy.

Another first occurred in October as Navy pilots struck the Phuc Yen Airfield, the largest in North Vietnam. Situated twelve miles north of Hanoi, the field was hit on 24 October by four consecutive strikes fifteen minutes apart, two from the Air Force, and one apiece by Constellation and Coral Sea air wings. Home to nearly twenty-five MiG-21s and seventeen other aircraft, the base welcomed Navy and Air Force pilots with defense from an estimated seventy-two 85-millimeter and 120 37/57-millimeter guns, and approximately thirty-five known SAM sites in the target and approach areas.

Ho Chi Minh and friends feverishly expanded their surface-to-air missile batteries throughout the year. There was an estimated jump in visual SAM sightings from 990 in 1966 to an incredible 3,500 in 1967. On average fifty-five SAMs were required to down one American aircraft in 1967, compared to thirty-three in 1966 and thirteen in 1965—testimony to the increased experience of U.S. pilots in handling the deadly foe and to effective countermeasures such as the Shrike anti-radiation missile. Brought to the fleet in March 1966, the Shrike was designed to home in on radar beams, tracking them to their source and destroying the radar-guidance van in the missile's battery with a 390-pound "surprise package."

At home, a secret Pentagon study released in early 1967 (and published in *The Pentagon Papers*) revealed the air war had become the main topic of civilian controversy. Public dissent over the bombing was rising, said the study, with reports from Hanoi by Harrison E. Salisbury (assistant managing editor of the *New York Times*) generating "an explosive debate about the bombing. His dispatches carried added sting," the study stated, "because he was in North Vietnam as the bombing moved close to Hanoi."

Salisbury had visited the North a mere two weeks, from 23 December 1966 to 7 January 1967, and what he had seen and written about had been well orchestrated by the Hanoi government. Writing for the *Washington Quarterly,* John Colvin said that Salisbury's articles "were based almost wholly on North Vietnamese propaganda pamphlets and on statistics provided by DRV [Democratic Republic of Vietnam] officials. His description, for example, of Nam Dinh as a cotton-and-silk town with no military objectives, when the city in fact contained POL storage, a power plant, and a railroad yard, and was surrounded by antiaircraft and surface-to-air missiles, ensured Salisbury received no Pulitzer prize. But the articles and their implication, drawn chiefly from North Vietnamese falsehoods, that the United States was deliberately bombing civilian targets carried worldwide conviction." Evidence of Colvin's testimony was borne out by a massive 1967 anti-war march in New York which attracted 300,000 to 500,000 protesters.

Another report, this one from the CIA, indicated that in Operation ROLLING THUNDER, the total number of individual flights against North Vietnam had risen from 55,000 in 1965 to 148,000 in 1966 and total bomb tonnage from 33,000 to 128,000; the number of aircraft lost had increased from 171 to 318 and direct operational costs from $460 million to $1.2 billion.

For 1966 alone, Seventh Fleet statistics showed Navy pilots flew more than 30,000 attack sorties against North Vietnam and 20,000 in South Vietnam. In only the North, the sum total of the thousands of sorties was 17,832 targets destroyed and 21,718 damaged. By specific target, the avalanche of figures included the destruction of 18 SAM sites, 3,903 POL areas, 10 railroad yards, 2,067 motor vehicles, 4,941 buildings, and 38 communication sites. Even though the figures were modified by the fact that some of the fixed targets "were restruck numerous times and damage may be reported more than once," their impact was something of a joke to pilots flying day in and day out. Lieutenant Frank Elkins of VA-164 wrote in his diary *The Heart of a Man:*

Radio Hanoi yells about the numbers of aircraft shot down in a given day, and we laugh and call them crazy, wild propagandists. Then we tell about the bridges, trucks, barges and POL storage areas which we've blown to hell every day, and our releases read worse than the Hanoi crap. Hell, if you took the combined estimated BDA reports from just the time we've been here, a total like that would cripple the little nation.

Another Navy pilot said,

I'd hate to be an aviator's mother back in the States reading Hanoi's evaluation of antiaircraft successes, but I'd hate worse to be a truck driver's mother in Hanoi reading the American estimates of trucks blown up—it reads like a Detroit production figure.

On the U.S. side eighty-nine airmen had been killed, captured, or reported missing in 1966—including Frank Elkins—and over 120 aircraft lost on combat missions.

The 1967 CIA report also stated that while the air campaign had significantly eroded the capacities of North Vietnam's industrial base, those losses "have not meaningfully degraded North Vietnam's material ability to continue the war in South Vietnam."

Chapter 19
Shrike

Summer came quickly and early in 1967. As the month of March unfolded, the wet chill of winter suddenly, and without benefit of spring, gave way to one hundred degree temperatures and stifling humidity in the urban population centers of North Vietnam. Just as suddenly, the tempo of the air war shifted into high gear over Haiphong, Hanoi, and other targeted areas.

"April was a dandy—two alpha strikes a day, plus nights and regular assignments," recalls Gary Scoffield, then a lieutenant commander with VA-192 aboard the carrier *Ticonderoga*. "We started that month with fourteen good aircraft, and came out with six still flyable. Of the other eight, four, I think, could be repaired and we lost four."

Two of the "lost" A-4E Skyhawks were piloted by Lt. Cmdr. Michael Estocin, "the one he brought back aboard 20 April and the one he went in with," notes Scoffield. Both missions struck targets at Haiphong, and posthumously earned Estocin the Medal of Honor, the nation's highest combat award.

A gregarious and demonstrative individual, Scoffield had become acclimated to Vietnam duty by virtue of three consecutive tours. "I was the CAG landing signal officer for Air Wing 5 in 1964 when we got caught up in the events of the Gulf of Tonkin incident," says Scoffield. "The PTs came out on August 2 and we started flying cover twenty-four hours a day for the destroyers. We worked three days straight, and I can clearly remember spending all three days on the landing platform. I slept in-between recoveries and had my flight gear on, so anytime they needed a tanker I could just jump in the plane. I picked up [Cmdr. James] Stockdale the night of August 4, he was one hundred miles north of the ship and out of gas. I pumped him and his wingie and brought them back to the ship."

Scoffield and the *Ticonderoga* returned home in November 1964, followed by another Vietnam deployment for both man and ship in 1965.

The Utah native's orders to VA-192 came in 1966, this time to be primarily involved with flying.

I left CAG-5 in March of 1966 and joined VA-192 as the admin officer. The squadron left for Vietnam in October, and on December 2 took part in the first alpha strikes to hit the Hanoi area, or at least very close to the first. There had already been alphas to the Kep POL, down at Thanh Hoa, Hon Gai, all the regular places as far as POL, bridges, crap like that. But this was the first to the Hanoi area. I carried the Shrike missile, and there were six of us in VA-192 Shrike trained, and by trained I mean we'd carried a dummy warhead in Lemoore. The first time I actually shot one was in combat over the North, so I really got trained up. I guess they looked at second-tour people for the Shrikes, and the group included Les Sanders, Jud Springer (Squatty), myself, Rick Millson, Mel Moore, and Mike Estocin.

On that first alpha strike, the target was a truck facility at Van Dien right out of Hanoi. Mel was leading Squatty, Les Sanders, and myself. The four of us hit the beach right there at the armpit [a coast in-point north of Thanh Hoa and south of Nam Dinh], while the strike group headed south to Thanh Hoa and came up through what was called the slot, little mountains straight south of Hanoi. Within a minute-and-a-half of hitting the armpit, twelve missiles were fired at us and we split up. Mel went southwest of Hanoi; Squatty was south; I went southeast; and Les east. That day each of us carried a centerline Bullpup, two Shrikes, and two rocket pods. The Shrikes were in short supply, tough to get aboard ship, and in some cases the only way to get a Shrike was fly an airplane to Cubi, load it up, and bring back four. Shrikes were dear to everyone's heart, and you didn't fire them unless really locked on a SAM site.

One of the SAMs fired at us hit Squatty. I was yelling, "Break, break, break!" But he didn't move in time, and I saw him get hit. What saved him was the impact went into the fuel tank and missed the engine, and I got him headed for the karst ridge south of the delta and out to the beach. Squatty was streaming, really leaking fuel; but the ship had a tanker on the way; his gear was down, and I knew he was okay. Back I went, and no sooner do I arrive than a SAM is fired at me from the same site that got Squatty. I pitched up, fired a Shrike, and they fired a missile, and both went by each other at the same time. I hit the site and the missile rolled me over, but that wasn't a problem. I picked up and fired at another site. I got that one too, and knew it because I saw the site burning while [I was] heading in to fire rockets at it. About this time the strike group came in, hit the target, and was never fired at by any missiles. Flak sure, but no missiles. Out of the Shrike group that day, Jud was hit, Les took shrapnel from a missile, two of us were hit, and the other two did a lot of dodging.

The Shrike people also bombed, and I led one mission to the Thanh Hoa Railroad Yard, catching 109 railroad cars, a bunch of engines, and cutting the road in seven or eight places. I remember that count because I led the strike. A good target, I planned it, everybody followed through, and the strike worked out nicely.

As an air wing, we started plowing, as I called it, around Vinh shortly after getting out there. We wore the North Vietnamese down, bringing in the F-8 Crusaders as flak suppressors, carrying 1,000-pounders with daisy cutters and weapons like that. By the time the weather got real crappy, you could fly unhampered from up above Thanh Hoa south. At that point, early January, I went to the beach as the Seventh Fleet representative in Tan Son Nhut for two weeks, a period when Dick Stratton, our maintenance officer, got bagged and taken prisoner. The Navy sent two fleet combat types into Tan San Nhut to work with CTF-77 Det Charlie staff. We stood watch, coordinated the strikes, sent messages, really a lash-up because this Navy lieutenant commander is standing watch with an Air Force one-star general.

When I came back out, the air wing hadn't been flying for squat; hell, they hadn't flown an alpha strike that entire two weeks, which really ticked me off. I didn't miss a darn one of them. I flew back to the ship, the weather was clear, and the COD [carrier on-board delivery plane] had to hold because the ship was getting ready to launch. I landed on another ship, they helped me aboard the *Ticonderoga,* and the comment was "Boy, you've been away for two weeks, you've got to catch up." I said, "What do you mean catch up, you guys haven't been doing anything." And I caught up real fast, flying something like eight straight alpha strikes. That's when we started the movement up North again, when the weather opened back up. Had Washington let us keep going, there wouldn't have been a missile left, the North Vietnamese would have fired them all.

The ship came off the line in March, and arrived back out in late March or early April with fourteen new airplanes. What I mean by new, they were all up, all in good shape because all the shot up A-4Es had been traded off. By this time, the Shrike group was escorted by the F-8s because of the need to keep our heads in the cockpit to watch where the North Vietnamese were shooting from. We'd hear the warble and watch. At the time they supposedly had over 150 sites, although only thirty or forty would be shooting. Maneuverability against the SAMs was important; we took the A-4 in as slick as possible, just a centerline tank and four Shrikes, because not only were the missiles fired at us, but all types of AAA. One particular day I stayed in and covered both our ship and another ship's strike. I was on one side between Hanoi and Haiphong, and the BARCAP was beyond me, and we took thirty-one missiles at the Shrikes that day. There were only four shot at the strike groups, which ticked me off, but that was our job.

A SAM site could fire one missile or two, depending on how many they had and where you were located. Generally just one was fired and if the operator did fire two, they were usually tracking just one target. The sites were camouflaged because as soon as the missile went off, the dust and dirt was visible. With the camouflage, and the North Vietnamese were pretty sophisticated in hiding the sites, the first sight was the smoke trail from the burning missile. If you didn't catch that, the booster dropped off in three to four seconds, and then there was nothing to see except picking up the missile itself. By spotting the SAM, you could outfly it, I thoroughly believe that. I've seen them zip right past me with their canards full tilt and sideways trying to turn. I'd just laugh because the SAM couldn't make the turn with that speed. But you had to see it, and if you didn't, the SAM was in your back pocket.

I saw two or three pilots get bagged by SAMs, trying like hell to get away. Squatty, there is no reason he wasn't bagged that day except the tank protected his engine, and he was pulling. The folks down below were pretty smart with the SAMs and radar-guided flak. In other words, if you didn't move, three shots and they'd be in your back pocket. That's why guys got bagged—they didn't move, or rolled in twice in the same direction, or some dumb thing like that. If you didn't move—jink—in three, they'd be in you. It was that simple; hell, you could watch them walk. I was very methodical, and the only time my wings were ever level in a high-threat area came while making a Shrike shot.

You had to level the wings and get it right in there. But by golly, the rest of the time I never stopped moving, changing altitude, shifting here and there. A lot of guys got busted straight and level.

When the squadron had enough Shrikes, we started shooting at any site that came up on the air, and pretty soon there were no radar-tracking guns. If the North Vietnamese turned the radars on, they'd have a Shrike on their heads. We did that for a while, and boy did it get quiet. Pretty soon the North Vietnamese were firing visual.

After Mel Moore went down, that left Estocin and me as Shrike lead. We'd flip, one of us going in the afternoon and one in the morning. Once in a while we'd let some other people lead. José [Joe] "Oklahoma Slim" Tully, we let him lead once because he didn't have a DFC yet, and he got shot down. Things like that would happen, we'd send somebody else on one and sure enough they got bagged too. One airplane, double nuts, had never come back from a big strike. Every time we put on an alpha strike, somebody would get nailed in that aircraft, or somebody would jump out. I took it; I was assigned it; it was a Shrike bird and away we went. I brought it back, and maybe there're mysteries to stuff like that. Joe Tully always carried a big old Panama hat to the airplane, another guy had a bugle. Everybody had a charm. Some people went in with two pistols, fourteen knives and nine hundred pounds of stuff on them, which did nothing but throw off an arm or break their neck as they went out. My theory was get your radio, a gun, lots of tracers, signaling devices, and medicines. No food or any of that other crap. I threw away all the ball ammo, only tracers, I wasn't going to duel it out with anybody. Tracers were just fine, and I wore my pistol down on the side, with nothing around my neck. I really think a lot of people got hurt with all this crap hanging around them.

I also had a lucky watch and lucky water-bottles, two or three of them. Everybody said, "Hit the ground and you're dry," so I said, I wasn't going to be dry when I hit the ground. I considered filling up one with scotch, but finally thought better of the idea. The watch was Navy issue, one I'd worn for I don't know how long. When I came back from my third cruise, I threw it over the side when we pulled into port in San Diego. I'll never forget it. I didn't need it, but I don't know why I did it. I gave my water bottles to Jim Busey and they did him well.

Mike's Medal of Honor was for two separate missions. On the first, we took him into the fence [barricade on the carrier deck]. He'd come around, plugged into the KA-3 [tanker], and was streaming fuel, just like a sieve. The KA-3 dropped him off and he went straight into the fence. He'd taken a SAM, and you could look through the airplane any direction and see light—there was no way to count the number of holes.

The night before April 26, the hop he went in on, we were briefing another alpha and flipped a coin down in his room while having a Kool-Aid. The flip was to see who was taking the morning or afternoon alpha. I took the morning and he took the afternoon. He had some problems on the 26th, came back out once, and then went back in and got hit full, dead in the head with a SAM. The F-8 was right on his wing, telling him to get out, he went in inverted, going through the clouds, and all that stuff. Of course, we never found anything indicating whether he got out and the area was off the coast of Haiphong, off toward these islands beyond the lighthouse. The clouds in the area were down about 6,000–7,000 feet and it was hard to get in until a day or two days later, and then we left the line. We did get in, going through at 400 or 500 feet with a flight of four, flying two SAMs into the water while looking around trying to pick up something. The barges down below were unloading the SAMs, and all the targets we couldn't hit were right there in the harbor. Never found a thing.

Mike had walked on [board] a week or two before the squadron got underway. He and his roommate "Pappy" [Noel] Morton were close, real close, but Pappy is dead now too. I didn't know Mike well, or his wife and family. [VA-] 192 was a different squadron, we were running pretty fast in those days. What I mean is that I popped in there [in the] April–May time frame, and there wasn't any time. We were always gone, working hard, and we played very hard, very hard. You got to know people in a working atmosphere, but you were coming and gone. You'd have two nine-month cruises under your belt in a little better than two years, with a six-, maybe seven-month turnaround. It wasn't unusual to get 200, 250 traps on a cruise, and before the war started you were lucky to get 100.

McKellar and I wrote the Medal of Honor report for Estocin. . . . Between the time the ship left the line and [reached] Hong Kong, we wrote up 247 medal citations, something like that, even staying on the ship in Cubi. McKellar and I sat up for two days and nights at Cubi, and I was dying to get off the ship, but we had to get that work done.

Events had been recorded, guys had really done something, and we just never got around to writing it down. Then we had Estocin's two missions, same guy, and with him gone it was different. At the time, a special award could be fired off by message, so we, along with the ship's awards board, took the separate missions and off they went to Seventh Fleet as a Navy Cross. The message came back and I'll never forget it, the word was upgrade and resubmit. I pretty much took the information, jammed it all together, everybody nodded, sent it through the ship's awards board, and fired it off.

For conspicuous gallantry and intrepidity at the risk of his life above and beyond the call of duty on 20 and 26 April as a pilot in Attack Squadron 192 embarked in USS *Ticonderoga* (CVA-14). Leading a three-plane group of aircraft in support of a coordinated strike against two thermal power plants in Haiphong, North Vietnam, on 20 April, then Lt. Cmdr. Estocin provided continuous warnings to the strike group leaders of the surface-to-air missiles (SAM) and personally neutralized three SAM sites. Although his aircraft was severely damaged by an exploding missile, he reentered the target area and relentlessly prosecuted a Shrike attack in the face of intense anti-aircraft fire. With less than five minutes of fuel remaining he departed the target area and commenced in-flight refueling which continued over 100 miles. Three miles aft of *Ticonderoga*, and without enough fuel for a second approach, he disengaged from the tanker and executed a precise approach to a fiery arrested landing. On 26 April, in the support of a coordinated strike against the vital fuel facilities in Haiphong, he led an attack on a threatening SAM site, during which his aircraft was seriously damaged by an exploding SAM; nevertheless, he regained control of his burning aircraft and courageously launched his Shrike missiles before departing the area. By his inspiring courage and unswerving devotion to duty in the face of grave personal danger, Lt. Cmdr. Estocin upheld the highest traditions of the United States naval service.

The award wasn't actually made until 1978, 1979, somewhere around there because the family fought changing Estocin's status from Missing in Action [MIA] to Killed in Action [KIA]. I was the Navy senate liaison executive director in the mid-70s, and couldn't find out whether the Medal of Honor had been approved or not. I left Washington, D.C., and went back out to sea as executive officer of *Kitty Hawk,* and I don't recall if it was the *Navy Times, Stars and Stripes,* or what, but boom, there's a picture of Marie Estocin receiving the Medal of Honor for Mike.

Chapter 20
MiG Kill

Theodore R. "T. R." Swartz, fighter pilot by training and mentality, attack pilot by decision, reached the war early in 1967 as a lieutenant commander with Attack Squadron 76 aboard the carrier USS *Bon Homme Richard.*

Swartz's cockpit background was uniquely different from virtually all of his VA-76 counterparts. He'd previously flown the F-8 Crusader, and made a conscious and deliberate choice to fly the A-4C Skyhawk "because the attack guys were doing most of the work. They were going over the beach and getting all the action, while the fighter guys were out in the BARCAP once or twice a day not doing a damn thing except flying circles. Basically, what I wanted to do was go where the action was.

"My thought when I was doing this was, It's nice to be a fighter pilot, and nice to be an attack pilot, but for Christ sake it's tactical air warfare. The job was going in and stirring up the enemy, making them burn, bleed, and blow up."

Buoyed by previous experience in the A-4 as Air Wing 3's landing signal officer, Swartz made the unique request of asking his detailer to "do me a favor and send me to Lemoore" rather than an F-8 squadron. "I didn't care where or who, just send me to Lemoore. Lemoore was the heart of the attack community. If you went to a Lemoore squadron, you were going west."

Swartz believes most members of naval aviation's tactical cadre wanted orders to Vietnam "although there are a number of naval aviators who even managed to get to flag rank by avoiding the God damn war altogether. They don't even have an air medal, and some of these guys are absolute true, fine naval officers and bureaucrats, but they're not warriors. A warrior just wanted to get in the airplane, and do as good a job as he could. He was as good as he could get in that airplane, he tried to get everybody else around him to be as good as possible, and he didn't hesitate to go and take on the enemy and make them burn, bleed, and blow up because that's what the hell he was getting paid for."

The Spirits of VA-76, assigned to Air Wing 21, reached the coastal waters of Vietnam in January 1967. As the monsoon season faded, the air war's intensity rapidly ballooned and sites around Hanoi and Haiphong that previously had been off-limits felt the sharp sting of American bombs and rockets. Those same bombs, or more correctly, the aircraft and pilots that dropped them, piqued the interest of North Vietnamese MiGs which rose to meet the enemy challenge. Seventeen MiGs fell prey to Navy jet aircraft in '67, and ten of the kills were earned by Air Wing 21 pilots, certain evidence of the deadly pace of activity over Hanoi and Haiphong that spring and summer. Six kills of MiGs were recorded in May, one of which went to Swartz, the only pilot of any service to down a MiG while flying the attack-designated Skyhawk.

Two-and-one-half months later on 21 July Swartz nearly recorded his second MiG kill during a noteworthy seven-minute exchange that occurred as a strike group from the *Bon Homme Richard* approached the Ta Xa POL site. Eight MiG-17s attacked the Shrike–armed Iron Hand A-4s of VA-76 and VA-212 and the F-8 fighter cover of VF-211 and -24. One MiG was destroyed by a Sidewinder fired by Cmdr. Marion H. "Red" Issacks; a second was downed by the 20-millimeter fire of Lt. Cmdr. Robert L. Kirkwood; a third was destroyed by air-to-ground Zuni rockets and 20-millimeter guns from the Crusader flown by Lt. Cmdr. Ray "Timmy" Hubbard; and the fourth was probably downed after impact with a Sidewinder launched by Lt. (jg) Philip W. Dempewolf.

Swartz's May shootdown, while certainly a boon to his reputation, created its share of controversy.

"T. R. was saving ordnance he was assigned to deliver for a specific purpose, and he was not using it so he might get a chance to shoot a MiG down," reflects one former A-4 pilot on-line during the same period as Swartz. "He got lucky, and a MiG came. But that's all he had on his mind, and he could have gone the whole cruise and never saw a MiG.

"Now the guys on the bombing run, they didn't care if the son-of-a-bitch got a MiG or not; he was there to suppress the flak. There were some bitter people, taking flak because T. R. wasn't using his ordnance. He was not doing his assigned mission, to their hazard, so he could have the opportunity to shoot down a MiG. Granted, suppressing flak in Vietnam was like peeing against the tide, but it was the thing you did."

Swartz received a Silver Star for the MiG kill, an honor his A-4 contemporary vehemently disagrees with. "We gave T. R. a Silver Star for shooting down a MiG, and then we had half the attack pilots running around looking for MiGs. I'd have never given him a Silver Star, I'd have court-martialed him for failure to obey his lawful order. But our system doesn't have enough bastards like me in it."

For Swartz, the difference between the air-to-mud and fighter worlds came down to emotion. "When you're in a no-shit dogfight with somebody else—who can put a weapon on you and blow you out of the sky—it's kind of like just before you go out on the ballfield or get in the ring with somebody," said Swartz. "Whereas, I never really got apprehensive flying over the beach.

"I would feel more comfortable once the guns started or the SAM came up because you knew they were worried and awake and you knew where they were. I was always worried when nothing happened, and was always waiting for something to happen because then it was time for action, the adrenaline ran, and you were ready and working."

In VA-76 we had some real warriors, guys like John Waples, Les Jackson, and Paul Hollingsworth. We lost the CO—Guy Fuller—to a SAM and the XO, Ken Cameron, went down early; and as far as I was concerned, the squadron was Hollingsworth as operations officer, Jackson as maintenance, myself as admin, Waples, and four or five other pretty God damn good bombers and airplane fliers. We were calling the shots, leading the alpha strikes, the maintenance was getting done. We believed we could go out and beat the hell out of the North Vietnamese on the ground with the airplanes, take on the SAMs, dig them out, and dig out the guns if we had to. Our sister squadron, VA-212, had some good people—Homer Smith was the CO—and Jack Monger was one of the best CAGs around, an old attack pilot.

It was kind of fun over the beach, like pro football where you take the ball, get on the field, kick everybody's ass, and come home. We weren't concerned with what the hell the war was all about; we were more concerned with getting it done right, getting everybody back, and doing some good damage to the enemy. The shots, of course, were still called by somebody way higher than us, but we were able to go up North of the 20th Parallel, into the Haiphong and Hanoi area, and targeting was fairly well open.

You don't forget how to be a fighter pilot, and I didn't let anyone in the squadron forget there was a real possibility one day they might have a MiG on their ass, and they ought to have an attitude developed in a training frame-of-mind that takes them to the point to not only get the son-of-a-bitch off their ass, but blow his brains out or at least scare him. A MiG pilot had no idea the A-4 didn't carry weapons that could hurt him, and he probably felt as apprehensive as we were. I think if you go up and meet somebody in the air and just act aggressive and point the airplane at him, and push him out in front of you, and shoot at him regardless of what the hell it is, he's going to think twice about who in the hell you are. I believe that is what I was pushing for in the attack community, because while we had gone through defensive tactic drills and offensive business, it wasn't getting sponsored a whole hell of a lot.

Spring and summer of 1967 were alpha strike business. We were up there, *Oriskany* was up there, and another couple of big carriers. We started seeing MiGs, and getting MiG calls and opportunities in April, and flying alpha strikes every day into the south part of Route Pack 6B and Route Pack 4. On the evening of April 30 the squadron had a big get-together in the ready room, and I just got up and felt like I had to say, "Hey guys, if you ever get a MiG behind you, here's the way you ought to take care of this whole thing. Push him out in front of you, execute whatever you have to do, and remember he doesn't know whether you are Barnie Oldfield or not. Just push him out in front and shoot the hell out of him." I even got on the blackboard and with a little chalk, kind of drew a picture of the gunsite, and here's how you go about shooting a rocket.

The next day Paul Hollingsworth led, I was a flak suppressor, and John Waples was my wingman. We went over the beach up north of Haiphong, heading to Kep airfield, which is kind of in and around Hanoi. Our job that day was just to beat up the air patch, and I think somebody had spotted a MiG-21 either flying through a flight, or just go whizzing by earlier in the day. We all rolled in on the airfield, a lefthand roll, and our specific job was to pound some flak sites on the north side of the runway. The bombers took the middle of the runway, and there were flak suppressors up on the other end also.

We all rolled in together, and Waples and I saw a couple of MiGs taking to the runway, shooting at them as well as the flak sites. I think we got two of those guys on the ground, and just as we pulled off, my eye caught, coming from right to left, a pair of MiG-17s. There wasn't anything we could do about it at the time because our paths were going to cross, and I was going to cross right in front of them. I couldn't slow down; if I turned right to meet them head on, I'd run into the whole strike group, and if I turned left, which I had to do to stay the hell out of the way of the strike group, I had to accept them back, on the inside of my turn on the lefthand side.

Waples called in and he said, "T. R., there's two MiGs down there," and I think, to quote him, he said "Let's get those sons-of-bitches." I said something like, "Hang on," and I had three Zunis left. The Zuni package carries four rockets that can be fired single or ripple, and the load says fire all of them at once. I put one package on single and saved three; I kind of felt naked in there without God damn nothing and the MiGs around. The Crusaders were there, but I felt the odds were in the MiGs' favor. If they got down in the pack, they could pick one of us off before the Crusaders got into it. Nevertheless, my ass was chewed out and the CO of the boat damn near wanted to court-martial my butt about saving the Zunis, although it turned out all right.

I accepted the fight with the MiGs inside my left hand turn. I looked back over my lefthand shoulder and saw the two of them shooting with their big God damn cannon, a 37-millimeter that really gets your attention. They were shooting the 37, plus the 23s on the side of the airplane. I can remember seeing those sons-of-bitches spark and saying to myself, this is all kind of interesting—two MiGs at close formation, shooting guns, and the old 23s sparkling on the side of the fuselage.

I did a high-G, barrel roll at 425 knots, which is very difficult to follow, putting the slats out—the A-4's little aerodynamical slats—and as the airplane came over the top, the MiGs were off my right shoulder. I poked one Zuni at the wingman and missed, poked another one and missed, and then poked the third. Blind ass fucking luck because all this skill and science about the gun sight was garbage, there wasn't enough lead on the sight. On the Zuni I fired, the gun sight was in-between my feet.

After getting the one guy—and I was working so God damn hard it took only three or four seconds of thought before it was all over—I went after the leader with my little gun, the 20-millimeter, which had just a few bullets in it because most of the space had been used for the electronic warfare stuff. The gun kept jamming, and you're not supposed to recharge the gun, but I recharged it about four times, shot a couple of rounds at him, and finally said this is incredibly dumb because I can blow up the front of this airplane and I'd really be in deep shit. The

North Vietnamese would be pissed because there's one guy on the ground, and they'd probably get me with a pitchfork. So I turned right and got the hell out of there.

Back on the ship, and I was glad to get back, some guys were happy as hell, and there was a little bit of professional jealousy. I was never really approached head-on by anybody who said, "Why didn't you have all your Zuni tubes set?" but it was kind of inferred and I heard there was some grumbling. The Navy can only tolerate a moderate amount of independent thinking.

The kill was no classical dogfight from the point of getting the radar vector, or seeing somebody five miles out and meeting them head-on, and turning and burning for a minute or two before you shot at him or he shot at you, but it was a unique moment.

A more interesting strike occurred in the early morning on July 21 when VF-24 and -211 bagged four MiGs. Mike Cater from VA-212 had the lead and I was Iron Hand, and Iron Hand was a good mission. Jack Monger was a good CAG, and he let a lot of us junior guys lead, and by junior I mean middle of the road lieutenant commanders. It gave us a lot of experience and a lot of confidence. As a strike lead, you got to look around and were pretty busy. As Iron Hand, you got to look around and duel the big red SAM.

At the time, we had the Shrike, and the little scope in the airplane that gave you targeting of the SAM. We didn't have many Shrikes; in fact, some of the missions were flown carrying the Shrike with orders not to shoot the damn thing, just go up and listen. For a while, we carried Zuni rockets, smoking them off to see if the jerks on the ground would shut down their radar, and I have no idea whether that worked or not.

The little A-4 was about as good an airplane as you could get to go out and duel with the SAM. It was maneuverable, and as long as you kept your heart going, your eyes out of the cockpit and saw all the SAMs, you'd stay alive. As Iron Hand, our job was to attract the SAMs, so we just went out and chummed, got the SAMs in the air, called them in the air, and protected the strike group. I flew a lot of Iron Hand and had only two or three close encounters, usually because I became triangulated. One site would shoot at me, and I'd turn into it; then another would shoot from behind, and you'd turn around to look at that one; then there'd be a third lift-off. The guys on the ground knew what Iron Hands were doing, and if the system worked right, they could get you. One particular day, I was worked down to about five hundred feet trying to get away from them. Fortunately it was a pretty non-defended area for guns, or else they would have eaten me up. The guys on the ground were good; they'd try and fake you out by bringing up the missile command guidance linkup, which really scared the hell out of you. The warning lights came on, and you'd think they're steering a missile when they weren't.

That morning I was Pouncer One, and because of our limited Iron Hand resources, Timmy Hubbard, an F-8 Crusader pilot, flew cover for me. I was up in front of the strike group about two or three miles, with my head in the scope and listening to the noise, the radar frequencies, and telling the guys information like there's a SAM site over in the valley to the right. Timmy Hubbard is on my right wing, and a pack of these bombers are behind us. Incredibly, a flight of eight MiG-17s crept between Timmy Hubbard and myself, and the strike group. They're all in a God damn column, like they're out for a Sunday parade. Waples saw them first, and Mike Cater looks up and says, "Jesus, they're dropping bombs." Well, in fact, they dropped fuel tanks. Waples said to me, "T. R., check your six, you've got a couple of MiGs back there." I looked around and said "Two, shit, there's eight of them," and I call out something like "Get 'em Crusaders!" Red Issacks was in the strike; Phil Dempewolf; and Bob Kirkwood was the other MiG killer—all from VF-24 flying the F-8. In the melee that followed, four MiGs fell out of the sky, one of them Hubbard's.

[His plane] loaded as the morning flak suppressor, Timmy carried Zunis and poked a couple of those at the MiG, then put every bullet he had into that damn airplane, and the thing didn't fall out of the air. Timmy hollered "I'm ammo minus, and I'm running out of fuel. I've got to go." I said, "Okay, Pouncer Two," and I figured, Shit, here's number two. I've got a cripple and another God damn MiG. Well, Hubbard drives up beside this guy, and I'm one thousand feet from him, and about the time he gets beside the MiG, the guy gets out of the airplane, and the airplane blows up. So it was a confirmed kill for Timmy.

In all the confusion—and I'm taking pictures, doing a little Iron Hand, flying the stick, and listening to the bombers roll in—I end up kind of tailing the strike group. The Crusaders are milling around; they've managed to get four MiGs, and there's still four left. Red Issacks, he has two 17s behind him and they're both shooting at him, and his God damn left wing is on fire. He's burning bad and he said, "This is Page Boy Two. I'm hit, I'm burning. I've got two MiGs behind me." I said, "Okay, Red, turn right," because we were pretty close to the border, and I don't want him to go into China. I said, "Turn right, and I'll take care of the MiGs behind you." I came smoking across the circle we're flying with a Shrike on one wing and Zunis on the other, and arm up the Zunis. I poke two Zunis at these two airplanes at about one thousand feet, God damn near head on. [The Zunis] whizzed right through them, just scared the shit out of them, and they got off Red's ass. Red's wingman was some kid on his first God damn strike or something—lost the whole thing, never saw anything, and finally made it back to the ship.

One other incident took place that day between Bobby Kirkwood and Phil Dempewolf. I'm on top of these two when Kirkwood shoots a Sidewinder and gets a MiG. Dempewolf also shoots a Sidewinder, and it heads straight for Kirkwood's tailpipe. I'm looking down on this incredulously, and I'm saying to myself, Self, I know what I'm going to tell Kirkwood as soon as he's hit. I'm going to say, Hey Bobby, you've just been hit with a Sidewinder, that's your problem, better get ready to jump out of that thing. Just as the God damn Sidewinder approaches his tailpipe, Kirkwood launches another one, and the Sidewinder headed for him goes after the one he launched, lops off the starboard horizontal stabilizer of his airplane, and puts roller markers on the underside of the wing.

One of the missiles hit the MiG, and the other flies through the debris. Kirkwood keeps on going. Meanwhile, I've got my hands full and decide not to say shit about the whole thing because Kirkwood is still flying the airplane, and he doesn't have utility or hydraulic failure.

We got back, had this big debrief, and I said, "Okay, now I'm going to tell my story." They said, "Impossible," and I said, "Go out and look at the airplane." We went up on deck and the [plane's] starboard horizontal stabilizer was sliced off, and there's a big God damn line down the underside of the wing made by the stainless steel guidance and balance fins of the Sidewinder. Kirkwood about shit, and Dempewolf tried to claim a half kill. He's lucky he didn't get his ass kicked, but it was funnier than hell.

I don't know why I happened to get so lucky. I won one, had a draw on July 21, and saw some for the third time over the Hanoi lake. I guess it was being at the right place at the right time—there was a helluva lot of fighter pilots that never saw a MiG—and it was pretty active in 1967.

Chapter 21
Must Pump

An ever-expanding Southeast Asian air war generated significant problems for naval aviation. Shortages were evident in pilots—one source said the Navy needed almost seventeen hundred aviators—as well as in ordnance, survival gear, and qualified personnel to maintain jet aircraft, virtually every necessary element to carry on the air war effort efficiently.

"[Neither] the Navy nor the nation had geared up to the fact this was a real war," relates a retired Navy captain who served four Vietnam combat tours in the cockpit of an A-4 and A-7. "We didn't want to end up pumping all these pilots out of flight training, taking all these new people, because no one thought the war would last. That was the mindset that was working."

The pilot crisis really had two components, the need to produce new pilots and the need to reduce the risk for the men still flying and willing to stay in the Navy. The Department of Defense [DoD] believed naval aviators were simply making too many trips into the face of danger, with the combat loss-rate escalating, as more squadrons deployed to Southeast Asia and the North Vietnamese defense network became more proficient at spewing out SAMs and AAA. Concern about pilot and flight crew loss prompted a DoD investigation, which revealed pilots were flying an average of sixteen to twenty-two combat missions per month over the North, with some pilots going as high as twenty-eight. To rectify the situation, DoD issued a declaration stating no pilot could fly more than two complete deployments in a fourteen-month period.

To increase the long-term pilot count, efforts were undertaken to speed an ample number of prospective aviators through the training command and fleet replacement squadrons at Lemoore, Cecil Field, Miramar, and other naval air stations, and onto the decks of carriers deployed in the Gulf of Tonkin. Many of these young "must pumps" (the term for the aviation version of the 90-day wonder) became nothing more than cannon fodder—bodies to fill combat cockpit seats—and squadron commanding officers would sometimes find it difficult to write consoling letters home to Mom and Dad when they barely had enough time to shake the young pilots' hands before sending them off into the deadly Iron Triangle.

To fill the combat cockpits quickly, the ranks of tactical aviation were opened to other elements of naval aviation. The results were certainly mixed. "The Navy scraped up anybody who'd flown before and told them if they wanted to transition to jets, they could," says the retired captain. "It was dumb, and sad. We took a lot of people that should have never been in jets. There were rotor pilots, Spad pilots, S-2 pilots, and many were disasters because their mindsets were at 125 knots, and they could never get over it."

William Morris Siegel required slightly over a year to earn his Navy wings, an unexpected gift, if you will, from the venerated Adm. Hyman Rickover.

"Coming down to my senior year at the Naval Academy," said Siegel, "it didn't look like I could fly because everybody that stood ahead of me [in class ranking] was picking aviation, so I was going to be a boat driver. But then Admiral Rickover came out and said the top two hundred guys in the class were going nuclear power. He didn't go to the Navy with that, he went to Congress, and they backed him. All but three guys in the top two hundred went nuclear power, which meant Siegel goes aviation."

Graduating from the academy in May 1965, Siegel entered flight training three months later. "I wanted to fly the F-8, but nobody in my class got to fly the F-8. One guy got P-3s and everybody else went to A-4s and A-7s."

The diminutive Siegel arrived at Lemoore in October 1966 to complete his training with VA-125, the West Coast A-4 training squadron. As a must pump, his training syllabus was somewhat abbreviated. It culminated in a night carrier-landing on the USS *Oriskany* off San Francisco Bay. Siegel's aircraft was the first to approach the carrier "with the deck really pitching," said the New York native. "I knew I was out of my league, the landing ball was going out the bottom and out the top, and when I tried to land, the deck came up and smacked my hook as I made a move at the end to try and get aboard. I did arrest, there was no damage to the airplane, but I didn't handle it well.

"After my incident, they closed down flight ops. I knew we shouldn't have been out there, but I was a student and didn't have the savvy yet to say I'm not going to land. The head of the det came looking for me later and asked, 'Are you all right?' My reply was, 'Heck no,' and he said 'It was our fault, we shouldn't have let you land.' It was nice of him to say that, whether it was true or not I don't know. But it sounded good to me."

Originally scheduled to join NAS Lemoore–based VA-155 and complete a full squadron workup cycle before heading to Southeast Asia, Siegel went immediately to VA-55—the "Warhorses"—when another pilot failed to carrier qualify. He joined the squadron in mid-May, just days before its departure for the Gulf of Tonkin aboard the *Constellation.* Half the squadron's pilots had completed one combat cruise, the other half had spent at least six months in the squadron.

I walked onto the *Constellation* docked in San Diego and had my first terrible experience with squadron life. There's a bunkroom of six guys, but only five are living there. And these five guys have been together a minimum of at least six months, through the whole training cycle. In I walk, dressed in khakis, all sweaty, sat down and said, "Hi guys, Bill Siegel. I'm the new guy." Their joint reply was, "New guy! We don't need a new guy! We're not getting enough flight time as it is."

I ask which rack is mine, then look around and see every rack is made except one in the back, loaded with all their stereo gear. I ask, "What do I do?" and they reply, "Isn't there another room you can go to?" These guys are really shitbirds—there's no joking around; they were all serious. Nobody stood up, shook my hand, or nothing. They wanted me out of there because I was screwing up their room. Eventually, some commander got me situated, but that's my first welcome to the fleet.

Two weeks later the squadron started flight operations, and the senior people were trying to decide who'll fly with me. Rudy Kohn, the squadron maintenance officer [said he] will—he's the first son-of-a-bitch to even smile at me—but the decision was made to give me a tanker hop first.

I saw the assignment as a chance to show that Bill Siegel is a good aviator. My thoughts were, I'm going to kick ass in the tanker; it's going to be the best tanker hop anybody ever had. I don't say any of this, but that's what was going through my mind. I read every bit of literature ever written about the tanker, maintenance of the tanker, the maintenance of the refueling drogue. I knew every wire and switch. Unfortunately, I made a few mistakes.

For starters, the first mistake was going to the back of the ready room and pulling out a card with a bunch of frequencies on it. Our radio had twenty channels on it, with every channel set to a different frequency. Every week the frequencies were switched, but I didn't know that and picked up the wrong frequency card, probably a card some guy was using for scratch paper. Not only that, but the tanker radio had not yet been channelized. [It had] nothing but the old channels, which were garbage; nobody was on them. The problem could be fixed by channelizing in-flight with the right frequency card, but I didn't know how to do that. It was something I hadn't learned in the RAG—it was not in the book; it was a maintenance procedure.

There was an overcast that day, made worse by the fact [that] the ship steamed under a cloud after I was catapulted off the deck. I knew I was going around and around, and I knew I was on top of the ship because the TACAN was on, which picks up a beacon put out by the ship. I kept calling and calling, and nobody would talk to me. I tried all the frequencies and finally figured we were at some type of EmCon [emission control conditions], although it didn't dawn on me if we were at EmCon, they wouldn't have the TACAN on either.

I decided to play the game and not say a word, taking my mask off to avoid inadvertently saying something that might blow the cover of the ship. There I was, steaming around, making a perfect circle around this boat in case someone wanted gas. An hour goes by, two hours by, two-and-a-half hours. As a must-pump, I'm in the dark about the concept of cyclic operations. During training you go through a period where the flight deck is open. You go down and trap, shoot off the catapult, and then go home. There wasn't a concept of cyclic ops, where a part of the air wing is launched, operates, then those guys land, and the other half goes off. I had never been briefed on cyclic ops, and while everybody just assumed you were born with that knowledge, my group went through the RAG real fast. We didn't even know it existed. Someone had always told me when it was time to land, and the ship was now trying. But I had the wrong radio frequency, the day was overcast, all the worst situations.

At the three hour mark, an hour-and-a-half after I'm scheduled to be back aboard ship, an A-4 from our sister squadron finds me. He came along the side, ripped off his mask, and signaled, "I've got the lead, you get on my wing, and we're going down." I signaled no because I read all this literature and knew the tanker takes the lead. My reply to him was, "I've got the lead, you plug in, and get some gas," and I was smiling the whole time, so now he was pissed. He grabbed hold of his collar, pulled up his lieutenant commander's leaf, and replied, "See this, I've got the lead." I figured the guy is just an asshole, gave him the lead, and we headed down through the overcast. He lands, but I'm heavy fuelwise and hit the dump switch to unload the extra fuel, which goes all over the deck of the Connie because I'm right over the ship. I thought it would dissipate and wouldn't make it to the ship—a real rookie's mistake.

The landing was my first on the *Constellation*—previously I had only been on small boats—and it's a little weird and different. In fact, it scared me on the first pass and I bolted, so the ship, unbeknownst to yours truly, was still waiting on me.

I came back around with still no clue there's anything wrong and land. Some guy says the captain wants to see me, which I thought was great; he's going to congratulate me on a first trap. Up [to] the island I go, and on the bridge is Capt. John Thomas with CAG Gene Tissot; my skipper, Bob Holt; Kohn; and the squadron ops officer, Hardy Rose.

They were all standing there, and I said something like, "Hey Skipper, how you guys doing?" Well, Captain Thomas started ripping ass—first CAG, and then right on down the line. He came to me, and by now I've got the idea I screwed up. "Siegel," he says, "you know how much it costs"—and he was right in my face—"to keep this ship in the wind for one jg for two God damn hours?" I said, "No sir, how much?" and he screams something like "I don't know how much either, but it's a lot of money. Now get out of here, you asshole, and don't ever come back." I left there heading for the fantail. I was going to jump off and swim back to San Diego because this was bullshit. Well, Rudy and Hardy grabbed me, took me downstairs, and there was a bottle of scotch. They poured me a couple of drinks, and that was my second welcome to the fleet.

As we neared the Philippines, the guys were starting to like me because I'm not very pretentious and I'm the new guy, and you could always laugh at the new guy. Then we get to Yankee Station and go to war.

Our first mission is this bridge, and I'm twenty-four years old and scared to death. I had been through this training cycle, I had about ten or twelve hops under my belt. I had flown a lot at Cubi and I was proficient. But the realization came to me there's a whole lot I don't know about. I didn't know what to expect, but I just knew I was going to die on the first flight. There were a lot of guys talking macho, except no one felt it. Guys get scared in different ways. Some are quiet, some boast a lot, but everybody felt scared.

Before that first launch, the skipper called an all-officer meeting in the ready room. I looked as nice as I could; my boots were shined—I wanted to die with good looking boots on—all my possessions were squared away. My locker was cleaned; anybody who had to clean up my stuff was going to have an easy job.

Well, the skipper gives this fantastic combat speech. He says "We're going to war, and we're going to be doing this for nine months. When you go into combat, and I've been there a lot, you're going to have losses. Some guys die, some guys screw up and die, some guys die by chance. So we're going to lose a couple of guys in the room. But we're not going to lose anybody today. It does not happen on the first day, you do not die as soon as your nose goes over the beach. There's not a wall of bullets waiting there for you. It's just a sleepy country with a bunch of sleepy people, and when they see you coming they're going to start shooting. But you have a lot of things going for you. All your training, plus you're in a little airplane. It's hard to see the A-4, and you're flying with bigger airplanes, so the Vietnamese are going to want those guys first. There are things you can control in life, and things you can't. Concentrate on things you can control. Fly good wing position, don't get sucked in, keep your lookout, don't make multiple runs, spend minimum time over the beach, drop your bombs, and get the hell out. Those are the things you can control. Don't sweat it, do as good a job with the things you can do and get the hell out."

On that first mission, I flew wing for Rudy, and he told me "I don't want you to do anything fancy. Don't protect me, don't do anything except lock yourself on my wing and just make it like I have a bigger airplane. Don't make the run yourself; when my bombs come off, just drop yours. Put them on manual. I'll make the run, I'll do the aiming, you just fly."

Rudy's green light was about three feet from my face during the entire flight. That's all I saw. We launched, I rendezvoused. I put his wing right there—and I can fly good wing—and off we went. By God, he had one airplane. When he rolled, I rolled. When he rolled inverted, there I was. We rolled in, off came the bombs. I never saw bullet one, I never saw missile one. We came into the ship, and I happened to see it go by in my peripheral vision, and that's the first time I saw anything but that green light.

We get down on the deck, and this newspaper reporter is aboard the ship, and he picks me out to interview. I don't know this guy, he was just somebody out there. And he asked me "How did it go?"

Now you have to remember I'm a consummate smart ass who had just completed his first combat flight and didn't die. Since 1961 I had been training to do this, and for the first time I [had] dropped a 500-pound bomb, and Rudy said we hit the target. At that time I also had about twenty traps on the ship; guys liked me; I was getting a little bit of respect and starting to feel pretty good.

So I told this guy we napalmed a school yard. The deal was [that] Rudy put lollipops in the speed brakes of his plane. The first pass over the school yard was made just to get their attention; on the second pass he dropped the lollipops out on the school yard, and when the kids ran out to get the lollipops, I was right behind him with the napalm smoking them all.

After the June Gulf of Tonkin arrival, the *Constellation*'s air wing initially flew only division-strikes over North Vietnam.

"When we'd get to the target, we'd split into two, two-plane strikes," recalled Siegel. "In we'd go, drop four or five 500-pound bombs, meet up, and then go back out over the water as a four-plane group."

The purpose, said Siegel, "was to get the wing flying together. You had a bunch of guys that didn't know each other, the new guys and the old hands that could do anything, and you needed everybody working together."

As the combat deployment progressed, full-scale alpha strikes involving all the Connie's attack, fighter, fueling, and other assets were staged and sent into strategic locations.

The hottest areas during the 1967 June to October combat missions included Hanoi "where you could get everything—missiles, MiGs, guns," notes Siegel. "The next little town down the road was Hai Duong, which had no missiles but an incredible amount of bullets. And Haiphong had everything."

During the month of August, sixteen Navy aircraft were shot down over Haiphong alone. On one particular day—21 August—some eighty SAMs were fired by the North Vietnamese in response to strikes off the Connie and fellow Yankee Station carriers *Oriskany* and *Intrepid*. The carrier air wings' targets included railroad yards, supply depots, and airfields, which were struck by bombs, rockets, and Walleyes.

One Haiphong mission was described by Siegel as "one of the most frightening moments I ever had."

We were in a thirty-plane strike going to bomb Haiphong, and the Navy was a little early to the target and the Air Force a little late in leaving the target area. The day was hazy. We were at fourteen thousand feet and traveling at four hundred knots, and here comes the Air Force. We didn't see them in time to move, nobody had time to yell. All you had time to see was them whiz by, and they were gone. We flew right through each other. God knows how many airplanes might have collided, but nobody touched and nobody said a word because once it was gone, there wasn't a reason to talk. I looked over to my roommate Jim Steele. He had this little thing that whenever he was scared, he'd take his mask off, put his visor up, take his helmet off, and scream. So that's what he did, took everything off and screamed.

On that same flight, I've got these two 500-pound bombs that didn't release during the bombing run. I pulled up, immediately stalled the wing, and boom, I'm upside down in an auger over the top of Haiphong. I'm dropping like a rock and seeing the city get closer as I come through the smoke and the clouds. I was able to reach over, throw the switch again, pickle the bombs, and off they came. Of course, the drop meant I was alone and there's two SAMs coming toward me. I went right down to the ground because I had no airspeed to maneuver with, and in order to save myself, I got down low to the deck where the missiles couldn't find me. While on the deck, I got this idea that Steele had been hit, after I spotted a burning plane that actually was an F-4. I went down to the crash site, circling about ten feet off the ground. I saw a guy on the ground, so I started looking around for assholes coming to get him. There weren't any, but then I started getting buffeted around and it's Steele on my wing, rocking the aircraft. I looked at him and told myself if he's there, who's that below, and why do I care. I look up and there's F-4 guys covering for their buddy, so off we flew.

Another particularly scary hop, about my thirtieth, came on a flak suppression mission. Up to this point I was fairly cavalier, with a pretty good attitude my ass was golden, and with my smoothness and combat experience, I could evade anything. And I had evaded missiles, making a few turns on MiGs and getting a couple of shots off.

The mission was near Hai Duong, and we were going to try and knock out some of the flak sites before the strike group arrived. Flak suppression had two sides; it could be scary, but the bad guys also knew you were a flak suppressor. They didn't care about you, they wanted the strike group. Finding the flak sites was a cat and mouse game. We knew about where they were from intelligence, but that was just a pin on a chart. An hour-and-a-half later, you're looking in the jungle or whatever, and it's a lot more difficult, so we had to get the sites to shoot at us.

To do that, we would send one guy down low, and if we could get the site to come up, the other guy would be up on top, ready to go in and smoke'm. On this mission I was loaded with bombs, bullets and Zunis. Steele was the low guy. He goes in over this flak site, and they come up and fire a few rounds. So I roll in and it's a trap. They're playing games with a quad mounted 30-millimeter gun, and unload on me. I was nailed, and I mean nailed. But I was high enough so the shells had lost their velocity and the slipstream of my airplane caused them to deflect and go around me. While they weren't coming through, I'm thinking, Hey, one of them could be directly on the nose of the airplane and could come right through and kill me. I'm a grape, I'm done, I'm just waiting to die. But I disarmed my bombs, and armed and fired the Zunis, which went right to the gun site and knocked it out. One minute I was scared to death, but as soon as it was over I was feeling eighty-feet tall. I had seen Matt Dillon do this for years on TV, and now it was me doing it.

In the middle of the first cruise, a buffer zone was reinstated around Hanoi. If you flew in there, they'd take your wings and bars and send you back home. We felt that was bullshit. From the Navy's point of view, we felt it was all political from Cubi on back. Every decision that was made was bullshit, and one of the reasons we felt like that were the stand downs. Here they were needlessly risking our lives because we finally had the North Vietnamese defenses knocked back. I could fly almost anywhere in North Vietnam, drop bombs, and not get shot at. But after the buffer was lifted, sure enough we'd go back in and it was hot again.

The target areas we couldn't hit were another real source of frustration. There was a place called Phu Ly, a bridge complex south of Hanoi.

On my first large alpha strike, the strike leader screwed up, picking the whole group up real slow, and my aircraft took a large round that blew off my wing tip. I still rolled in, got my bombs on the target, and made it back to the ship. I received a Distinguished Flying Cross for it, and the citation said I continued to the target after being hit. Hell, there was no place else to go but down, and I released the bombs just to save my ass. Anyway, we ended up going back to Phu Ly, and the reason was these four bridges that all went across one river, all feeding one road. We bombed three of the four bridges, but the fourth was a dam, and because it was a dam we weren't allowed to hit it. So we keep going back into Phu Ly and someone keeps taking a few rounds. So I told Steele this was bullshit, they're screwing us again and we're going to lose somebody.

So we just missed it. We were supposed to hit one bridge and we hit the dam. The RA-5 photo plane flew over, took the pictures, and there was hell to pay. A big meeting was called in the wardroom, wanting to know who dropped the bridge, but the end result was we didn't have to go back to Phu Ly. We beat their ass a little bit.

My second cruise from June to January 1968–69, I assumed the role of flight leader. I'm still scared, but for a different reason. The randomness of taking a round and being shot down scared me more than it did before because I'm aware that no matter what I did, or every bit of skill and experience that I had, it didn't matter. I could still get shot down. I was back to the I'm-as-good-as-I-can-be thinking, but that still wasn't good enough because there was a 5 or 10 percent chance I was going to get nailed.

The bombing halt up North put us into Laos, South Vietnam, and other places where we weren't supposed to be. It was futile really. One incident really stands out in my mind, one of those flights where the intelligence officer said it was very critical to the war effort. Like, if you do well on this one, the war may be over. That kind of bullshit.

The target was a road intersection, about five roads that came together. And they weren't roads, but trails, and there's already a million pock marks. I mean the place has been completely wiped out already, and there's no people in sight to shoot at us, no nothing. So we decide to go in and do some bombing practice.

In the midst of this little session, I hear "A-4s over umpty-ump checkpoint, stand down to the south, we've got an Arc Light coming through."

I don't know what an Arc Light is, so I said, "Arc Light, why don't you guys stand down to the side, we're just about done here."

The reply comes back, "We're a little short on gas, do you mind if we drop our bombs?" I said, "No problem," thinking we're all in this war together. We move to the south, and all of a sudden it gets dark. Here comes this big aluminum overcast, about forty B-52 bombers, and they're coming to bomb our target. Every B-52, flying at about 40,000 feet, has some 105 500-pound bombs and they start bombing at one end of the jungle and go to another. It was unbelievable.

As they leave, the call comes to me, "Okay, Garfish, you guys go back and clean it up." Well, there wasn't much before, but there is absolutely nothing now. Not even an aim point. I just told everybody, Forget it, let's go back to the ship.

The second cruise, and even the first, I continually asked myself, What are we doing here? I finally decided—and I was a pretty junior officer then—that we blew it. We had no national objectives, and I was very skeptical and cynical about everybody back in the United States.

I still believed that what I was doing was right, but I did not believe in any of the boffos that were making the decisions. I believed we were right in fighting Communism in Vietnam, showing them we were not going to put up with that crap. But we needed to do it with a defined objective.

As a pilot I was a wasted instrument, and that meant my aggression became less and less toward the people I was fighting against. I would always fight for the important hops because that was good for my career. However, I wasn't a maniac. There were some guys over there that were maniacs, who would take every last bomb they had and try to hit the target.

I would never make a multiple run. I would do my mission and be as aggressive as I could be. But once the mission was over, I was out of there. I always remember a pilot, a friend of mine, who was shot down and taken prisoner in 1967 trying to drop a bridge with one Mark 81, a 250-pound bomb. Had he hit the target right in the middle, the bridge would have still been standing there. He spent five years in jail for that.

Chapter 22
FAC

Summer and fall of 1967 proved more than memorable to the men who flew off the aircraft carriers based at Yankee Station.

On 29 July, only five days after arrival on-station, disaster struck the Atlantic Fleet–based USS *Forrestal.* Just before eleven that morning a Zuni rocket, accidently fired from an F-4 Phantom, struck the fuel tank of an A-4 Skyhawk, resulting in the death of 134 men and the destruction of 21 aircraft and damage to 43 others. Cost to repair the carrier was set at $72 million.

In the sky, bombing of the central areas of Hanoi and Haiphong was limited in June and July to single attacks on the power plants in those two cities. By late July approval was given to attack road, rail, and waterway segments in the formerly off-limits area around Hanoi and Haiphong. During the next month, major industrial and military targets previously spared were approved. The thirty-nautical-mile radius around Hanoi and the ten-nautical-mile radius around Haiphong were lifted, although special permission for strikes within a ten- and four-nautical-mile radius was still needed.

With the new guidelines, U.S. pilots dropped bombs on the Longbien Bridge in downtown Hanoi, railyards near the center of the capital, the Port Wallut naval base sixty-one miles northeast of Haiphong, and numerous targets along the Chinese border. New targets continued to be authorized in September and October. North Vietnam's third largest port, Cam Pha, was struck on 10 September, and planes hit additional highway bridges, warehouse areas, and railroad facilities in the heart of Hanoi and Haiphong. The latter became the focal point of a concerted effort to cut all land access routes.

The Haiphong isolation campaign began 4 September when A-4s and F-8s from the *Oriskany* knocked down four spans of the Haiphong Highway Bridge located two-and-one-half miles southeast of the city's center. Other bridges were also hit and on 21 September, the isolation of Haiphong was complete when two spans of the Kien An highway bridge, 1.7 miles southwest of the city's center, toppled into the water.

Haiphong's shipyard also came under attack—although the port and dock areas remained untouchable—and 30 September found previous off-limits airfields at Phuc Yen, Cat Bi, and Yen Bai under attack. In September alone, an average of five hundred Navy and Air Force planes hit North Vietnam every day and at one point—after five successive days of bombing—Haiphong simply ran out of SAMs, much to the amazement and amusement of American pilots.

By October, inclement weather gave the North Vietnamese cover to rebuild the bridges, although the Communists had found other means of getting the much-needed imports—estimated at 85 percent of the country's incoming goods—from the ships in Haiphong harbor out into the countryside. Truck and supply-boat activity increased, and the number of boats on the waterways from Haiphong to Hanoi doubled in the last half of September, and tripled by the middle of October.

North Vietnam did not sit idly by while the pace of American activity quickened, responding with a wicked barrage of SAMs and AAA. Sixteen naval aircraft were shot down in August, six by SAMs for the highest monthly SAM-loss rate of the war. Pilots counted 249 SAMs during the month, with a single day total of eighty on 21 August as aircraft from the *Constellation, Intrepid,* and *Oriskany* pushed their bombs toward targets. By late 1967 Hanoi was defended by fifteen occupied SAM sites, at least 560 known AAA guns of all calibers, and MiG-17s and -19s from nearby airfields.

As ship's company aboard the aircraft carrier *Bon Homme Richard,* Air Wing 21 landing signal officer Lt. Cmdr. Joe Ausley was regaled with stories of MiG kills and bridge strikes. Much to his regret, Ausley couldn't participate over the beach, and that bothered him. But the Air Force provided an alternative flying assignment.

I was upset not to get any combat time, so I wrote a letter to Seventh Fleet, with the captain's approval, requesting an exchange tour with the Air Force as a forward air controller [FAC] when the ship went off the line. Seventh Fleet thought the idea was great, the message went to the Seventh Air Force, and I found my young ass on the ground at Da Nang flying O-1s with the Air Force. In three weeks, I flew fifty-four missions, starting at Da Nang and then moving up to Dong Hoi just south of the DMZ.

The hops were about two hours long, covering [Route] Package 1 at fifteen hundred feet in the O-1, a Cessna 150 with a fabric skin over the frame. The ground crews would just cover the bullet holes with ordnance tape and the plane was ready to go. Our protection included a flak vest, we sat on a flak seat, and a flak vest was wrapped around our feet. We also carried an M-16 with three hundred rounds of ammunition. There was a high mortality rate, and just after, or just before I came, one of the O-1s got smoked by a SAM. Can you imagine wasting a SAM on an O-1?

The mix in the outfit was every type of Air Force pilot imaginable— B-52 drivers, many-motored props, F-106 folks, attack people. All these guys thought it was sort of purgatory to be there, like they're being punished. But, boy, there were some brave guys.

The tour was fun, watching all the different airplanes and their tactics, especially down South watching the little Army helicopter gunships attack pill boxes. At the time, we were still using napalm, and it was always exciting to watch the napalm drop, just unreal. Near Da Nang, we had one-bird flights, and I sat in the back, while up North there were two airplanes, primarily to have a spotter if someone went down. First flight I made out of Da Nang was with this Air Force captain. I can't recall his name, but I do remember him saying, "Hey asshole, what are you doing over here? Why would you volunteer for this dumb mission?"

"Well, all my counterparts are getting combat and I haven't had any combat."

"Oh, you want to get shot at."

"I didn't say that necessarily."

He took me out, saying he's got this one crazy down in a little pillbox who always shot no matter what. So down we go, he drops a smoke grenade out the window—there were smoke rockets on the wings, but you dropped the grenades out the windows which were always open— and the guy below shoots. Back we come, there's holes in the airplane, and his comment was, "How did you like that?"

In Package 1, the only way to get the air strikes was to have the sites come up. You'd just sort of troll, the site would start shooting, and you'd call in the strike. The FACs really loved the Navy A-4s, preferring a flight of A-4s at that time over any Air Force plane. The Skyhawk could really put the bombs on target, and the hits were good. The only plane better than the A-4 was the South Vietnamese Air Force Spads; they were really good at close-air support.

I remember going up one day, riding in the back seat because I wanted to get pictures of the Freedom Bridge, which went across the river from North Vietnam to South Vietnam, with flags of each country on both sides. We get to the bridge, taking all kinds of small arms fire, so I can have pictures for my scrapbook. We get back, and the film wasn't wound. The pilot called me a stupid SOB, I felt like one, and no, we didn't go back. But why would anyone risk getting shot at to take pictures of a bridge? I think a lot of people have the attitude, if it's going to happen, it's going to happen, and there's nothing to be done about it. Do your best, and don't worry about getting smoked.

Chapter 23
POW Summer

Summer 1967 was not the time for an American pilot to fall into the hands of the North Vietnamese. "A madness was said to be in the air, an eagerness to hurt, to cripple, to create the kind of groveling fear that would induce a 'cooperative attitude,'" wrote John Hubbell in *POW: A Definitive History of the American Prisoner of War Experience in Vietnam.*

Commander Bill Lawrence, a future three-star admiral, was shot down over Nam Dinh on 28 June. The commanding officer of VF-143, flying off the *Constellation,* Lawrence had not been aware the North Vietnamese were torturing POWs. He soon found out, suffering five consecutive days of gruesome misery.

In many respects Lawrence was lucky—at least he survived. Commander Homer Smith, skipper of VA-212 aboard the *Bon Homme Richard,* was shot down 25 May. Smith simply disappeared.

"I think he knew he was going to get shot down," related T. R. Swartz, who flew with VA-76, another Bonnie Dick A-4 squadron. "He was worried about the area we were going in—it was up North, just north of Haiphong—and in his brief [briefing] he didn't look good, smoking away on his God damn cigarettes. Sure enough, he got tagged with a gun, and he died or was killed in captivity."

Nineteen sixty-seven witnessed several major changes in the POW housekeeping and mutual support system. On 2 February Briarpatch was closed. Two dozen of the prisoners went to the Zoo and the remaining thirty-two, including Bill Shankel, a POW since 1965, were moved to a relatively new area of the Hoa Lo compound known as Las Vegas. Six individual cellblocks within Las Vegas were appropriately entitled Thunderbird, Desert Inn, Stardust, Golden Nugget, Riviera, and the Mint. Despite the best efforts of the prison authorities, the POW's Las Vegas communications network soon flourished.

More significantly, Thunderbird resident Jim Stockdale developed a policy to provide important guidance for areas not covered in the military Code of Conduct. Using the acronym BACK US, the letters represented:

B-Bowing. POWs were not to bow voluntarily in any fashion in public when anyone other than prison officials were present. If others were present, the bowing must be forced. The point was to show observers that POW treatment was not in line with the accords of the Geneva Convention.

A-Air. Stay off tapes and the radio.

C-Crimes. Admit no crimes and simply avoid the word.

K-Kiss. If forced to leave before the general departure of all prisoners, don't kiss the enemy goodbye. Make no show of gratitude to the captors.

US-United over Self. The POWs would stick together, placing prisoner unity over selfish interests. No officer would dodge responsibility to take command in order to protect himself from torture.

Bill Shankel and his POW counterparts utilized Stockdale's guidance to counter the mental and physical challenges of the North Vietnamese. But virtually nothing could combat the ill effects of malnutrition.

There were four guys to a room at Las Vegas, real small rooms, and initially Ralph Gaither and I moved in with Dave Wheat and Tom Collins. Gaither and Collins went someplace else after a camp shake-up, while Wheat and I were moved either to the Desert Inn or Stardust with Barry Bridger and Hayden Lockhart. From that time on, Wheat and I were either in the same room or the same building for something like six years.

At Las Vegas, people started complaining about pains in their feet and poor vision. The pain was so bad that Tom Collins and I would sit up all night long and keep our feet on the floor, hoping they'd get cold and wouldn't hurt. One night we even got a pan of water from the guard and tried sticking our feet in it. The problem reached the point where we could hardly walk, more of a shuffling gait to try and get around. It was all, I'm sure, due to a vitamin deficiency and only the guys from Briarpatch had the problem. We had a real crappy diet there, and a lot of the time meals were nothing more than a thin, watery wood soup. In other words, it [contained] a piece of bamboo. The bamboo shoots, I guess, went for the guards, although the food at Briarpatch was so bad even the guards had diarrhea all the time. By the time I reached Las Vegas, after over a year in captivity, I had yet to have a bowel movement that wasn't runny, and periodically there were episodes of bad diarrhea, maybe ten or fifteen bowel movements a day.

As for vision, Tom Collins reached the point where he couldn't read anything, and I developed huge cuts through my visual field. Eventually the gooks decided we couldn't live on just rice—as their most valuable piece of property, I guess they were afraid we might die—and started giving us bread. I was probably down to 110, 120 pounds, something in that neighborhood, before gaining any weight back.

Despite the sickness, either with bad foot pain, bad cuffs and irons, or whatever, I never wanted to die. I never, ever did, and I did not become a devout Christian or undergo a great religious experience, what's called being "born again" today. Robbie Risner, then an Air Force colonel, is one of the most inspirational and impressive individuals you'll ever meet. Guys told me he received the Air Force Cross for leading a strike on the primary target, and with ordnance left over, he went and hit the secondary target as well. One or the other was fine and he got both. When Risner talked, everybody just shut up and things would get straightened out. Certain people, you meet them and say this is King Wolf, this is the guy to follow. That was Risner. I was with him at Heartbreak, by ourselves for a couple of weeks, and Risner would say, "We've got to pray for this." Every day, I'd get down on my knees, and my right knee hurt something awful, but I'd do all this praying and nothing ever happened. I didn't feel saved, I didn't see any lightning bolts, and I did not feel any great forgiveness. One day it finally dawned on me that if there is a God, and he's all-seeing and all-knowing and everything else, he knows where I am, he knows what's happening to me, and asking him to get me out of here is just wasting his time because it's nothing but begging, and I'm not going to do that anymore. I decided if praying was the answer, just be thankful for what I had. So what did I have? I had all my toes and fingers and could still see, which is pretty good considering what I'd been through. Certainly I could have been killed out there, so from that time on I never did [pray] and I still don't pray for anybody.

The summer of 1967 was really bad because the North Vietnamese discovered, or at least knew, we were communicating, and the problem was more than just guys out speaking code. Notes were being passed, code flashed back and forth from building to building, and there wasn't a place in camp that wasn't covered. The gooks' biggest problem was they couldn't believe communication was so easy. Huge rooms had been cut up into little cells, built with two walls separating the cells and all that sort of stuff, so you couldn't talk, couldn't communicate. Well, we'd pass notes, cough by code, and so on. They started going through the cell blocks, room by room, and torturing people to tell how we communicated. This took time because guys were holding out, guys were being tortured for days and then giving little or nothing. It was important to push them as far as possible, to keep bad stuff off your buddies. Finally, this process got to be so long, or looked like it was going to take such a long time, they gave it up. The gooks never got down to my room that time, but they did later that summer.

I was asked to see a visiting delegation, and said no, I don't want to go see a delegation. So they put me out in the bathhouse in what we called portable irons, a long steel bar run through two U-bolts and padlocked. Portable irons and handcuffs, and just left out there in a bathhouse with food and water twice a day. The mosquitoes ate me alive because it was a wet and slimy place, and every so often the guards would come around and pound on me just for recreation. Just dumb-shit guards, but it was summer, and in summertime the guys were mean.

Finally, the gooks succeeded in giving me a black eye so swollen I could barely see out of it, plus I had infected mosquito bites and boils all over me. I figured it was time to talk to their delegation, and I had this master plan about going to the delegation and telling them how the treatment really was. The gooks, however, weren't interested in that, and they put me back in leg irons in my room, saying I had a bad attitude. Both legs were placed in stocks at the foot of the bed, and when your legs are in stocks, the knees can't bend. Then the right wrist was handcuffed to the left ankle and that's how you'd be left, sitting right on the two bones of your butt.

Fortunately all the cons had found a piece of wire someplace and ground it down and made a pick for handcuffs. Everybody had a handcuff pick, and we could all open a set of handcuffs behind our backs in the dark faster with a cuff pick than a gook could with a key. I was like that for a month or so and finally let out.

Chapter 24
Bloody 16

When the campaign to isolate Haiphong began on 4 September, the task of destroying the city's southern highway bridge went to the USS *Oriskany*'s Air Wing 16. Led by the air wing commander, Burton H. Shepherd, the twenty-four-plane strike dropped four of the bridge's five spans and returned unscathed to the carrier.

Not every bridge, unfortunately, was as easy to destroy nor every strike as anguish-free for the combat aviators of Air Wing 16. As the *Oriskany*'s final line period concluded in January 1968, thirty-eight out of seventy air wing aircraft had been lost, fifty-two were reported damaged, and nearly one out of every four combat pilots was either killed or captured, the worst loss rate of any carrier that served in Vietnam. And CAG-16, like her fellow air wings, also ran across one bridge that simply could not be destroyed.

During the three-and-a-half-year ROLLING THUNDER program, the Thanh Hoa Bridge—known as Ham Rung or Dragon's Jaw by the Vietnamese—achieved near legendary status because of its ability to withstand some seven hundred bombing sorties by CAG-16, by virtually every other Navy air wing to sail the waters of the Gulf of Tonkin, and by Air Force and Marine units. More than 1,250 tons of ordnance were dropped on the Dragon's Jaw, and eight aircraft lost in the quest to bring her down between 1965 and 1968.

Located seventy miles south of Hanoi and carrying part of the 165-mile rail line running from Hanoi south to Vinh, the structure, which traversed the Song Ma River, had been grossly overbuilt by North Vietnamese engineers. Five hundred and forty feet long, fifty-six feet wide, and about fifty feet above the river, Dragon's Jaw had two steel truss spans that rested in the center on a massive reinforced concrete pier, sixteen feet in diameter, and on concrete abutments at each end. Hills on either side of the river provided a firm bracing; between 1965 and 1972, eight concrete piers were added near the approaches to give additional resistance to bomb damages.

Despite bombing efforts that ranged from elaborately orchestrated strikes to spur-of-the-moment endeavors, no span dropped until 1972, leading Navy and Air Force ROLLING THUNDER pilots to speculate humorously that "the world was composed of two spring-loaded hemispheres, hinged somewhere under the Atlantic and held together by the Thanh Hoa Bridge. If the bridge was severed, the world would fall apart."

The bridge's mystique, however, had little to do with its purpose as a transportation conduit. When it was finally brought down by an Air Force laser-guided bomb, the North Vietnamese made no effort to rebuild it since alternative methods of rerouting supplies had long been implemented. The survival of Dragon's Jaw had represented a symbolic triumph of will for the North Vietnamese.

"Bryan Compton was convinced we could knock down the Thanh Hoa Bridge," remembers Dean Cramer, who called Compton "skipper" during VA-163's 1967–68 deployment, "and he was right, we could.

"It would have been a piece of cake if we had been able to get anybody to focus on it, but we never did. We focused like little kids; there was no leadership, no planned or calculated endeavor that would advance the war and therefore we're going to take the bridge. It would appear on the target list from Washington, but whimsically. It might be there one month, and not the next. We never addressed it, never dedicatedly, cold-bloodedly decided we are going to bomb the Thanh Hoa Bridge if we have to chip it away brick by brick."

When the bridge was given to the *Oriskany* as a target, Cramer reflects, "Burt Shepherd says, I'm CAG and I'll lead it. Bryan says, I'm going too, and we went."

We coasted in north of the bridge, headed for Laos, then turned south. It was only five miles, maybe ten from the coastline. We're tooling along and Bryan says to Burt, who's got his head in the cockpit, "It's off at ten o'clock, come left," and he starts giving him [Burt] vectors. It's a gorgeous day, and you can see it [the bridge] for miles. "Come left, come left, it's on your nose." Burt says, "I got it." We all roll in, dump, and thought we sunk it. You can't see the bridge for all the bomb debris, it's got to be gone; and the clouds disappear and there's the damn bridge.

Bryan decided to go back even though the bridge is the secondary target, and I said, "I'm going too." He launches, gets his strike rendezvoused, starts for the coast, and calls up, "My target is Flipper

Frankenstein," our code word for announcing the target is weathered in, "I'm going to my secondary target." This time there's just a little bit of flak and of course the same outcome—there stood the bridge when it was all over. He cobbed it, came back, and the next strike of the day is getting ready to go. He bumps the leader, and the Al says, "This is your primary target and the secondary target." And Bryan says "My tertiary target is the Thanh Hoa Bridge."

Bryan is told to stay away from the bridge, and he's not even out of sight of the *Oriskany* and comes up on the radio and says, "My primary target is Flipper Frankenstein, my secondary target is Flipper Frankenstein, I'm taking the tertiary target." He gets there and [there is] no flak, and that was his argument. If we kept hammering, they couldn't resupply fast enough, and we could lay down the God damn bombs if we needed to. But we never did."

Dean Cramer desperately wanted to fly jet aircraft in combat. Vietnam brought that desire to fruition, a desire not wholeheartedly shared by all his Navy counterparts.

Some people handle war well; they thrive on it. Other people have a helluva time with it, and some people can't do it. We had a helluva loss of people, endless numbers of lieutenant commanders turned in their letters because they were afraid, and it became a very sensitive issue. One of them lived next door to me, a baby lieutenant commander, an instructor in the RAG. He was the ready room tiger, with every God damn patch known to mankind sewn on his jacket, always smoking a big fat cigar, and a pretty good stick-and-throttle man.

We lived in base housing, and one day he's sitting out on the picnic table in the backyard, and there's just a board fence between us. He tells me [to] come on over and I'll buy you a drink. "I've had to make a helluva decision," he says. "I've decided to go ahead and get out. Now, I don't want people to misunderstand, but my brother is in the bridge building business, and he and his partner have been after me for years to get out and join them. I haven't been paying much attention, but they sent me another letter, and I just scrawled in the margin my price, what it would take for me to leave the Navy. They said, 'Okay, we'll accept it.' With that kind of an offer, I don't know how I can turn that down with my family and all that."

I said, "Hey, if somebody made me a helluva offer I'd get out, except I don't really want to do anything else. This is my bag, so for me it's different. But for you, do as you please. Yeah, maybe somebody will bitch, but six months from now you'll never see them again. You'll forget about it and know what you did was right.''

He left the Navy three or four months later, and another month goes by and his wife wrote us a letter. They're in San Francisco, and he just went to work for Pan Am. The whole story was bullshit. About five years later, probably longer than that, I walk into the VA-125 ready room, and there he is, same outfit, same routine. He'd gone to work with Pan Am, signed up for the reserves, and was now a commander getting ready to be skipper of a reserve squadron up in the Bay Area. He was playing the same old role, right there in the God damn ready room where I'd seen him before.

When I walked in, his face kind of froze. He smiled and said "God damn, Dean, it's good to see you." He stuck his hand out, and I just looked at him. Everybody was watching us, and I just stood there and looked at him. He put his hand down, I walked over to the coffee pot, and he just evaporated. Just disappeared.

I didn't care if the guys felt like they couldn't handle the war; that was their prerogative I guess. But it seemed unfair to the Navy, the nation, and the taxpayers to draw a salary for ten, twelve years while just training and playing grab ass, and when the time came to do your duty then say I'm not going to do that, and bail out without even trying. That really offended me, and still offends me.

Combat operations for the *Oriskany* and VA-163 began 14 July and by 4 August, two pilots—Lt. Cmdr. Don Davis and Lt. (jg) Ralph Bisz— were dead, while another went home after injuring his neck during an ejection. Saints' skipper Cmdr. Bryan Compton, nicknamed "Magnolia" for his southern drawl, led his squadron that first three-and-one-half-week line period on nearly five hundred combat sorties, of which 35 percent were alpha strikes. Dropping nearly 1.5 million pounds of bombs, VA-163's target list included railroad yards, bridges, POL, transshipment areas, and SAM sites.

Dean Cramer was getting the combat action he long sought and a taste of unique leadership.

Bryan is an unbelievable person, literally unbelievable. He's got a genius IQ, I think number two in his class at the academy. When they sent him to Postgraduate School at Monterey, the story goes half the time he ended up teaching the instructor. They'd say Mr. Compton, what do you think about this, and he'd go up to the board and show the instructor where he screwed up. But when you met him, you'd swear he just stepped out from behind a plow in Alabama. He's got that drawn, skinny, lanky kind of look of a farmer, and he uses every colloquialism found in the state of Alabama. He's absolutely oblivious to dress code, we had to follow him around to make sure he was dressed properly.

He's a fearless pilot. He'd fly into the hinges of hell and get away with it. Bryan's totally and absolutely satisfied he's in the hands of God, so nothing was going to be wrong. If he died, that was God's will. He felt God was going to take care of him. Half your survival is not losing control, and because he had such iron emotions and control of his fears, he got away with a lot of stuff. He also had a superb sense of humor and could take the hairiest hop, and have everybody laughing in the ready room with his off-color comments. One time the squadron was going up North of Haiphong, right on the Chinese border, to hit a railroad bridge in the pass. Cutting the tracks, we'd stop the supplies coming out of China. Washington finally authorized us to go up there, but were so scared about bombs falling into, or planes going into, China, that along came a truckload of instructions. Compton says okay fellows, blah, blah, blah, and then adds, "I want you to remember, penetration, however slight, constitutes an offense." Everyone just looked around and started laughing.

People would fly with him because they had faith that he could pull it off, but we also lost people right and left. My memory tells me the squadron started out with fourteen airplanes, and struck or lost nineteen, and we started out with twenty-one pilots and struck or lost eleven. At one point in the cruise 163 was down to something like six airplanes and twelve pilots, and we called ourselves Det Charlie.

The losses were nobody's fault, just a weird situation. Certainly we could probably blame Bryan with his overaggressiveness to a degree, but it wasn't always Bryan people were shot down with. Sometimes it was in twos, sometimes in another strike. So it wasn't Bryan per se. By fate, we ended up getting the primary targets over and over again. *Constellation* would go in, they wouldn't get the target, and we'd go in the next day when everything was stirred up and get the hell shot out of us, but we'd get the target. Whether it was true or not, we were kind of a sweep up. When all else failed, just assign the target to us, and we went to some God damn targets. Three alphas a day, and all of them to the delta. God, forty or fifty SAMs were not unusual.

There were alpha strikes, and there were alpha strikes. It depended on the target. To Haiphong, hell, it was a big deal, but also no big deal in a sense. Unless the North Vietnamese blew you out of the sky, water and safety was right there. Whereas if the strike was inland in any direction or distance, you were going to be captured because the chances of the airplane holding together were marginal. Now, a lot of people leaped out of their airplanes before they really should have— that's a fact. I've seen it. If the plane was still flying, you'd just have to gut it out, and again, the word is control. Hang on and not lose control. As long as the plane was flying, there was a chance. Walk away and all your options were gone. Maybe it might blow up, maybe it won't, but eject, and it's a given you're either dead or a POW. A lot of people just couldn't hang on. If they had, I think they might have made it, or at least had a helluva lot better chance.

Burt Shepherd, our air wing commander, was a very fine aviator and a helluva stick-and-throttle man, but he didn't have that iron-like control. Burt couldn't control himself—[he was] probably closer to the average aviator—and the problem was he had Bryan Compton, Jim Busey, and others, who could control themselves. He was compelled mentally to continue—he couldn't and wouldn't quit—and although he tried, Burt just couldn't come up to that level of performance. The way he'd try, Burt just went to instruments as he'd cross the beach. He didn't look out of the cockpit, almost strictly using instruments until getting to the target area, and usually somebody else found the target. I flew with him a lot, and on one flight to Hanoi I saw SAMs come right by him, one on each side.

Burt could not control Compton, there were very few people that I know of who could control Bryan. If he considered a request to be a stupid decision, he wouldn't do it. It was an acknowledged but unspoken fact that if the target was a really tough place, Bryan should lead because he could do it better. Never spoken, it just happened. As a result, our squadron then effectively led the war during that cruise on the *Oriskany*. We tried to spread the joy, but the natural tendency for Bryan was to ensure his people were with him. The squadron pushed availability—if the aircraft lighted off and dropped bombs, it was up. So we had a little better availability than other squadrons; we'd get more planes in the show. We had a lot of aggressive people, and those who weren't aggressive were forced to be players whether they were or not. You can't come back to the ready room after regularly downing the airplane, just can't do it. They were forced to play along.

I lost three wingmen. Another came to my room one morning and said, "I've got to quit." Jack, and that's not his name, said, "I can't handle it." The problem was he'd gotten himself so emotionally screwed up with this woman that he was an absolute disaster, and was hanging on by his fingernails. I said, "You can't quit, not for that reason. That's called cowardice in the face of the enemy, and Bryan will charge you with that. You can quit by telling me you can't fly, that's legal. You can always turn your wings in, but you can't quit because you don't want to fly in combat, that won't work. But you can't even do that. You've got a problem, a helluva problem. Your father idolizes you and you idolize him. If you turn in your ticket, you'll never forgive yourself. The old saw about a coward dies a thousand deaths, that's what you're going to do to yourself. You just can't quit."

"Then what am I going to do?"

"I'll tell you what, are you scared to fly with anybody?"

"I don't mind when I'm flying with you because I know I'll be okay."

"All right, you'll be scheduled to fly with me and you'll always fly with me. Just stick with me; that's the deal. Whatever I do, you do and you'll be fine."

In my mind, I'd get us out of any trouble somehow. I never stood still in the plane, always moving, jinking and so forth. With my good eyesight, most of the time I could see the SAMs coming when other people didn't, and I just seemed to be able to survive.

I was and am a very aggressive person. I was a small child, so I had to think to beat the other guy whether it was a physical confrontation, mental confrontation, any sort of confrontation. I had to use my mind, and I continued to do that. I had to think, and I had to have control. I couldn't lose control; I can't lose control. Occasionally I lose control and it embarrasses the hell out of me. I accomplish my goal, but it's overkill. Busey could stay in control very well, and some of the younger ones came along in that direction.

Because the air wing was losing so many people, teams were sent out from Washington, D.C., to find out why. They came up with nothing except the argument we flew line abreast, which was nothing but an expression we used. It was not a line abreast, God, if I defended this once I've defended it a hundred times in BS sessions. Initially, we, the wing, didn't have a tactic to handle the SAM; [We were] groping for an answer to handle the SAM and the awesome amount of opposition. What solved the problem, and created this line abreast thinking, was a discovery I made on one of our early strikes. I was the spider, the flak suppressor, and the job was to accelerate away from the strike group, get out in front, and have bombs impacting on the flak sites just as the strike group rolled in. That's the way the book read; yet there were a helluva lot of *ifs* in it. But regardless, that was the plan.

On this particular strike, I'm maybe two, three miles in front of the strike group and about that time I saw these two fireballs and I think, Uh, oh, that's the SAMs. I had thought about them a lot, and VX-5 [a test squadron] had come up with various spirals, high-G barrel rolls, and all kinds of crap to evade a SAM, none of which made any sense because most were impossible in a fully loaded airplane. Something told me the only way to handle the SAMs was play chicken with them, let the missile get as close as possible, make a violent maneuver, and cause it to miss by a couple hundred feet. On this day one of the missiles was luckily ahead of the other. The first one came, I waited, waited, and evaded. Here came the other one, and I evaded again.

I went back to the ready room and said, "I've got the solution, the way to evade the SAM." I explained [that] it's going to miss you at six o'clock, so no way can you evade to six o'clock. Bryan liked the idea and we began to plan our strikes in a very wide V, each of the groups of four and the entire strike. When the SAM came up, we were in position to descend, accelerate, build up energy, and duck the SAM as it came toward us. If there was a flight of four, if the leader pitched to the left, you didn't follow him, you pitched straight up. Some people didn't do it and, as a result, got shot down. But that's where the story came about as a line abreast—Bryan described it that way while briefing. Everybody then immediately thought of it as a full square line, and we could never get through it was a very loose description of a very wide V.

Our losses really were the work of three elements: the hot part of the war, *Oriskany* always ended up with the tough missions, and the wing had some very aggressive people.

I made four different combat cruises, and in that 1967 cruise alone I flew 125, 130 missions out of a total of 397. The real concern was complacency, and I constantly reminded myself not to get complacent.

I've seen guys die just because of plain, absolute, sheer stupidity. Others were just way over their heads.

One pilot—I'll call him Sam—just chickened out. He cold bloodedly created an injury. Sam was one of those way over his head, just absolutely petrified of this whole damn mess. We were going up the back door of Haiphong July 20, cutting up by Cam Pha and going in along a ridgeline headed towards Haiphong. Once past Cam Pha there was nothing, no flak, no targets, no SAMs, until the end of the ridgeline. We're about halfway in, and Sam comes up on the radio and says "I've been hit." But what the hell, there's no fire, and we're at 10,000, 12,000 feet, so it can't be small arms. He says I'm hit, I'm leaving the flight, and he breaks off and starts back, which is something you normally don't do. Sam went back out to the water, went to the north SAR station, made three turns around the north SAR, and ejected. Nobody could prove that he had not been hit because the airplane was in the water; then, he said, I've hurt my neck. We sent him home and he stayed in the Navy.

My best friend was killed because he was too aggressive. It was a night mission, July 25, underneath the flares, and flares were about as useless as a candle. You couldn't find anything with a God damn flare. He dropped the flare, and theoretically, you'd see things under it. Well, you couldn't see anything but shadows, everything else was a guess. He was sure he found a couple of trucks, but to this day we'll never know. He was with another guy. They dropped their bombs and decided to do night, low-level strafing runs under the flares. Strafing with 20-millimeter was another joke, and did nothing but get people killed. My friend was convinced he could fly anything, anytime, anywhere, and he was not that good, just overly aggressive. In peacetime I had conversations with him—"You silly bastard, one of these days it's going to bite you." He'd just grin and say it didn't. One time, to drop a 2,000-pound, inert bomb on the practice range in Fallon, he cleared the range and told the tower to hold the runway open because he was in a low fuel state. He delivered the bomb, chopped the power to idle, and coasted to the runway with about 200 or 300 pounds of fuel in an A-4. If the runway had been clobbered, there was no alternative but to eject, and all to drop a practice bomb. He did the same thing in Vietnam, night strafing, and flew the plane right into the God damn ground.

Losing a best friend tears you up. I had been on the flight ahead of him, landed, and he took off. All of a sudden we had word that he was down, and then the wingman over the radio said, "I saw the crash. He went in on a strafing run, there was a big explosion, and he does not answer." There was no doubt in our minds. I was really broke up about it; in tears and all that crap. I went out the back of the ready room to the catwalk and was crying. Jim Busey came out, but I took control of my emotions like I always do eventually and went back in and said, "I've got that off my chest." Busey's saying, "Why don't you go relax," and skipper said, "Go on and go to your room," and I said, "No, I've got my job to do. I've got to get his records and get a message out." And as his roommate I cleaned his gear out.

His death was the first loss that really impacted me hard, and I'd been through a lot of losses. In the old days you'd go on a peacetime cruise and lose five or six guys. He was close and had been for years, and losing a friend could really cause people to be relatively ineffective for a period. Most of the time, after a couple of days, they came out of it, although some didn't. Sometimes we'd ground them because the guys were too shook up, but other times, when short of pilots, the luxury wasn't available.

We had our share and more of wild raids, like the strike to Haiphong on August 31. Three guys were shot down, two from my squadron, and another from 164. One was an active duty reservist, and he had an alligator mouth, a real ready room tiger. He didn't believe anybody would pay attention, so he ran around and volunteered to come on active duty, never believing they would agree to it. They did. As a baby lieutenant commander, he'd ordinarily lead at least a section, maybe a division. The reserve was not permitted to lead anything. We very quickly learned he was incompetent, totally and absolutely petrified. I tried to get Bryan to pull his wings or send him home—he was dangerous. And he cost us two people and two airplanes.

Bryan came up with the idea that instead of going straight at Haiphong, we'd penetrate south of Haiphong about fifteen miles, aim towards the delta, go in three or four miles, make a hard right turn, and hit the target. It worked, we faked them out, and so we did it three days in row, the exact same damn maneuver.

The third time we went in, Compton had a flight of four, VA-164 had a flight of four; I was supposed to have four, but only had two, and I was between the flights of four. Bryan's leading this line-abreast maneuver, and as we turned to go into Haiphong, I called out two SAMs lifting off from north of Haiphong. I said, "Okay, they're tracking you, Bryan, and one is tracking you, Ghostrider,'' [to the pilot] leading the other group of four. The SAM in front is tracking Bryan. He pitches up and to the right, and the reservist [flying with Bryan]—call sign Old Salt Three—breaks the rule and turns down, and the missile blows up right in front of him and his wingman, Old Salt Four. Pieces of airplane went everywhere.

In the meantime, the other SAM headed for Ghostrider's division, and he froze in the cockpit. All three planes in the division left him, and he continued on, straight and level. The guys could see him moving the stick so rapidly the control surfaces were flapping but not responding because he didn't leave them in any one position long enough. The missile came right up and zapped him. Ghostrider came across my bow trailing smoke, but still generally in a whole airplane and heading for the water.

I told Bryan I'm going down with his two playmates [Old Salt Three and Four], and I trailed one of these hulks, waiting to key the mike to say eject. As a general rule, you didn't tell anybody to eject because you didn't know the situation. But in this case, if he didn't eject, he died. Just about the time I'm going to punch the button to say eject, out comes a chute. I go down with the chute, and it hangs in a tree by this little village. It's Old Salt Four, and I ask him if he's okay.

"Yeah, I'm okay I guess."

"All right, there's not a God damn thing I can do for you. I can't get a helo in here. I'll see you."

"Okay, I'll see you."

I went on out to where Ghostrider was just about to go in the water. The chute came down, collapsed right on top of him, and nothing. We screamed for heloes, finally got one in, and the crewman jumped in the water. Ghostrider was underwater, and of course, dead. He had suffered massive chest wounds, according to the crewman, bleeding and torn up. Whether he got hit in the chute or in the airplane, we don't know. But to get his body out was just too dangerous because the North Vietnamese were mortaring the helo. They [the crew] hoisted the helo and beat feet. Ghostrider's remains came home in 1987.

In the meantime, Bryan went right to the target, bombed it, and returned to see how his chicks were. On his way back he looks up, sees a chute in the sky, and a voice comes up on the radio, "Sorry boss, I blew it." The reservist always said boss. The reserve was either blown out of the cockpit or ejected, and to this day he doesn't remember. All of a sudden he was in the chute, one arm shattered. He knew he'd blown it and said so.

I came roaring back to the boat, ready to go through one of my horror shows. For about two weeks, we'd been told not to attack SAM sites unless [they were] a primary target, and we all said that's dumb. The North Vietnamese knew they could shoot and guide the missile without fear of retribution, and now we've lost three people. I'm totally out of control and bitter because I blame someone for this. We should never have not been able to attack SAM sites. I can't blame Bryan. It was dumb to go the same way three days in a row, but that's Bryan. The admiral has to be the one. He's the only one around, and he's the one who made this dumb rule. I was not emotionally prepared to consider that CARGRU didn't make the God damn rule; it's coming from Washington.

I hit the break, wham into the wire, and out of the airplane. I roar into the ready room with Bryan right behind me, throw my helmet into a chair, and head down to the war room where the leader goes to debrief the target. I wasn't the leader, but I'm going anyway; and the chief of staff, admiral, and Burt Shepherd are standing there when I fly into the room yelling something like "You son-of-a-bitch!" to the admiral. The admiral was a superb man, he really was. I was grossly insubordinate, and if he had acknowledged anything I said, he'd have had to accept that I was insubordinate. But it was like I never spoke, just wasn't there. He turned around and left the room. Bryan physically grabbed me, and I'm cussing out the chief of staff. Burt Shepherd and Bryan are trying to calm me down. "All right," I'm shouting, "I can tell you right now that if I'm leading an alpha and a SAM comes up, I'm going to take that SAM site out. And there isn't a God damn thing you can do about it except take the alpha strike lead away from me. If you do that, and give me a division, I'll break off from my division and attack the damn thing. If you take that away from me and make me a section leader, I'll take two [planes], and if you make me a wingman, I'll go myself. But I'm never going to pass up another SAM site." Bryan then dragged me out.

They did knock the SAM ban off. The admiral went in on the message track, I'm sure, and got it relieved.

The two "Old Salts" came back at the end of the war. One was an academy kid, on his first operational assignment, about as green as grass. We're up at San Francisco, and he meets a typical, good looking blonde and falls madly and passionately in love. We're all saying, "Hey, nice girl, but it's a big world." This doesn't bother him, but he won't marry her, he didn't want to bind her to anything because he believed he might get shot down. She's willing, so they're semi-engaged. She's in love with him, and none of us really believed that, but she is. After he gets shot down, she starts coming to all the squadron affairs, driving down for the wives' meetings. So when we get back from cruise, here she is. I grab her at this big party at the club in Lemoore and take her out by the pool.

I tell her "I know how you feel and all that, but God knows when he's coming out of there and that's *if* he comes out, if they don't kill him first. You're young, you ought to march on."

"I don't care, I'm going to wait."

"Well, do what you need to do, but if you change your mind, don't feel people will think otherwise because most of them don't know enough to think anyway. And I will think you've done what you needed to do."

"Well, I want to wait."

About two months after he got out they were married. She sat back, saved money, waited, met him, and two months later there was a wedding.

One of the most memorable raids of the cruise took place 21 August when Cmdr. Bryan Compton led a six-plane strike on the Hanoi thermal power plant, a mission that produced two Navy Cross recipients. Flying with Compton that day were future four-star admiral Jim Busey, as well as Cramer, Lt. Cmdr. Jerry Breast, Vance Shufeldt, and Lt.(jg) Fritz Schroeder.

"Each of us had a different location on the main generator to aim our weapons," remembers Busey. "Two of us were hit on the way in to the target area."

"I kept on going in, got my weapon, a Walleye, TV-guided glide-bomb on the target, and came back with an airplane full of holes and on fire."

Five Walleyes were fired and five bull's-eyes resulted, three striking the generator hall and two the boiler house. Thirty SAMs were fired at the strike aircraft, joined by 85- and 57-mm guns and small arms fire.

Official accounts of the strike report Busey's aircraft totaled more than 125 holes ranging from an inch in diameter to one eight-by-fourteen-inch gap, plus the plane was on fire.

Cramer, who never reached the target, made it back to the ship, on fire and with an assortment of aircraft damage, including a hole in the port wing measuring thirty-eight by eighteen inches.

In order to knock out the power plant, we needed to put four Walleyes on the target. Figuring to lose a couple of people in the process, [we took] six pilots. Ideally, all six would select a window to put the bomb through from all points of the compass.

We came across the beach as a flight of six—the fighters hung out over the karst in case the MiGs came up—and hit the crotch, went up by way of the ridgeline, and turned in towards Hanoi in two flights of three, splitting up individually to come in from different angles.

I was hit in my dive, my glide, by an 85-millimeter that exploded underneath and blew the plane inverted. I got back level, but the Walleye screen was all screwed up, and I could hear the bomb, with a thin, tin-like skin, tearing away from the plane. The 85-millimeter, and I didn't know this, put a hole in one wing, a small hole, which was bleeding fuel and leaving a white vapor trail behind me. Every God damn SAM and flak site in Hanoi, I'm convinced, was shooting at me. I ducked six or eight SAMs, controlled SAMs. I flew up, there'd be one, and I'd go down, and there'd be another. All the SAMs were in close, reasonable range and finally they just ran out. Then I got complacent, flying straight and level, and a 37-millimeter shell blew a hole in the port wing, which caught fire. The wing's burning merrily and I say, "Okay, I'm hit, I'm on fire and coming out." We're on a tactical frequency, over Hanoi, and I think nobody else can hear. Wrong.

The admiral knew the raid was going to be a tough one and was worried about it. So he put up a middle man, an E-1, to pipe our transmission back to the war room to follow the raid's progression. He thought about it more—hell, the whole ship knows this is not a normal raid and it's no secret. He put it on the 1MC, and that's the speaker you hear even in the john.

I'm saying [that] I'm hit, I'm on fire, and it would be nice if one of you bastards would come over and join on me so when I get out of the son-of-a-bitch I can be found. I headed for the karst, and an F-8 driver eventually found me. The plane's still burning a little, none of the gauges work, and the stick is moving, but it doesn't feel right, and I can't get anything out of it because the whole ass end is all shot full of frag.

The fighter pilot doesn't want to tell me this because he's afraid I'll eject. Of course, by then I had no intention of ejecting. I'm obviously short on fuel, all that's left is one thousand pounds in the fuselage, and the rest is all falling out the wing and burning. A tanker's waiting at the crotch, and he gives me two gallons and that's it, the package is screwed up. A second little A-4 tanker can't get his hose out, but by now I'm over the water and not too sweaty any more. If all else fails, I'll jump out of this God damn thing and be okay.

I start working my way back to the ship, and at the same time asking if a big tanker is up. The reply is "Wait one," and I come back and say, "Wait one, my ass. God dammit, do you have the big tanker up or don't you?" The reply is "Stand by," and I yell to look up on the board and tell me if you've got a big tanker up or not. Then I see the big tanker, and say, "Aw forget it, I've got him in sight." I get two hundred pounds, but no more because my pipes are all screwed up.

The ship clears me straight in, but unbeknownst to me, Busey's cleared straight in on a different frequency. So here we are both coming straight in, and I've got another problem. If I come in on a normal approach, the plane's going to flame out right over the fantail. So in my head, I decide to shoot a precautionary flameout. But I can't tell the *Oriskany* because nobody will ever approve it. I plan to come in at 2,000 or 3,000 feet, chop the power to idle, dump the nose down, and flare myself into the wire. As I decide, Okay now, out from under my nose comes Jim. "Aw shit!" I pull out, say, "Okay Jim, you've got it." He says, "No, I'll take it around." "No Jim, you've got it, and I'm already doing a 360 because I expect my wing will fall off when I trap and clobber the deck." Jim comes in and bolters, and I call up and say, "Sorry about that Jim, but you had your chance." By now, I'm back in position, drop the nose, flare the wire, and land. I look around, and the God damn island has people all over it, and they're all waving. It's like family day, and on the flight deck is the admiral and the captain of the ship, and they're both waving. I park the airplane, climb out, and they're beating me on the back. Then I find out it's all been on the 1MC.

The admiral gave all of us medicinal brandy, Christian Brothers' brandy with cokes, two or three of those. A kid who had been a public affairs officer on Second Fleet staff is now a PAO on the Seventh Fleet staff, and I know him and he knows me, and he says, "Mr. Cramer, did you think about ejecting?" I said, "Eject? Hell no, the liberty's piss poor over there.'' Everybody laughs and I don't think anything about it. That night I write a letter to my wife—another day, a couple of hops—and about a week later I get a letter from her saying she just heard about me on television. Walter Cronkite picked it up.

I received a DFC for the strike. The awards board put the medals together. Bryan received a Navy Cross and Busey was put in for a Silver Star, later upgraded to a Navy Cross. Jerry Breast got a Silver Star, and the board wasn't sure how many of those would be available, and I'm asked what I thought I should get. Well, I ought to get something, I'm pretty satisfied I did a pretty damn good job of flying. A Distinguished Flying Cross seemed fair, so they put me in for a DFC. That was my first DFC, and I ended up with five. The damn award ceremonies for 163, 164 took almost two hours. But it wasn't hard to get a medal; all you needed to do was just stay alive. And if you didn't stay alive, you got one anyway.

Chapter 25
Corsair

The aircraft carrier USS *Ranger* and Carrier Air Wing 2 (CAG-2) arrived in the Gulf of Tonkin 3 December 1967, bringing the all-new A-7A LTV Corsair to combat. Designed to replace the workhorse A-4 as the Navy's primary light attack aircraft, the Corsair was flown by the Argonauts of Attack Squadron 147 (VA-147).

"It was a big deal to be part of the squadron," relates Rusty Scholl, then a lieutenant (jg) making his first operational deployment. "The luck of the draw got me there; I just happened to get into flight training at the time they were looking for the initial group of nuggets to go to 147."

Joining the F-4B, A-4, and A-6 as the carrier's strike-fighter element, the Corsair's first taste of combat came on 4 December, and within two weeks, A-7 pilots were bombing the Hai Duong rail and highway bridge between Hanoi and Haiphong. On 22 December the first A-7 combat loss occurred, and over a month later, the *Ranger* and its Corsairs arrived in the Sea of Japan. Eighty-two American crewmen from the *Pueblo* had been taken prisoner, and the focus of American military attention, for a brief period, drew away from Vietnam.

"One day we're sweating and dropping Mk-82s off Vietnam," remembers Scholl, "and three days later we're freezing, it's snowing, and we're dropping Mk-76 practice bombs on an island off Korea or Japan."

The *Ranger* soon returned to Vietnam, with the A-7 and its VA-147 pilots continuing to draw attention as the Navy's newest and finest light attack unit.

The squadron, commissioned in early summer of 1967, was treated differently, not outwardly, but babied along. We deployed in November, going on-line in December, with us and an A-4 unit providing the light attack role. The A-4 guys weren't too hot about being out there with us because of all the attention the squadron received. The newsmen would always come and talk about the A-7, pushing the A-4 off into a corner, and I was so green I didn't realize the attention was anything abnormal. The only plus the A-4 squadron had over 147 that first cruise was a better ready room. Selected [according to] the seniority of the skippers, ours was underneath the arresting gear in the back of the ship.

Skipper [of the squadron] Jim Hill was quiet, always had a soggy cigar butt in his mouth, sometimes lit and sometimes not. It'd gross you out, plus he always had a cup of coffee. You'd get to his stateroom at three o'clock in the morning to wake him up, and the first thing he'd do was grab the cigar, stick it in his mouth, and grab that cold cup of coffee and start drinking. He was demanding, but not overly so. He knew what he was doing; there was no question about that. And there's no question that all the pilots in the squadron knew what they were doing in the airplane by the time training was completed.

We started out bombing in Laos, South Vietnam, making toothpicks out of trees in order to get experience and go up North. All FAC-controlled, and I don't know whether there was anything down below or not, but the nuggets would pull off the target, jinking all over the sky because the enemy had to be shooting at us. After a couple of flights, the senior people told us there was no need to maneuver quite that much.

The FACs loved the A-7, especially in North Vietnam. Whenever A-7s were around, they'd try to get us because of our ability to put the ordnance right where it was supposed to be. Our accuracy had nothing to do with pilot technique, it was the bombing computers onboard at the time. LTV, the Corsair manufacturer, had as many tech reps aboard the ship as we did pilots, and I mean they had those airplanes tuned just perfect.

A-7's were also great on fuel. You could fly all day, come back, and still have plenty of gas. That ability just amazed everybody. Here's a plane that launches off the ship with ten or twelve 500-pound bombs, goes out and comes back, and has enough fuel to miss that recovery and get to the next recovery four or five minutes later. The F-4s and A-4s had just enough fuel to make one or two weapons passes, then leave. We'd come in there, and the FAC would ask, "How long can you stay?" We'd say "I've got ten bombs; we can give you one bomb each run, and then there's the 20-millimeter, we'll give you five or ten runs from there." And we'd still have plenty of gas left.

[As for] combat, the first cruise never got hot, and the second that started in late 1968, well, the bombing halt had been ordered. Our first and only combat loss—and the A-7s' first loss—was Jim Hickerson. My section leader, he got bagged by a surface-to-air missile up near Haiphong. I didn't see the missile; in fact, I didn't see a missile in my first two cruises. I saw a lot more action later in 1971–72 on the staff of Air Wing 15. But I enjoyed the hell out of the uniqueness of being [in] the only A-7 squadron in Vietnam. LTV provided patches, peel-off stickers proclaiming Jason is Here and Jason and the Argonauts. I mean those stickers were all over Hawaii, on bathroom doors, light posts, sign posts, you name it. We also picked up a new nickname, the "Farcuts." Some journalist or senior officer was talking about the officers in 147, and he said these officers are obviously a far cut above the average officer. So we became known as the Farcuts.

Right before we headed to Korea, January 22, 1968, the *Ranger* was coming up on its one hundred thousandth landing. Three of us were coming back from a bombing mission, fooling around and having a good time, and this F-4 screams into the break and cuts right in front of me. Really shitty. I try and slow down, and the air boss came up and asked the F-4 driver what he was doing.

"I didn't see the A-7, and I'd like to go ahead and land."

"No, take it out and bring it around."

I came up and said, "I can make room for him," but the air boss said, "No."

The F-4 driver then says he's low on gas. "I'd really like to go ahead and land."

"Take it out and reenter the break."

All throughout this entire conversation, it still hadn't dawned on me what was going on. Well, the first guy in front of me traps, [then the] second guy, and then it comes around to me, and I roll into the groove, call the ball, and someone tells me "better make this a good one." Then it dawns on me, the *Ranger*'s one hundred thousandth landing. So I land, the skipper of the ship comes down from the bridge, and there's this humongous cake and everything. I ended up with a plaque, and the tailhook was taken off my airplane, but what sticks in my mind is the next day, the *Pueblo* incident occurred and the landing never got in any of the newspapers.

We came home in early summer, had a four, maybe five month turnaround, and went back out. It was like you're gone before turning around. We came back, went on leave, started workups, went to Fallon, came back to Lemoore, went to sea, came back, and then went on cruise.

The ship started up in North Vietnam; then it was nothing but South Vietnam, Laos, and Cambodia. That second cruise, Dave Carroll and I had the biggest stateroom on the ship, located right near the ready room. We'd walk right out of the room twenty feet, turn left, go down another twenty feet, and there was the ready room. The place was next to a dead-end passageway, and nobody else wanted it because of the possibility of fire and no place to go. Plus, one end was next to the catapult machinery room, another side was the steam accumulator for the catapult, and the other end a bomb elevator. During flight ops, you didn't want to be in our room. It was ridiculous. I used to try and sleep with Mickey Mouse ears on, and it would still be too noisy. The catapult would fire, the steam accumulator hiss, and the bomb elevator make this real screeching whine, and the room would shake. But when there was no flight ops going, it was great. The place used to be the ship's administration office, and we'd show movies, skin flicks, and such; put a sheet at one end and get thirty or so guys in there. God, it was a great time.

The combat environment of the second cruise wasn't too tough. Everybody knew the war wasn't being fought to win; and putting all those restrictions on where you can bomb, and can't bomb, isn't my idea of going out to win.

Part Five
1968

There are wars that are inevitable under the circumstances. The war in South Vietnam is one. The U.S. could not ignore the challenge. . . . We can and should think in terms of the defeat of the North Vietnamese. . . . To say that the United States cannot do this is a counsel of despair.

Drew Middleton, *America's Stake in Asia*

Introduction

Khe Sanh, Tet, the *Pueblo,* the 31 March bombing halt. Events and names that dominated the attention of millions of Americans in early 1968.

The Tet offensive, initiated one day before the Vietnamese lunar new year holiday, marked the psychological turning point of the war as the Communists launched attacks on every major city in South Vietnam. While the offensive was unsuccessful militarily, the television image of North Vietnamese soldiers entering the US embassy in Saigon played havoc on the American psyche. Of no help to American morale or military credibility was the request by General Westmoreland for another 206,000 troops to launch a new offensive.

Khe Sanh, an isolated Marine camp some six miles from the Laotian border, came under assault 21 January. The seventy-seven-day siege saw Navy pilots join their Air Force and Marine Corps counterparts in beating back North Vietnamese troops from the embattled camp. CTF-77 aircrews flew sixteen hundred attack sorties in March alone, striking a wide array of targets in Khe Sanh's immediate area.

If Tet and Khe Sanh were not enough to occupy U.S. military forces, North Korea joined the list of American tormentors. The Navy spy ship USS *Pueblo* was surrounded by North Korean patrol boats and boarded 23 January after a brief exchange of fire. In reaction, the carrier *Enterprise,* which had been docked at Sasebo, Japan, en route to her third Vietnam deployment, rushed to the Sea of Japan where she stayed until early February.

The pace of Task Force 77 strikes on North Vietnam during the initial months of 1968 was a far cry from the hectic schedule of 1967. The previous twelve months had found naval aircraft flying a record seventy-seven thousand combat and support sorties, resulting in the destruction of thirty-three SAM sites, fourteen MiG aircraft in the air and another thirty-two on the ground, almost two thousand antiaircraft sites, thirty power plants, and nearly fifty-six hundred motor vehicles. The cost for these spoils of war was quite steep—133 aircraft shot down, and two-thirds of their crews killed or captured.

In essence, 1967 might best be remembered as the year that could have been. John Colvin, British consul general in Hanoi, observed that the strength of the American bombing campaign of summer 1967 had rested not only on its weight but on its consistency, hour after hour, day after day. The strategy . . . for the first time, allowed the North Vietnamese no time to repair warmaking facilities. No sooner were they repaired than they were struck again; Tonkinese ingenuity had been defeated and, by the remorseless persistence of the campaign, their will eroded to near-extinction.

But although some spasmodic bombing in the northeast quadrant took place after September, it was on a greatly reduced scale and frequently interrupted by long periods of inactivity during "peace initiatives," all illusory if not contrived, and anyway occasions when the campaign should have maintained, even increased, momentum. Above all, that factor—the persistence of the campaign—which had sapped North Vietnamese endurance was discarded. . . . Victory—by September 1967 in American hands—was not so much thrown away as shunned with prim, averted eyes.

Early 1968 activity was limited in scope because of poor weather, and the bulk of the work went to the aircrews of the all-weather A-6 community. Visual bombing in January and February occurred on only 3 percent of the days, thanks to the Northeast Monsoon. The weather showed little improvement in March. April operations up North were never realized.

The evening of 31 March—the morning of 1 April to the aircrews on Yankee Station—President Johnson announced his decision to decrease the war effort.

"Tonight," said the President, "I have ordered our aircraft and our naval vessels to make no attacks on North Vietnam, except in the area north of the demilitarized zone where the continuing enemy buildup directly threatens allied forward positions and where the movements of their troops and supplies are clearly related to that threat.

"The area in which we are stopping our attacks includes almost 90 percent of North Vietnam's population and most of its territory. Thus there will be no attacks around the principal populated areas, or in the food-producing areas of North Vietnam."

With all bombing limited to below the 19th Parallel, Navy aircraft during the next seven months focused their attention on attacking supply lines in the southern panhandle of North Vietnam and Laos. On 1 November all bombing in North Vietnam came to a halt. ROLLING THUNDER, long-running and ill-conceived, was over.

Chapter 26
Back as CAG

Two years and a totally disparate war marked Cmdr. Paul Peck's return to Vietnam in 1968 as the commander of Air Wing 9 based on board the carrier USS *Enterprise*.

"It was literally a different war," relates Peck, who left NAS Lemoore–based VA-94 in late 1965 after leading the Mighty Shrikes on the initial combat missions of the conflict. "The war was serious, much more political, and the opposition very sincere—you were susceptible to everything from thirty thousand feet on down.

"Our performance was much more professional, and so was [that of] the Vietnamese. Their warning system worked very well; they kept pretty good track of your airplane, your heading and location; and the fighting was a lot tougher and the losses, correspondingly, a lot higher."

At Lemoore, home of the Pacific Fleet's A-4 and A-7 light attack element and several air wings, including CAG-9, the mood of the community had taken on a gloomy hue during Peck's two-year hiatus.

"Lemoore had changed just unbelievably," remembers Peck.

When I got back from the first combat cruise, it was kind of a happy community. My second cruise, many of the quarters were occupied by ladies with husbands missing in action [or] POWs, and [by] unaccompanied wives. A little melancholy, not totally so, but the overtones were certainly there.

Lemoore was bearing the brunt of the war, and [for] anybody who riffled through the names of the killed in action, missing in action, or prisoners of war, there was no question Lemoore outnumbered them all put together. We took our hits, but there was a little bit of pride that went along with that too. But it was a totally different atmosphere from two years earlier.

The Navy lost 195 A-4 Skyhawks in combat during the Southeast Asian conflict—more than double the losses of any other fixed-wing aircraft—plus fifty-five A-7s were also blasted from the sky. The cockpits of a good percentage of those airplanes were manned by Lemoore-based pilots.

Peck found the responsibilities of leading an air wing quite different from his previous combat cruise as a squadron CO.

The mission of CAG is a lot different than CO. CO is primarily a flyer. CAG has got to be a flyer, but at least 50 percent [of his job] is planning and negotiating with various people at the staff and fleet levels as to the employment of the wing. I didn't have the latitude to take the flights that I could and did take as CO, because of the five to six hours of daily strike preparation and planning work.

But CAG has got to be the best job in the world in the flying sense. I flew the F-4, A-6, RA-5, A-4, even the E-2 a little bit. Off the ship I initially flew the F-4, A-4 and A-6, but a rule came out you could only fly two off the ship in combat, which for me was the F-4 and A-4.

In combat I thought the wing did a pretty good job, although we took a lot of losses, particularly my A-6s as misfortune would have it. The A-6s were doing a lot of the heavy work just prior to the stand down, flying daily at night into a lot of missiles and flak. As I understand it, VA-35 flew over 50 percent of the night missions the A-6 community made into Hanoi. For one squadron that's big stuff, and we lost half the squadron including the CO and XO. To get into a target at absolute zero visibility at four hundred feet and four hundred knots on solid instruments is pretty tough. Almost half our A-6 losses were operational—flying into the ground—but to come in above five hundred feet, you were getting the [SAM] beeper all the time. At one point, another squadron was sent in to check our losses out. That group launched four airplanes, none of which made the target. They were all shot down, every one of them. The squadron went in at one thousand feet and it was impossible to live up there. Living safely down low was tough, but you couldn't live up high. I was still flying the A-6 at that point and there was no way to make the target at that altitude.

In the bad weather, we decided the only way to take A-6s in was one at a time. Unfortunately, the planes had everybody's attention. We tried very hard to get the planes coming from different directions and crossing the target in close proximity, but it wasn't like a Blue Angels' show. Separation was mandatory, and by 1968 the missile work down below was very, very good. The North Vietnamese, or whoever operated the sites, were just excellent.

Despite the losses, there was no problem in motivating the A-6 types. I remember the night we lost the [A-6] skipper, Glenn Kollman. He was very popular, a very experienced and capable CO. His plane had a malfunction of some sort, [and] dumped in right off the catapult on probably one of the worst nights I've ever flown. I was out with a group of four that had gone in on a strike, and to spot the weather—which was absolutely solid, the type the A-6s liked—and over the radio I heard him go in. He was a close, personal friend, and it kind of takes the heart out of you to lose someone like that. We finished the damn mission, a real pyrotechnic display because the Vietnamese were shooting low and bending the trajectory of the SAMs. These great big orange puffs were coming up above the low overcast, really a sight to behold, and all I could think of was Glenn. I wanted to get back and find out what had happened, whether the helo got him out or not.

I barreled back to the ship in this F-4, one of two times in my Navy career I came aboard without ever seeing the meatball. Absolutely never saw it—they talked me in and all of a sudden I was on the deck. I got out, thinking this was going to be a really bad recovery, so instead of going down below and finding out what happened, I went out to the tower, the pri-fly. We made sixteen approaches, sixteen landings, nobody took a wave-off, and the airplanes weren't even visible from the tower, just popping out on the deck. We'd been flying a lot at night because *Enterprise* was the large deck carrier out there at the time, and the conclusion I drew was that if you practice, get good at something and get the emotional edge out, it's easier.

When the recovery was over, I went below and found out both Kollman and his BN were gone. I went over to 35's XO, Herm Turk, and said, "You know, XO, its been kind of a hard night and I think we're going to kind of wrap it up." He looked at me and said, "CAG, we've got to get started sometime, might as well be the next launch." I said, "Good for you, Herm, go get 'em and we'll see how it works out." He did just that, took the first airplane off, and [the squadron] never stuttered.

That era was supposedly the height of revulsion towards the war. In my experience, it never hit out in the gulf at all. Guys, at first, were a little goosey about going into combat, but all they had to do was get their pink body shot at two or three times and a personal interest in the North Vietnamese began to grow.

Our basic schedule was flying 12 hours on, 12 hours off. Initially, the wing flew the "Polish" schedule, flying from midnight to noon or noon to midnight. Of course, that was really a terrible mistake; we became very stylized about getting over the target, and the Vietnamese knew it. Take an hour-and-a-half flight, for instance, which everybody adhered to. Take off at 8:00 A.M., meaning you'll hit the target no sooner than 8:30 and be off the target at 9:00, and back to the ship at 9:30 when the next flight would take off. The enemy knew our schedule, and they'd have an hour or more of free time to work on roads or whatever. So it became patent to everybody that no matter what we did, don't take off the same time every day. On the *Enterprise,* and I don't know about the other ships, we'd fly from 11:32 to 11:32. Rear Adm. [John] Weinell was very good about giving us that kind of latitude.

As CAG, I had a lot of control over target selection in the interdiction work, which was mostly road recce. I'd have a pack of roads, and apportion them out to the squadrons to get a little competition going. A lot of people in road recce work would hit choke points, pacifying one point. The problem was the enemy would concentrate their road fixing equipment right there, and to only bomb that point would just make it easy for them. Our idea was to keep it varied, spread the bombs out, make a cut at one point; another, eight miles down the road; and another cut twelve miles; and maybe drop some mines in between. I thought it worked out very, very well, our indications were it did, and the competitive concept was a good idea because road recce can get to be a little dull. "Hey, 56 shut off route fifteen last night, only one truck got through; and 113, eighteen trucks came through their route and the fighter squadrons did this, that, and the other thing."

On alpha targets, once in a while we had flexibility. At Vinh there was a beautiful cathedral built back in the good old days. We just knew something was going on in there, and kept tabs on it. One morning an RA-5 goes out at the crack of dawn, zips across Vinh, and lo and behold, there's a SAM missile transporter backed up to the nave loading an SA-2 missile into the cathedral. I grabbed that photo while it was still wet, ran up to the admiral, and said, "Here it is," and he said, "Go get it." We previously had infrared photos showing lots of truck traffic around the cathedral, and you don't have truck traffic to that degree around a cathedral. The antenna went up, but the question was to get the goods on them.

Off we went, I dropped one bomb, and the damn thing went up; in fact, it was a little embarrassing. The secondary explosion went up eight thousand feet, and pretty much engulfed the second wave heading to the target. Nobody was hurt, but it sure scared the beejesus out of them. The flaming debris from the cathedral also hit some nearby buildings; they started blowing up; and we dumped bombs on those. The incident occurred about 8:30 in the morning, and I went on a night flight about midnight and the fire was still burning. Our claim later was we turned the most beautiful cathedral in Vietnam into the largest outdoor swimming pool. Nothing left but a hole.

The wing had the latitude to hit targets like Vinh, and I was fortunate enough to have an admiral I could talk to about anything. He, of course, had a much greater latitude in target selection than we did. If the wing had targets, we could always submit them to CTF staff and talk them around, and sometimes they came back. But a lot of the non-targets were inexplainable, like the docks at Haiphong. We wanted to mine the harbor at Haiphong in 1968, I begged them to let me put that place out of business. The main characteristic of the war in 1968 was the indecisiveness at the upper levels: Who was running the war? Why were they doing it? When you let civilians run a war, it's almost as bad as letting military people run a country. War is war, it's like love, all is fair. You've got to go out and do it, you can't sit around and play at it.

While the situation was frustrating, you had to concentrate on the positive, which we did. Our interdiction campaign was helping the troops down in South Vietnam, there was some pretty good proof to that. We took out Route 15, and the North Vietnamese quit on Route 15 for almost two months, and that was never done during the war. The squadrons were given great latitude to do whatever they wanted. Instead of the whole wing doing the same thing, there were four or five ideas getting thrown out and discussed. Morale was good out there, I didn't notice anything wrong. Aircraft availability was good. Our losses—with the exception of the A-6 squadron—were acceptable.

Fighter guys, I think, suffered from a morale viewpoint. In Vietnam, like Korea, the fighter role was limited; they weren't getting with it to the same extent the attack people were. I always had to work with my fighters in order to keep them going because a lot of what they did was deadly dull. For years, twenty-four-hours a day, we had the BAR-CAP—two airplanes, going around in circles. That's an awful lot of flight hours, and it was pretty dull stuff. Vietnam was an attack war, the attack people were the heroes and the ones who bore the brunt of it all, at least around the carriers. I went through three cruises, and I'd say 75 percent of our awards and decorations went to the attack people. And probably not rightly so, it should have been 80 percent.

In 1968 it was truly not unusual to fly three missions in one day. I often did it, and I did less flying than others. The dangers involved were just part of the job, and only once can I remember ever worrying about it. I don't know why, but I got the feeling right before one mission that, boy, this is a tough one, my number is up. But I flew the mission, it went fairly routine, and I came back and decided I wouldn't worry about it. A real ho-hummer. As a group, the guys that were in the squadrons in 1968 were all combat experienced, very professional. It fell off in 1969. The Navy was pumping new guys in, and there was a difference, because as the British used to say, "The regiment was blooded." There's also a confidence factor, and a capability factor.

In November of 1967, right after I relieved as CAG, we went out on the ship for buildups and received a message stating President Johnson was coming aboard. "He'll be on board for forty-eight hours, so please put on an air show and blah, blah blah, and oh, by the way, include day and night operations." Nobody had been aboard at night for the last three months, but the visit worked out just fine. Johnson was a guy I didn't cotton to at all, I wasn't pleased with the way the war was being run. He came aboard with Secretary of Defense [Robert] McNamara, who as it turned out, was fired on this little visit, and everybody who had a stateroom with a john attached had to give it up because of the ladies in Johnson's party. I went down and slept in sick bay. Anyway, we had a very nice meal for some of his staff, and I was with them finishing up the meal. Dessert was Baked Alaska and I was in the midst of a nice heaping helping when the telephone rang. I picked it up and the voice said, "Paul, this is the President. Could you join us for dinner?" Of course, I said, "Sure." I was absolutely unprepared for the personality and charm of the man. I think most anybody would have liked him.

That evening the entourage went up and watched the night recovery. It was a crappy night, and as I said, my guys hadn't seen the night

deck for months. I had all the COs out, the first team, and they did
very well until the last guy, an A-4 pilot, came aboard and had a poor
pass, really bad, and boltered. When he boltered, the President and
McNamara applauded. I see this guy shaking off the end of the ship
into the quag and crap and they, the President and McNamara, thought
it was a nice show. I told them that's how we do the bolter, and now
we'll have him come around and do it the right way. I couldn't get
over the ignorance.

Overall, the ability of the attack community to respond to the war
was really phenomenal. Not that we didn't make mistakes; we did,
paying dearly for them because we lost quite a few airplanes to premature
detonation and impacts with our own weapons. But the numbers that
we lost were very small, and the mistakes, I think, reasonable, and
reasonably few. Remember, we came into the war totally unprepared
for a conventional battle. For years the concentration, almost exclusively,
was [on] the nuclear mission. I had to go back two or three tours to
get anywhere near an alpha strike, and only on rare occasions did I see
a multiple-carry bomb rack loaded with bombs.

Back in Lemoore, Howie Boydston, the CO of NAS Lemoore, was
one of the most emotionally tuned-in COs I've ever known. He handled
what was a fairly desperate time in 1967–68 with a lot of understanding
for what a CO could do for the survivors of somebody in trouble. He's
the one who broke the logjam in the Bureau of Personnel, and I don't
know whether he's ever gotten credit for it. There was a rule out that
if a guy was killed or missing for X number of days, his family could
no longer occupy federal quarters. Boydston said "I'm not going to
follow that, and if you don't like it, relieve me." Of course, about
that time everybody said that's good. But he also did a number of worth-
while things in the CACO [casualty assistance call officer] program,
and he was the guy people at the Bureau of Personnel in Washington,
D.C., turned to to get straight insight into what was going on. Lemoore
was at the forefront, the heartland, of where the war was fought.

Chapter 27
Up North

John Nicholson required three-and-a-half years to complete his second combat mission over North Vietnam.

The first, as a lieutenant commander with VA-144, was launched in response to the reported attack on the destroyers *C. Turner Joy* and *Maddox* in August 1964 while he was flying from the carrier *Constellation*. His second did not occur until February 1968, this time off the deck of the *Enterprise*.

"I flew out to the *Enterprise,* which was operating off the [West] coast in December of 1967, as executive officer of VA-56," says Nicholson. "We left for Vietnam on January 1, 1968, but stopped first in Sasebo, Japan, and while in Sasebo, the *Pueblo* incident occurred. None of the squadrons had any winter clothing, and we spent a couple of weeks in the Japanese Sea, then headed to Vietnam and relieved the *Oriskany*.

"That was Burt Shepherd's air wing, and she had taken tremendous losses flying up into Hanoi and Haiphong. The MiGs were coming out, there was tremendous flak, tremendous missile activity, really hot."

On-line in February, the *Enterprise*'s Air Wing 9 and her strike element called upon to assist Marines under siege at Khe Sanh. "The siege was an intriguing operation," notes Nicholson. "Khe Sanh sat up on a hilltop, and the bad guys were all around. We were brought in to bomb the perimeter area, and the concern from down below was the North Vietnamese or Viet Cong tunneling under the perimeter.

"We dropped 2,000-pound bombs with delayed fusing to get the bombs in the ground and blow the gophers out. That was really harrowing because if you slipped, and the bomb went on the wrong side of the barbed wire, there went the Marines."

The *Enterprise* soon moved up to North Vietnam, bombing major targets within Hanoi, Nam Dinh, Hai Duong, Hon Gai, and Haiphong before horrid flying weather closed in all but the A-6 missions. "The alpha strikes lined up for Hanoi and Haiphong were cancelled and delayed, so we

226

ended up flying piddly flights down to the South instead," Nicholson recalls. "But all of a sudden on April 1, the weather was going to break. I was scheduled for the first go, a pre-dawn launch and first light strike against Hanoi."

We all knew, of course, the North Vietnamese had been moving in equipment because we'd been unable to hit them hard for some time. They knew, and we knew they knew, that we're coming as soon as the weather broke.

The morning of April 1 was very tense, and I didn't sleep much that night because for some reason—for the only time I can remember in my combat career—I felt my number was up. There was reason, I think every one of us had reason, because we knew the strike was going to be a donnybrook; there was going to be bloodshed supreme. The North Vietnamese had everything lined up, they'd been resupplied, and our strike was the first go.

I don't believe my apprehension showed, at least I hope it didn't, but I darn well know I didn't sleep that evening, tossing and turning. It seems like I just lay there awake in bed, finally getting up for the brief about 1:30 in the morning. You could cut the ready room air with a knife, not a word was said, and I was very, very nervous.

Information from air operations, such as weather and divert briefs, came to the ready room by way of a big screen fed by the teletype machine. As we're getting ready, all of a sudden across this screen came the message. "All flights north of the 20th Parallel have been cancelled until further notice." We all looked at that, and what followed was this tremendous relief, like stones had been taken off our backs. But then on the next line, someone had typed April Fool. I mean that had to be the lowest point of my life, going from tense, to this ecstatic joy, back to the depths of despair. I just wanted to get up and kill, I mean I wanted to go right up into air ops and tear off someone's head.

But a guy came on the squawk box and said, "This is no joke; all strikes north of the 20th Parallel have been cancelled; negate the April Fool." Of course nobody would believe the announcement, it had to be confirmed and was. We never went, and the atmosphere was like Christmas. On April 1, most years since then, I always remember that feeling of relief.

Following the president's decision not to bomb up north of the 20th, we took up this great, exotic maneuver to bring the North Vietnamese to their knees, called the interdiction program. South of the 19th we divided the country into packages, and the concept was to cut all lines of communications heading south and, therefore, starve the enemy to death. In reality, the interdiction campaign was frustrating; I think that's the word to use. Every once in a while you'd find a truck park, that was exciting, or petroleum storage, or something that went up in a big ball of smoke and flames. Otherwise, the targets were rice paddies, wooden footbridges, dirt roads—really frustrating, especially if you're losing pilots. We weren't allowed to hit the big metal bridges, we weren't allowed to hit anything that looked like a community, but show me a wooden plank across a creek and we'd devastate the site. Every target was dictated from on high, the big puzzle palace telling what wooden footbridge to hit.

Certainly it was combat, but routine combat. There was none of the tenseness of the morning of April 1, none of the hype. Even worse were the high altitude hops over South Vietnam or Laos. The FACs, or whoever, would fly you in straight and level, and when they'd say, "hack, hack," you'd push the button and the bombs dropped. That is the ultimate of stupidity, really dullsville, but that's how it was after April 1. For all intent and purpose, the SAMs were nonexistent, I can only remember seeing one or two. Now, the flak was there, but the April, May, June timeframe was not a real high threat like it was up North.

I kept myself busy with an interest in photography, spending hours in the intelligence center finding targets. We did a lot of road reconnaissance, and the beauty of road recce was you weren't assigned a target; there was an opportunity to get out and use your imagination. I spent hours looking at RA-5 photography and working with professional sailors who were photo interpreters, trying to locate targets like petroleum storage or truck parks. It was intriguing, and I developed a sense of accomplishment by locating and hitting these targets.

The cruise was over in July, and we were home in August. The squadron transitioned to the A-7B, and in 1969 I took VA-56 back as CO for another combat cruise. By this time the combat was even more routine, duller than even the year before. There was a lot of flying down South, in Laos, on the Ho Chi Minh trail, and easing down into Cambodia. The war had dropped out of North Vietnam, and we were down in the South, and I left the squadron about two-thirds of the way through the deployment.

Routine is the best way to describe combat after April 1, 1968, but I can't say I was sorry we weren't going up North. In the month we did fly to Hanoi and Haiphong, the atmosphere was real tight. I can remember the last strike we made against Hanoi; the North Vietnamese threw everything at us. I mean SAMs—these telephone poles—were coming up all over the place. You came back from a strike like that one and others, and just looked at the wall, drank a cup of coffee, and didn't say much. The *Oriskany* had caught all kinds of hell; then we came on catching all kinds of hell. The SAMs made all the difference in the world, just unreal. The first time I saw one it was unbelievable. The missile looked so slow, lumbering up, and all of a sudden it was right by me. I had one, I swear, within ten feet of me one time. I could almost read the writing on the missile. Why it didn't go off, why I survived and others didn't, I'll never know. I think the ones that got it, some were in the wrong place at the wrong time. Like that missile—why it didn't go off I'll never know, but if it had I wouldn't be here today.

I believe a lot of the young ones who got shot down were guilty of doing things maybe they knew better not to do. Just like when I went for the Russian Swatow in August of 1964—I shouldn't have gone that low, there was no need to go that low because the missile I was shooting would have covered the territory. But in my mind, when it finally came to the point of pressing the attack, I was not thinking logically. I believe the Navy lost one helluva lot of pilots who pressed the attack a little closer than they should have, or who, in not thinking, went back for that second time.

Chapter 28
Interdiction

As the war up North tapered down, then died with the November bombing halt, the focus of U.S. Navy pilots turned toward interdiction, stopping the flow of supplies down the maze-like Ho Chi Minh trail.

The effort proved enormous, frustrating, and useless—akin to quelling a forest fire with a garden hose. Ho's trail, really a series of trails, ran through the heavily forested, mountainous region of Eastern Laos and Cambodia, and provided the avenue for weapons, ammunition, and food supplies to reach Communist troops operating in the South. The thick forest of jungle provided a natural canopy of protection, in many cases three layers thick, for the trail and its beneficiaries.

Strategically, there's no doubt the trail keyed the North's success in the South. "Our failure to prevent North Vietnam from establishing the Ho Chi Minh Trail had fatal consequences," states former President Richard Nixon in his book *No More Vietnams*. "Hanoi could not have waged the kind of war it did in the South without a free run down the Laos panhandle."

After reaching office, Nixon tried to destroy the trail by way of massive bombing. In 1969 the daily average of sorties in Laos was nearly 400, up 280 from two years earlier. The amount of bombs dropped by B-52s increased from 93,199 tons in 1968 to 218,250 tons two years later. By war's end, over two million tons of bombs had been dropped on Laos, with all but a quarter of that figure coming after Nixon's inauguration. The bombing destroyed thousands of trucks. But with every truck destroyed, two, three, or four Russian-made trucks were off-loaded at Haiphong and began their trek down the trail. And a price was paid for the interdiction in human terms; 130 American naval aircraft and their crews were lost from November 1968 to early 1972.

The seven hundred thousand tons of bombs dropped by the aviators of CTF-77 between late 1968 and early 1972 fell along the Ho Chi Minh trail, especially in the Mu Gia, Nape, and Ban Karai passes of eastern Laos. "At the Mu Gia pass, coming out the western side of North Vietnam, there were about three main roads that came into this one area," remembers a Navy pilot who flew in the region during 1971. "You'd go in there at sunset, and everybody had been bombing that pass trying to make it impassable all day long. That's at least one carrier and half the Air Force that was anywhere around—flying either from Thailand, Laos, or wherever—dumping a lot of shit in one small area.

"The place would look like a ten-by-ten-foot sandbox in a schoolyard that had 120 kids playing in it all day long. I mean it's nothing but sand, but it wasn't ten-foot-by-ten-foot. Say, ten miles wide and twenty miles long. And at daybreak the next morning, there were roads back through the pass again."

Speculation has it that fifty thousand men, women, and children worked in capacities as diverse as engineers, truck drivers, and antiaircraft crews, to keep the trail open and supplies moving. And the bottom line is they succeeded.

"Much of our time was spent in the marvelous interdiction program," remarks Linn Felt, who served as XO-CO of VA-27, the third West Coast A-7 squadron, between 1967–69. "Interdiction was dumb, absolutely useless. Here we are trying to interdict this long pipe that the North Vietnamese were so clever in establishing. And it wasn't just one pipe, but a series of parallel pipes and intercommunications that was the Ho Chi Minh trail, pushing little packages at a time. There was always a constant flow [of supplies], but no place to get them where [they were] concentrated. Those guys down South, the North Vietnamese army and the so-called Viet Cong, couldn't have done what they did without that pipeline, and we were incapable of turning it off."

Felt arrived at VA-122 in August 1967 with orders to be the first XO of VA-27. By January 1968 the squadron was operational, and six months later flying combat missions over North Vietnam.

My squadron was commissioned in September with George Pappas, an A-1 pilot, as the first CO. The squadron pilots were a mixture of A-1 and A-4 types, plus fighter people and ASW guys who generally turned out to be pretty good. The good A-1 drivers transitioned well; the ones that were average A-1 drivers never fully made the transition.

Both 27 and [VA-] 97 were scheduled to deploy on the *Constellation*, and our squadron became fully operational in January. I thought the buildup time was awfully short, but it worked out okay. We went to the ship for the first time in April and deployed in May, starting combat at the end of June.

Our mission was interdiction, and you didn't stop the constant flow south by trying to hit these little pipes. You hit it back where the stuff was coming in. We should have leveled Haiphong. I think we could have really killed the economy of North Vietnam to the point where they would have been so busy building themselves back up, there would have been no time to go down and finish off the South in 1975. A lot of other military options existed, and I'm not saying win from the point of view of total capitulation of the government of North Vietnam; that never would have happened. I think they'd have dug holes, gone in, and emerged at some later time. I also don't believe, [even] given the full brunt of our airpower, we could have ever won the war with air alone. But we could have accomplished a lot more given liberal targeting, going after the source, getting tough, and getting the Russians the hell out of North Vietnam.

Totally political decisions ran the war—very frustrating to us—and of course, the more one contemplates it as a matter of history, the more you can philosophize in various respects. Most of the pilots, I'd say, did carry out orders. But the rules of engagement were such that you couldn't hit civilian populations unless a military target existed. There were occasions where intelligence had a truck park or transshipment point on the edge of, or in, a village, and you'd go at it. If the bombs blew up the rest of the village, you didn't do that intentionally; you went for the right aim points and missed a little bit. That's war.

Very seldom did we get gratifying results from interdiction. Armed recce in the daytime just gave nothing—like bombing the moon. Night work was good, laying out flares and going after trucks. My perception is we focused a lot on flak sites and the few SAM sites that popped up every once in a while. Late one afternoon we discovered a SAM site near Vinh Son—generating a small twelve-plane alpha strike the next day. The flight leader was the XO of one of the F-4 squadrons; I led a division from 27, and 97 had a division. There were some clouds around the target and the fighters didn't see it, so I called up, "I've got it, I'm going in." I head in, followed by the fighters, and I look up and here are the God damn bombs from the fighters above me. I pickled off my bombs and started getting out of there when the flak started, and it was pretty fierce. To tell you the truth, I think it was a gunnery school, since there is nothing else over at Vinh Son. There were a lot of road intersections, something you normally stay away from. But since we'd seen the SAM site, the decision was made to go get it. As it turned out, the BDA photography showed the SAM site was moved the previous night, so we missed. But here we generated a twelve-plane strike to absolutely no avail.

Other than few and far between good deals, it didn't get too exciting. We probably took a few more chances than we would have in some other situations; hopefully, to do something positive. Generally, it failed. Many times the weather wasn't cooperative, and once you're airborne and can't get over the target, all you can do is dump the bombs in the ocean.

There was some opportunity to go south and provide close-in support for the in-country people, but most of the first cruise was North Vietnam, and too much of it was Mk-36 destructors that disappeared in the mud and hardly got any results. We tried to bust a few bridges to no avail, although Mace Gilfry, our Walleye expert, destroyed one bridge.

We returned to Lemoore in January of 1969, I took over as CO in February, and left again in August for Vietnam. Being a squadron commander was a big deal. That's the goal most naval aviators are serious about. In my first squadron, we were always critiquing policy, and the word was always "when *I'm* CO, I'm going to . . ." It's an ambition, and I think it's probably the strongest ambition. To be the commanding officer of a squadron was the goal; yet to be CO in combat was even a notch above that.

While I was XO, George's [Pappas] plane got hit in the wing over North Vietnam. A fire started, but as he climbed, the fire went out. The decision was made not to bring him aboard and he diverted to Da Nang, making a straight-in approach. As he got down to about ten thousand feet, the fire started again. George put his gear down, went whipping in, and he couldn't get his flaps down, so he's going too fast; and as he got lower, the fire became stronger and stronger. George landed on the runway fast, I'm not sure how fast, and he's not either. He lost control of the airplane. There was no lateral control, and he ejected on the runway, still going fast enough and still within the envelope. The plane went off the side of the runway and went over by a hangar, not hurting anything else; and about a swing and a half in the parachute after George ejected, he hit the runway. The helicopter came swooping in, picked him up, and took George to a field hospital where they stripped off his clothes, put him on a slab in the operating room—and at the same time they're bringing in wounded Marines. The doctor washes up, turns to George—and George is lying there naked without a scratch on him—and the doctor says, "What is this, a psycho case?"

Well, we got George back, and he couldn't get up and down the ship ladders because of his knee. So for the rest of the line period, about two weeks, I became the de facto CO. It was great. I'd trudge up and see him a couple of times a day on administrative matters; but as far as the leadership in the ready room, that was my department.

It was rewarding to lead in combat. A good CO has to be a leader, and he has to lead in the airplane. It's good, in part, to be able to motivate your maintenance personnel; but you've got to be able to fly with, if not better than, all your pilots. You may not be the best, but you have to be close to it, and that's the difference between leadership in flying and leadership in some other areas. Being captain of a ship is tremendously demanding in knowing all the elements that are going on and controlling the weapons systems. You have to be a seaman; you have to show you can handle the ship, which is akin to piloting—but not the same thing as day after day leading a group of pilots in the air. My view is if you can't fly with the guys, you aren't recognized so much as a leader.

My CO tour—a lot of time was spent in Laos, FAC-supported. I thought we did that pretty well; but there's also some real losers like Sky Spot—flying along under radar control, dropping on command, and going home. That sucks. Actually, my view of Laos rates with the interdiction program, although with the FAC-controlled missions there was the perception the guys down below were scouring targets. Whether we could see the target or not, and generally we could not, we felt the targets were valid, at least for that kind of operation. You had to have a little bit of faith in the FACs down below hanging their ass out.

The heavy flak work came at Mu Gia pass. We did a lot of night work there. As we'd turn the corner over the northern part of South Vietnam and head north to go to the pass, you could see guys getting shot at that were maybe fifteen, twenty minutes in the flight ahead. The U.S., through the Air Force, was losing people up there, and the word was the Laotians were not taking prisoners. As the squadron CO, I had to make some value judgments as to how much risk I wanted to subject my pilots to. I chose to minimize the risk, and not that I pushed the limits way up, but I said we're going to play this much like we played North Vietnam. The minimum pullout was four thousand feet, and other procedures were followed. It didn't seem worth losing a pilot or an airplane for the effort being made, and it wasn't. We lost two airplanes total on both cruises, and I came away very proud we didn't lose a pilot. In fact, we lost more pilots in peacetime when I was with VA-34.

But even having said I took a rather conservative approach as far as Laos, there were times I hung it out, and I know some of my guys probably did too when there was some value in the target. You never strafed at night; that was a general rule because the tracers pointed right up to you. Well, one time in North Vietnam I found some parked trucks and I was out of bombs, so I strafed them, and I strafed them from a safe altitude. I wasn't down in the weeds, and I knew what I was doing, or at least I thought I knew until all of a sudden the tracers started coming back up at me. These red balls were coming right back at me, right from where I was shooting. I thought, oh geez, and got the hell out of there. I probably shot more guns than anybody in the squadron, but I didn't do it regularly, only when I thought there was something to be gained. But after that incident, I never did it again at night. What I'd been told was true, and fortunately I got away with it.

Part Six
1969–1971

I can't believe that a fourth-rate power like North Vietnam doesn't have a breaking point.

Secretary of State Henry Kissinger, 1969, in comments to his staff

---

Introduction

The attention of naval air focused on South Vietnam and Laos as the fifth consecutive year of Southeast Asian combat unfolded.

Gone were the "hard target" missions up North that had characterized ROLLING THUNDER, the program of measured-response bombing which had lasted three-and-a-half years and which (if viewed with the benefit of twenty years of hindsight) had accomplished very little. Certainly the flow of supplies from North to South had been curtailed by the bombing, a major aid to the thousands of combat troops who trudged through the humid jungles and wallowed in the muck and mire of South Vietnam. Yet one full-scale alpha strike into Haiphong Harbor, well planned and without the onerous rules of engagement, could have accomplished as much, if not more.

Up North, relentless bombing had either destroyed or severely damaged the country's transportation system, above-ground fuel storage, main industries, and major electric power generating plants. Virtually the entire military complex, most notably the airfields, was rendered useless. But the cost for these accomplishments, when weighed against the results, was grossly disproportionate. In terms of dollars and cents, a study ordered by McNamara showed North Vietnam's allies had supplied the primarily agrarian country with $1.6 billion in economic and military aid during ROLLING THUNDER, some four times the losses North Vietnam incurred during the bombing. "If economic criteria were the only consideration," read the report by McNamara's systems analysis division, "NVN would show a substantial net gain from the bombing, primarily in military equipment."

ROLLING THUNDER's U.S. aircraft loss total (measured in billions of wasted dollars) included 918 planes from Air Force, Navy, and Marine units. Navy figures alone stood at more than three hundred airplanes destroyed in combat over North Vietnam and another one thousand damaged. The human losses included 818 U.S. airmen, who died during the more than forty months of fighting. Eighty-three Yankee Station pilots and air crewmen were killed, and another three hundred were taken prisoner or reported missing. In short, the impact of ROLLING THUNDER on the enemy was appropriately assessed by RAdm. Malcolm Cagle: "We had forced him to the peace table, but we had not forced him to make peace."

A final summation of ROLLING THUNDER is incomplete without a look at the politics that played a major role in the program. The pilots who daily risked their lives had good reason to object to the oppressive rules of engagement laid down by the Johnson administration advisors, the majority of whom seemed to have nothing but contempt for the military hierarchy. Yet civilians can't shoulder all the blame for ROLLING THUNDER. Another war took place from 1965 to 1968, but this one was between the Air Force and the Navy. It was a battle for post-war budget and public relations supremacy. Both services refused to establish a joint Southeast Asian command, one entity capable of guiding all air activity. Instead, Yankee Station aircraft were commanded from that locale, Air Force aircraft attacking from Laos were controlled from air bases in Thailand, B-52 bombers were controlled from bases in Guam and Thailand, and aircraft based in South Vietnam, but attacking the North, received their orders from the control center at Da Nang. While a unified command might not have made a difference because of the nature of the enemy, such a command could have eliminated the pointless sortie skirmishes.

Interdiction of the Ho Chi Minh trail remained the primary mission from 1969 to 1971. Nearly two hundred "protective strikes" were flown into North Vietnam during the three year span, and only one MiG kill by the Navy was recorded. Close-air support missions were carried out in South Vietnam, and in March 1971 three carriers—the *Ranger, Kitty Hawk,* and *Hancock*—backed up the advance of South Vietnamese troops into Laos. Late in 1971 Navy and Air Force units launched a five-day, one thousand sortie effort labeled PROUD DEEP. The raids, triggered in response to a North Vietnamese buildup of SAM sites and MiG aircraft in the southern portion of the country, struck fuel and supply depots, airfields, SAM sites and truck parks below the 20th Parallel.

Because of reduced responsibilities and fiscal realities, the monthly average of three carriers on Yankee Station in 1968 was reduced to two throughout most of 1969–71. Logically, the sortie total also decreased, but not its importance for the career aviators seeking to reach flag rank. From late-1968 to mid-1970, the number of monthly attack sorties ranged between 3,000 and 4,000. From then until the end of 1971, the sortie figure fell to an average of 1,000 to 2,500 strike sorties in Laos and South Vietnam.

"The flying was relatively safe over South Vietnam and Laos, mostly

Air Force FAC-controlled, although there were a couple of areas where the FAC couldn't work," remarks retired Captain Clarence S. "Scotty" Vaught, who flew two combat tours in 1969–70, then returned for a final brief tour in 1972.

We were playing sortie games, and that's one of the elements that made flag out of the ship COs—how many sorties the ship got off. It didn't make a shit what you did over there, as long as the aircraft got off the ship. We either went FAC-controlled, or if the weather was crappy, we'd go under radar control. Basically, they'd set us up at 15,000 to 18,000 feet, someplace high enough not to get shot at. You'd drive on a course, and at some specific point, the bombs would be pickled off. Other times, you'd be told go 350 degrees from some TACAN station, and within a five mile area, it was okay to drop on anything. You'd find a stream, something that might be a bridge, and drop. The bombs didn't go back to the ship, I guess, or the sortie didn't count. This didn't bother me to begin with, but after a while you got the feeling of, what the hell am I doing over here. It bothered me more after the war was over, thinking back about all the money pissed away.

On my second cruise in 1970 aboard the *America*, myself and another kid were launched after somebody thought a fast boat was coming out towards the carrier. Somehow we were confused with a RESCAP mission, and the end result found us in a holding pattern for an hour, carrying six Rockeyes apiece. Knowing our recovery time, I finally called the ship and I said, "Hey, folks, we've got one of two choices, either we tank, or get rid of the Rockeyes and come back to the ship." The decision was made to piss away six Rockeyes apiece, and I forget their price tag, either $6,000 or $8,000 each, so $36,000 or $48,000 from each plane was pooped into the ocean for no reason at all.

The on-scene American military commitment to a democratic South Vietnam waned dramatically during 1969–71. The strength of U.S. troops stood at 543,000 in the spring of 1969. By fall President Nixon's program of reducing American strength resulted in a force of some 475,000 in-country troops. A year later, 334,000 American servicemen remained in Southeast Asia, and as 1971 closed approximately 150,000 combat troops were left. Just over 44,000 American servicemen had died in combat, while the air war, according to a 17 December 1971 Pentagon announcement, resulted in the loss of 8,051 aircraft at a cost of roughly three, maybe four billion dollars. Over half the aircraft losses were considered noncombat, due to accidental or nonhostile causes, and the remainder were attributed to North Vietnamese guns, ranging from single-shot rifles to surface-to-air missiles.

Chapter 29
Transition

Scotty Vaught spent the early years of the Vietnam war teaching young Navy pilots how to fly the A-1 Skyraider in combat. The assignment was rather incongruous since Vaught had never flown in combat, nor did he possess attack aviation experience.

"I received my commission in 1960 from the University of Idaho NROTC program and went through the training command's prop pipeline," notes Vaught. "I originally flew Spads, then was put into the E-1, which did not make me happy, needless to say. After one cruise on the Bonnie Dick flying the E-1, I transitioned back to A-1s, followed by LSO [landing signal officer] training in the 1962–63 time frame. My orders to Lemoore came in 1965, and I arrived at VA-122 in February.

"The early years at 122 consisted of teaching folks who were going to war—which is kind of interesting because one, I'd never been in combat; and two, my background was non-attack. It was somewhat difficult instructing people to go fight a war in an airplane that I'd never really made a cruise on. I did that for about two years; then in 1967 we got the first A-7. Plaques were given to the first hundred people who flew the Corsair, and I was like the ninety-eighth."

The transition from prop aircraft to jets was significant for Vaught and other naval aviators in many respects, not the least of which was ego involvement.

I was a mid-lieutenant when the squadron transitioned from the A-1 to A-7, and there were a lot of senior lieutenant commanders in the squadron, a large group of which never made the transition from props to jets. They could never get their brains going fast enough to fly jets, and most were afraid, but being aviators they couldn't admit it. There were several that did make it through, and several ended up busting their butts because they wouldn't admit to the fact they couldn't make the transition. That was unfortunate.

The bad pilots were obvious, but they didn't have a career without going to the A-7. I mean, the Spads were going away, and if you couldn't hack it in the attack community, the choice was to go VC, VRF or wherever. Their egos would not allow leaving the attack community. Better to die than look bad, right? The unfortunate aspect of the individuals who transitioned but really didn't, some of them became skippers and their squadrons really suffered for it. It's all right for the skipper to be an average pilot, but he can't be below average, particularly around the ship. He's the guy who is going to lead you into combat. One individual, even though I dearly loved the man, was a shitty skipper just because he couldn't fly.

In all, I spent over forty months in 122, arriving there as the junior of three LSOs. Those two senior guys went to 27 and 97, and eventually I went to CAG-9 as the senior LSO in 1968. The normal tour in the RAG is maybe two or three years, and I spent nearly four, so I was ready to go, although familywise it was great.

Everybody wanted to go to Vietnam; it was the thing to do. I received my first taste of that during the Korean War as an eleven- or twelve-year-old. Everybody wanted to march off and go kill bad guys, and of course, nobody was going to die on our side. Instructors were volunteering, like Mel Munsinger, another guy who started in VAW and about a year senior to me. The advisors we had in South Vietnam needed a maintenance officer, and he was so hungry to get there, he went over and flew with the Vietnamese on the guarantee he'd come back and go to a fleet squadron.

Everybody was also certain the war would be short—two, maybe three years max—and everybody knew the people who went over there and got combat experience were going to be the skippers; and that's where the promotions were, and that's why we joined the Navy. There's a lot of words that we're trained killers. Well, there's a mental idea of that, and it's what the country trained [us] to do. The war was the time to go show it. Everybody wanted to go and prove we had the capability of doing the job. That attitude eventually changed for the senior people, especially the ones going back for the third or fourth cruise. It started out you could only make two tours, and when guys went back a second time, most really didn't want to go. The game was no longer fun, particularly up North, watching friends get blown away and dealing with the family separations.

CAG-9 deployed aboard the *Enterprise* for the 1969 cruise and I flew with VA-146 and -215. The ship departed for Vietnam, went first to Hawaii, and that's when the big fire occurred.

On 14 January 1969 prior to an exercise, the nuclear-powered aircraft carrier *Enterprise* was steaming off Hawaii when a Zuni rocket ignited on an F-4 Phantom. The resulting destruction reached major proportions within minutes and required nearly three hours to contain. Twenty-eight men died in the conflagration, fifteen aircraft were destroyed, and there was more than $56 million in damage to the ship and other aircraft.

The fire occurred just as the wing was getting ready for a practice alpha strike. The airplanes were loaded with bombs, rockets, the whole nine yards, and it was the second strike, with the first group in the process of returning to the ship, when it all went off. A huffer was parked by this Phantom carrying Zuni rockets, and the huffer's exhaust was blowing on the rockets. The ship was in the midst of an ORE [operational readiness examination], with a safety team aboard. One member of the team goes up to a first class and says, "See that huffer? The exhaust is blowing on the rockets, they're getting hot, and if you don't do something about it, they'll blow up." The first class goes up to the chief and says, "Look at the son-of-a-bitch; the huffer is going to blow it away." The chief goes to one of the safety observers and says, "If you don't have somebody move that son-of-a-bitch, it's going to blow it away." Within five seconds it sure as hell did.

I had just gotten up and gone to the CAG office, basically sitting there, minding my own business, when I heard this ba-boom, ba-boom, ba-boom, and nobody could figure out what the hell was going on. Were we chasing a submarine with depth charges, or what? Fortunately, when the explosions started, the ship was just minutes away from general quarters. Everything was manned, and I think had that not been the case, we might have lost the ship. Everybody was there, they knew we were going to have a general quarters at 10:00 A.M. and everyone was prepared.

My roommate, Jim Finley, a fighter LSO, was in the airplane next to the one that first blew up, without his gloves and mask on—his engine running, and the plane ready to taxi. He was burned, not bad enough to go to a hospital, but enough that we had to send him home for a few weeks. When Jim finally came back, he'd learned the first rule in the cockpit is to put the gloves on and hook up the mask. Those two acts would have made a big difference.

Most of the pilots, the aircrew, as soon as the fire started got the hell out of their airplanes and went to the ready rooms. I think that was probably a good idea. Later on in fire drills, and even after the war, the expectation was pilots would leave the cockpit and man a hose if a fire started. I finally convinced the powers-that-be the idea was stupid, because as happened on the *Enterprise,* there were pilots blown away or severely injured from the fire. In part, they didn't know what to do, and it's now a requirement to get the training. But the whole idea behind the carrier is striking power, and the only people who can do that are the aircrews. To go charging in on an airplane that is about ready to blow up, and in the process blow away half your fighting force, doesn't make any sense to me. Some say, well, if they don't go do it, then you're going to lose the carrier. If that's the situation, they're probably not going to make any difference anyway.

Basically all I did was sit in the CAG office—an observation stand-point—and kind of monitor what the hell was going on. When it was all over, there were two big holes on the deck, just in front [of] or right at the number one wire. The powers-that-be, of course, wanted us to get the hell out of there and go fight the war. Third Fleet, a blackshoe, his solution was just to put boards over the holes, pull the number one wire, and go for it. He couldn't understand why we didn't want to do that.

The air wing split up, the fighters went to Kaneohe [Hawaii], and everybody else to Barbers Point [Hawaii]. It took a relatively short period of time to repair the *Enterprise*—six weeks, twenty-four hours a day— and we were on our way to Vietnam. While [we were] there, the movie *Tora, Tora, Tora* was [being] made, which proved to be very interesting. The film was shot right by the *Enterprise,* and there was all kinds of explosions, which a whole lot of people didn't care for.

Believe it or not, we were back home from that cruise on July 3, and I know we came back the third because my son was born on the Fourth of July. This was the period when every ship was extended; you'd go out for eight months and stay ten. But this cruise was unique because the *Enterprise* could not be extended, she had to be up at Bremerton [Washington] for refueling. They couldn't slide it off. So the fact the ship had blown up—and we got six or eight weeks in Hawaii—that pissed me off because it was my first combat cruise, and there went two or three air medals and a chance to kill the bad guys.

In the squadron I flew with, VA-146, I'm not really sure if there was anybody who'd flown over Vietnam yet. I know for a fact there wasn't anybody who'd been over there in A-7s, maybe A-4s or A-1s. We were certainly green as hell, and everybody wanted to get over there because we were still in that "I got to get over there and get my share" mode. If there were any feelings about the experience of the ship blowing up, it was "dammit, line time has been taken away." We were ready to go and get on with it, and we'd just recently stopped going up North which kind of aggravated people because that's where the action was. For the guys who hadn't been there, shutting down the North really gave you a feeling of frustration.

Once we reached Yankee Station, the flying was over South Vietnam and Laos. There were no alpha strikes in South Vietnam at all. Typically, and [I'm] speaking from A-7 experience only, one squadron would launch four aircraft and another squadron launch two, then rotate. At night, primarily, it was a launch of two, flying from midnight to noon, basically six hours of daylight and six hours of darkness. And it wasn't 50 percent of the flying time during the daylight hours because the launches would go 4, 2, 4, 2, and at night it was 2, 2, 2. Night missions were a third of the time.

The first cruise was flown in the A-7A/B, basically a manual bomber. The position of the instruments, the size of the cockpit lent themselves to be more comfortable than the A-4. But with the A-7 on that first combat cruise, we didn't know what the system could do for us, and we didn't know when the system was bad. On one occasion, Mink Ehrman, one of the CAG's ops officers, flew a close-air support mission with troops and dropped two thousand feet short, or I should say, the airplane dropped two thousand feet short. Because of that incident, we went to a mode of not using the system if troops were around. Here's this multimillion-dollar system that's supposed to drop in a gnat's ass but can't be used because it's not working right.

In 1969–70 the motivating factor [when] going into Laos was if you went down, you were in big trouble. There were lots of rumors of pilots tied to trees with ID cards tacked into their heads. Definitely not the place to go down. In North Vietnam, no question about it, you were going to the Hanoi Hilton and live there for a while. Go down in Laos, no chance, although I shouldn't say no chance. If you went down during the daytime, you might survive the night and get picked up in the morning. But after that, forget it.

In South Vietnam there was also the feeling that if you got picked up by the bad guys, it was all over. They just didn't have the time to send you back up; you were a burden. When the Spads were going South, pilots carried machetes, pistols, and even the Russian M-1, the little rifle. Man, they were going to fight their way out, kill all those suckers. Someplace in there we found out that if you went down in the North and didn't fire, there was a possibility of surviving. But if you killed anybody on the ground, you were a dead sucker. I stopped carrying a pistol because I didn't want to piss anybody off.

A lot of people also stopped wearing their wedding rings, and remember we're still at the point when the only information you could tell the enemy was your name, rank, serial number, and date of birth. The idea was if the enemy knew you were married or had children, they'd have something to work on, like your wife is screwing everybody at NAS Lemoore, your kid is a whore. So we shed ourselves of anything that could give the North Vietnamese something to use against us. Thinking back on that, there probably was a little macho image of—I can outthink these guys, even though I won't have anything to eat or drink, and they'll beat me. But my mind is going to be better than them. Right.

I was very confident of the Navy and Air Force SAR capability. Head for the high ground, get into the mountainous terrain, and hide. We were taught, and I forget what the system was, but talk for X amount of seconds on the radio, listen for X amount of seconds, and go dead. We knew they had radios obtained from other people—listening devices, or whatever. It was a big deal to get away from the parachute, away from your gear, and hide. The helo community—talk about the feeling of being a piece of crap before the war—yet those were the guys that earned their DFCs. The feeling for the helo driver, feeling for the Jolly Green Giant pilots, those guys had big balls. I mean you really had a great feeling for those guys—they'd risk it, put it on the line to get folks out.

On the first cruise, we lost a Viggie [RA-5] crew and that was it. Second cruise we had a couple of engine failures, people had to jump out, and a couple of guys got shot up.

The squadron life in the 1969–70 cruises: there probably was a big camp of—isn't this great, it's just like going to Fallon. We were winning air medals, we thought we were helping the cause, slowing the traffic from the North to the South. We were convinced, about 99 percent of us, that we could win this sucker if the politicians would get off our asses and let us go back up North. Morale was good for the most part. The war was enjoyable and nobody was getting killed.

Fighter jocks were hating it because they got absolutely no action, even though the fighters were loaded up with bombs. Problem was the F-4 drivers couldn't bomb worth a shit; the plane didn't have a system to drop bombs. There was no gun-sight in the Phantom until the war started, and I think the system put in was the same gun-sight used in the Spad. The fighter guys didn't like to do bomb, it wasn't their job, and the only reason for bombing in their mind was that's the way to get air medals. Surely fighter jocks can't be walking around without air medals on.

There was a lot of hate and discontent with medals. We were one of the first boats to go over that just made the combat cruises down South. Now I won't say the guys going up North definitely earned their medals, but more [of them] nearly earned them. I think we made only one really long line period and everybody wanted their DFC or whatever. The thing about it, we were telling the public "aren't we great," and yet we didn't do diddly squat to earn some of those medals. I can't remember whether it was our first or second cruise, but one of the A-7 lieutenant commanders wrote himself up for an air medal. What really sold the air medal was the fact that it was a night mission, there were thunderstorms all around, and he had to go in and out of the thunderstorms to get to the target. He found the target, dropped his bombs, and that was it; but he knew this was his last combat cruise and had to get his air medal.

Another point which made us angry about air medals: what is a successful alpha strike? I guess a successful alpha strike is when you plan it properly, go in and surprise the enemy, drop the bombs, and get the hell out of there without anybody getting shot. What did you get for that? Zero, nothing. But if the strike went *wrong*, egressed the wrong way, or for some reason the North Vietnamese knew you were coming, and the strike group got the shit shot out of it, and [a] couple of guys were lost, then, everybody gets a DFC. Right? Makes no sense.

On my last cruise I went off the *Coral Sea* in 1972 with VA-94. It was either my first or second strike North—and I remember this strike so vividly because it was the first time I led a division—and the strike lead was a fighter RIO [radar intercept officer], if you can believe that shit. A guy in the backseat of a fighter, the XO of a squadron, leading an alpha strike. I know the A-6 and A-7 communities are a little prejudiced, but we felt very strongly the fighters should never lead alpha strikes, particularly the RIOs. In actuality, as far as being officers and leaders they're equal. But somebody in the backseat leading an alpha strike; the A-7 community was particularly against that.

The weather was kind of iffy, and this RIO leads us into Haiphong, one of the shipyards. We're going in underneath an eight thousand foot broken overcast, the lead can't find the target, so he makes a pass with the whole strike group, about twenty of us, in tow. Finally, the RIO's pilot finds the target, and the fighters are at one point and the attack people at another. The fighters go burner, pop through a little hole, and of course, the A-7s are chugging along carrying these Mk-82s. The fighters roll in on the son-of-a-bitch target, and we pull back on the stick, pop up at 1,000 or 1,500 feet, go in through the clag, and execute a low roll-in at 2,000 or 3,000 feet, pickle our bombs, and get the hell out.

We're fixing to debrief afterwards, and my skipper comes down, asks how the flight went. I basically told him what happened. So the RIO's pilot comes up to my skipper, who heads the ship's awards board. He says, "Skipper, I want to do a little politicking here."

"Yeah, what's that?"

"Well, as you know, my XO is brand new out here, and he doesn't have a DFC! I'd like to write him up for a DFC."

And he did. Medals had somehow become very cheap. By the time I got there, when we were only going into the South, the individual air medals and the DFCs started not to mean too much; you weren't very proud of them. It almost became a joke to see somebody walking around with two or three DFCs. Well, did he earn them or didn't he? But they were necessary, because if you didn't get one, what the hell had you done, because anybody could get one.

One other thing that pissed off the attack pilots about medals was if you go out, fly over the North, drop your bombs, and knock down a bridge, you get an air medal. That's your job, what you've been trained to do, and the reward is an air medal. A fighter pilot can go out and shoot down a MiG, which is his job and what he's trained to do, and then get a Silver Star. What can you say about that?

Chapter 30
Alcatraz

For two years and one month, from late 1967 through most of 1969, Cmdr. Harry Jenkins, the third ranking senior naval officer in a North Vietnamese prison camp, was put into leg irons at five o'clock each evening. He stayed in irons until seven the next morning, but only under normal conditions. After having been caught communicating with another prisoner on one occasion, Jenkins spent eighty-five consecutive days in irons; he was released for only fifteen minutes a day to pick up food, dump out the toilet bucket, and bathe.

Home for Jenkins was a camp known as Alcatraz, located some ten blocks from Hoa Lo [the Hanoi Hilton], the French-built complex that housed the majority of American prisoners in North Vietnam. Alcatraz, situated in a courtyard behind Hanoi's Ministry of Defense, consisted of thirteen windowless cells, all but two housing an American POW. The eleven men had been singled out for special treatment, and special it was. Each cell measured ten feet long by four feet wide; six of the ten feet were raised about eighteen inches, serving as a sleeping area. Situated above the door was a closed metal transom, dotted with several holes for ventilation, and the sole source of light was a dim bulb, probably ten watts or less.

In addition to Jenkins, the occupants of Alcatraz—all grounded aviators—included Jim Stockdale, Jerry Denton, Jim Mulligan and Howard Rutledge, all among the highest ranking POWs in captivity. They were joined by Ron Storz, Sam Johnson, Nels Tanner, Bob Shumaker, George Coker and George McKnight. Storz died in Alcatraz, while Stockdale's tenure was cut short after he organized a forty-eight-hour fast. As Alcatraz's senior officer, he had ordered the fast following what best could be described as a prison riot. The early morning hours of 25 January had found Jenkins in terrible pain because of a stomach ailment; the refusal by North Vietnamese guards to provide a doctor triggered the riot. The prisoners' efforts did bring a doctor to Jenkins's cell, although the doctor did nothing to ease the pain. The following morning Stockdale ordered the 48-hour fast. The next evening each prisoner was interrogated, and on the morning of 27 January Stockdale went back to Hoa Lo.

Another ten-plus months would pass before Jenkins and eight other Alcatraz "cons" would leave their desolate confines.

Pilots had been taught that [if you] hang in there long enough, the enemy will find you incorrigible and non-workable; they'll put you away and leave you alone. They put us away, but never left us alone. We think now we were in Alcatraz because Stockdale was the troublemaker, an organizer; Rutledge and I because we carried his [Stockdale's] message around and so forth; Denton because he was an organizer; Coker and McKnight because they escaped; and Shumaker because he was just too smart for them. I lived with Shumaker for a while, and I mean he was just shrewd. Shumaker devised all sorts of communication systems and never got caught. Tanner sold them up—he's the one who concocted the Clark Kent story. I don't know why Sam was there, but Sam was a diehard, so he probably gave them a lot of trouble.

Interrogations were held on and off, but nothing much happened until I got very, very sick. Something was wrong inside, I was bad, and I mean to the point where I asked if they weren't going to give me any morphine, then shoot me. It was that bad, hitting me in the middle of the night, the stomach area, and there was no position I could find to relieve the pain. I bao caoed [called out to the guards] and nothing happened. Finally, the whole jail was yelling. Stockdale called a fast that morning, and the next day they took him out of the camp. It happened on a Thursday, I think, and about Sunday the North Vietnamese hadn't done anything at all except hoot and holler and try to quiet me down. On Sunday they took me to a hospital for some X-rays, but by then it was just sore, the damn thing had gone, whatever it was. We rode in by ambulance to the hospital where they gave me barium, took X-rays, and back I came. Really, nothing was done.

The '69 interrogations started with Bob Shumaker, and there didn't seem to be any logic about how the North Vietnamese went about it. Shu was in the middle of the cell block. They wanted him to write a request for amnesty from Ho Chi Minh. He refused. While you think of Vietnam as tropical, it can be cold. About November, the temperature gets down to forty degrees and sits there until March. The walls of the cells give up all their heat, and it's like sitting in a refrigerator. You'd never freeze to death, but it does chatter the teeth. They left Shu in this room with no blankets, trying to wear him down. There was no progress after a week, so he was made to kneel, and that took another week. Finally, he was kneeling on broom handles with boards on his shoulders. Shumaker was tough, and he came back with his knees looking like hamburger. It took the Vietnamese a month to get him; then they went after the next guy. Nobody would submit voluntarily, so pressure was exerted.

About May, Ron Storz attempted suicide. An Air Force pilot, Ron was very, very ill. I guess early on he didn't eat, as a form of resistance; but in fasting, and this happened to a couple of guys, you reach a peak, get on the backside, and then you *can't* eat. Even if you eat, there's no way to keep it down, and it's very difficult to get back over the peak. Ron did this; he'd try to eat and he'd throw it up—so he tried to commit suicide. The night we left camp in November, he stayed behind, and I know he was making a ruckus about something, just giving them hell. He died there.

The North Vietnamese got around to me about August, and by now, amnesty was gone; the goal was complete a biography, a "Blue Book" biography. It was rather well prepared; someone very knowledgeable in our language had obviously developed it. I refused, but there was no screwing around—three guards were called in and just started beating me up. I was standing up against a wall, until literally there was no way to hold my arms up, they'd just slide down the wall. The guards would put them up, and back down they'd slide. I literally could not move my arms. Finally, I filled out the biography.

In September, Ho Chi Minh died, and the Vietnamese went into a mourning period. After that mourning period, George McKnight was called in, the last guy to be interrogated. George told them no, and he came right back to the cell. Early on, one of the new guys had asked, "Why do you take all this abuse when you know they're going to win in the end?" Rutledge passed the word to this guy that he was going to have to shave each morning and look at himself in the mirror, and [that] he should know he'd done his best. At Alcatraz, by all of us hanging in there, we prevented McKnight from being tortured, so we won one from them.

The first indications we had of a change in treatment was some guy would be going to take a bath, and he'd pass a guy going back. That had never, never [before] happened. Then we were allowed extra food, to sit out in the sun a little bit each day, and I went out one day and Coker's door was wide open, like the guard forgot. So Coke and I communicated the whole time. I believe that if treatment hadn't changed, many of us would have died. I weighed 180, 185 pounds in 1965, and by spring of 1969 I was down to about 110 pounds. Ron Storz looked like something out of Buchenwald—a piece of canvas hanging on a cage of bones. Watching him through the cracks in the door, [I'd see him] take ten minutes to walk fifty yards, just shuffling. And if he fell down, there was no way he could get up; the Vietnamese would have to lift him up.

After 1969 we started getting a third meal each day, and by 1972 everybody got just as much as they wanted to eat. For example, initially we received just a small portion of bread, and later on you could get a loaf-and-a-half if that's what you wanted.

I received one package at Alcatraz, during Christmas of 1967. It came from my mother, and everything was in it except a couple of items. The crossword puzzle was gone—I guess they thought there was a code in it—and two packages of cocoa. The box contained ten packages, and there were eight, so I accused them of stealing and boy, were they upset. Their claim was the packages had been tested for poison because our countrymen were so ashamed of us. I didn't get another package until 1972, and it wasn't a whole package, just a half jar of one-a-day vitamins and two strips of beef jerky. My wife, every month or whatever the allowance was, sent exactly what was allowed by weight. She sent soap and so forth, although ultimately we got the word back [home] of don't bother with anything but coffee and tobacco.

When questioned should I become a prisoner of war, I am bound to give only my name, rank, service number and date of birth. I will evade answering further questions to the utmost of my ability. I will make no oral or written statements disloyal to my country and its allies or harmful to their cause.

Article Five, U.S. Code of Conduct, 1969

We had our problems with the Code of Conduct. With one exception, Doug Hedghal, an enlisted man, the guys who came home early were told not to. Whether or not they could avoid it, I don't know, but they could certainly have done it under protest. I do know the Vietnamese scheduled John McCain to come home early, and he told them, "Hell no," and he wasn't forced to come. We considered coming home early as accepting special favors, which is a violation of the code.

There were a lot of discussions at some very high levels as to whether or not the Code of Conduct applied after we got involved in Vietnam, because it was an undeclared war. When the *Oriskany* left Hawaii in 1965, going to WestPac, Stockdale, my CAG, got all the pilots together in the ready room one day and said, "We're going to war, and the Code of Conduct will apply. If shot down, you are expected to follow the Code of Conduct." That was a very astute move on his part, because when I went down, there was no doubt in my mind to follow the code. When he went down, I know he did, and three or four others did also. Later on I heard from prisoners coming in there'd been a top level conference, CINCPACFLT level, to discuss the applicability of the Code of Conduct. The conference resolved nothing, so everybody was left on their own. A couple of things bothered me about that meeting. First, that there was any doubt to start with; and second, if a bunch of guys sipping coffee in an air-conditioned room can debate whether or not the code applies, what's some guy in ropes going to decide?

In prison a couple of guys went over to the North Vietnamese side. I didn't know them well. [One seemed to me to be] just an opportunist. I understand that up until the time he was shot down, he was gung ho. He made no bones about the fact he expected to be a general one day. When he got on the other side of the fence, it was better for him to play their game. He got favors; there was a time when he was smoking cigars and eating popsicles, and I understand in one camp he and [the other man] roamed freely in the daytime.

I don't think [the other man] was an opportunist; I believe the North Vietnamese convinced him the war was not necessarily wrong, but that a lot of innocent people were being killed. There isn't any war that innocent people don't get killed, but I think it bothered him. I'm not asking anyone to like war, but my contention was if an individual had reservations and, say, he developed these reservations after becoming a POW, the camp was not the right place to air them. An aviator opposed to the war didn't have to fly; he could have quit flying at any time. So any guy who wound up a POW, in a sense he became a POW by his own choice to remain in the war. And even if he discovered he was entirely wrong, the POW camp was not the place to say it. He could think it and do anything he wanted, but he was still a part of us and should have supported us; and those two didn't.

Because Stockdale had made it very clear we would adhere to the code, the first time I broke, and was all alone, that was the lowest point of my life. Everybody hit that point, and then they'd get into communication and find out everyone had been there, everybody understood it, and everybody knew that you did your best. The consensus was to do your best, you're expected to do the best you can, and there'd be no repercussion if you fell short as long as people understood you did your best. I guess that's what really kept you going.

The Vietnamese could take you in three hours, or an hour if they wanted. The point was to give them nothing for free, and Stockdale eventually devised the BACK US policy to go as long as possible short of losing one's mental facilities. You didn't want to be pliable before giving in. We also found that in going as long as possible, many times the Vietnamese would settle for less, or something different from, what they originally wanted. When the torture was over, certainly everybody, myself included, felt they might have lasted another two hours. Of course, at that point in time, you couldn't last another two hours, or didn't think you could, or you wouldn't have given in.

I found out several things about myself from the experience. I'm not near as tough as I thought I was, and most of us, I don't believe, are [as tough as we think we are]. There's a conditioned effect in this country that makes us think we're smarter, richer, better, tougher than anybody else in the world, and the media propagates that. The movies and TV do, with John Wayne getting beaten, and blood running from his mouth, that type stuff. When first exposed to the POW environment, you've got that attitude: "I'll hang in there, I'll bleed a little, but they're not going to get me." Then you discover you're not that tough, and the reality of the situation takes you down. Mentally, I'm not as tough as I'd like to be, or thought I was. I'm tougher than some, yet not as tough as others.

John Dramesi, an Air Force pilot [who on 10 May 1969 escaped from the Zoo only to be captured a day later], has been very critical of the POW hierarchy since returning. To understand John, you have to know him. I don't know John very well, but I know he is an extremely tough individual. Physically tough, mentally tough, the only thing wrong with John, I think, [is that] he wouldn't make a good leader because he'd lead by *his* standards, and people can't reach his standards. I speak on leadership, and you can be the finest leader in the world, but if you set goals nobody can reach, you're not leading anybody, because they'll eventually give up trying to get there. Dramesi was in on the only Hanoi escape attempt, and he was tough enough to survive some very brutal treatment afterwards. His partner, Ed Atterberry, wasn't and died. John was ready to go again, and he was very critical of Air Force Col. John Flynn for calling off his last escape attempt. I was privy to that decision and understand all the thoughts and rationale that went into it. I support not having gone, in view of the war approaching some crescendo and the price that would have been paid. Based on what occurred in 1969 when he [Dramesi] went, the price was not worth it to the entire camp. Now I don't take anything away from John. If we could have all been like John, we would have been a bunch of outstanding prisoners. But he makes no latitude for other people's weaknesses, and most of us aren't as strong as him.

I also learned from the POW experience that most events in our lives aren't worth the time it takes you to worry about them. In a lot of cases, you worry for three or four days, and the problem goes away. And in those cases where it doesn't go away, worry is not going to change it. Events take their course, and it's either going to have a solution or it's not. If something goes wrong, the hell with it. I enjoy life a whole lot more that way. I don't do things I don't like to do, and I made myself a vow—never to be hungry or cold. And I haven't been either.

Part Seven
1972–1973

I implore you, I beg you to consider what you are doing. There are peasants. They grow rice and rear pigs. They are similar to the farmers in the Midwest many years ago in the United States. . . . Are these people your enemy? What will you say to your children years from now who may ask you why you fought the war?

Actress Jane Fonda, during a July 1972 visit to Hanoi, asking American pilots to reconsider their participation in the Vietnam War in a broadcast over ''Voice of Vietnam Radio.''

Introduction

These were not the best of times for the U.S. Navy. Seven consecutive years of war had seriously cracked the morale and discipline of the seagoing service, leading to unprecedented problems.

In June 1971 Secretary of the Navy John Chafee labeled drug abuse out of control, and facts supported his claims. The Navy had discharged 170 drug offenders in 1966, 3,800 in 1969, and 5,000 in 1970. One West Coast destroyer scheduled to deploy in 1970 was reportedly forced to postpone the departure when over 10 percent of the crew were found to be involved in a drug ring.

Reenlistments were another major concern, with only 13 percent of the first-tour sailors choosing to re-up in 1971. "We have a personnel crisis that borders on disaster," proclaimed Adm. Elmo R. Zumwalt, Jr., the Chief of Naval Operations. Responding to the crucial need for retaining highly skilled technicians, Zumwalt's dictates (known as "Z-Grams") included disciplinary permissiveness, longer haircuts, fewer inspections, and other cosmetic changes designed to make the service more palatable. The changes of longstanding policy in the tradition-oriented Navy ordered by the Z-Grams widened the chasm between the career officers, both commissioned and non-coms, and the younger sailors. By 1972 it was not unusual for enlisted personnel to simply ignore the presence of superior officers in the passageways of Navy ships.

Racial tensions also surfaced. In March 1971 the National Naval Medical Center in Bethesda, Maryland, was forced to close its base enlisted men's club because of tension between blacks and whites. It was inevitable that racial problems would reach Yankee Station. Late in a grueling 282-day cruise, a race riot broke out aboard the carrier *Kitty Hawk,* forcing the naval aviators to take refuge in their squadron's ready rooms.

From a combat perspective, 30 March 1972 triggered a new era in the air war over North Vietnam. Tens of thousands of North Vietnamese and Viet Cong troops opened the Easter Offensive, a massive assault that broke across the DMZ, moved through the Central Highlands, and headed toward Saigon from the north. In swift reaction the administration of President Richard Nixon authorized Seventh Fleet aircraft to strike the area of North Vietnam closest to the DMZ. Over the following nine months, Navy, Marine Corps, and Air Force pilots poured megatons of bombs, rockets, and bullets onto North Vietnamese soil, literally pounding the Communists into submission. By year's end B-52 strikes into Hanoi and Haiphong, reviled by the U.S. media as an act befitting barbarians, convinced the Hanoi government the time had come to consider calling it quits.

The campaign started slowly, utilizing bombing practices that would seem familiar to the pilots. April witnessed the reintroduction of the interdiction campaign halted in November 1968. But as the tally of carriers in the gulf expanded to five—the Constellation, Kitty Hawk, Hancock, Saratoga, and Coral Sea, the largest carrier task force ever deployed to Southeast Asia—the target picture began to widen. By early May the entire country, excluding a buffer zone thirty miles along the Chinese border and several other sensitive targets, had been opened to Navy and Air Force strikes.

The LINEBACKER I campaign debuted in May; it was a full-fledged effort undertaken to isolate North Vietnam from outside support. Operation POCKET MONEY witnessed the 9 May mining of Haiphong Harbor by Coral Sea–based A-6 and A-7 aircraft. The mining of other ports soon followed, and between May and December, no large merchant vessel was able to enter or leave North Vietnamese harbors.

Yankee Station Navy units, unlike their counterparts during the Washington, D.C.–authorized ROLLING THUNDER campaign, were allowed to pursue their own mission objectives and target selections. Rail lines and roads between China and North Vietnam were cut, while ammunition and POL storage, power plants, bridges, and rail yards came under devastating attack. Loosened restrictions, advanced technology, and eventually the use of B-52 bombers brought down several longtime nemeses, including the Thanh Hoa Bridge—The Dragon's Jaw—which tumbled into the water 13 May, destroyed by Air Force laser-guided bombs.

Between May and September, Navy attack aircraft flew an average of four thousand day and night sorties each month, reaching a peak of nearly 4,750 in August. A typical flight schedule during June 1972 for an A-7 Corsair included two missions daily—an alpha strike loaded with eight Mk-82 bombs into Haiphong and a night recce that evening with bombs and parachute flares.

The exertion of Navy and Air Force air power brought a vicious North Vietnamese response. The same May to September time frame witnessed the firing of nearly two thousand SAMs and thousands of rounds of AAA, resulting in the shootdown of twenty-eight American aircraft. The activity in the air-to-air arena greatly intensified, highlighted by action on 10 May when forty-one MiG aircraft opposed Navy and Air Force fighters. Eleven North Vietnamese MiGs were brought down that day, including three by the F-4 Phantom aircrew of pilot Lt. Randy Cunningham and radar intercept officer Lt. (jg) Willie Driscoll, making the duo the Navy's only aces of the war. Six American aircraft were also "smoked" 10 May, certainly one of the most deadly days in the history of modern air warfare.

In July actress and political activist Jane Fonda appeared in North Vietnam, denouncing American military activity in the country and calling on servicemen to lay down their arms. Her itinerary included visits with POWs Ed Miller, Gene Wilber, and others, and posing for photographers while wearing a North Vietnamese combat helmet and examining an AAA battery. The latter act alone would endear Fonda to a generation of American pilots.

American airpower during LINEBACKER I made North Vietnam leaders much more amenable toward peace discussions, and by early October the Nixon administration felt peace was at hand. Strikes in the vicinity of Hanoi were called off, and by 23 October targets were restricted to ones below the 20th Parallel. The results, however, were all too predictable although not entirely the fault of the North Vietnamese government. Negotiations slowed down thanks in part to reluctance from the South Vietnam government of Nguyen Van Thieu in approving the terms of the peace agreement, and the North Vietnamese retooled and restocked up North.

Nixon's response to the peace delay came with the authorization of LINEBACKER II. Aided by CTF-77 aircraft in limited Iron Hand roles, B-52 bombers based in Guam and Thailand began a full-scale assault on targets within Hanoi and Haiphong on 18 December.

"When LINEBACKER II started," remembers Linn Felt, then a captain based in Washington, D.C., and planning contingencies for the cease-fire agreement, "the carriers primarily provided flak suppression, a support package without too much opportunity for primary targeting.

"We did have some Navy strikes in the Haiphong area following the B-52s, but it was the 'well, if you've got some leftovers go ahead and do it' type of approach. The focus was on B-52s, and unfortunately, the SAC pilots weren't very flexible. Until they varied the flight plan, the B-52s took a lot of losses."

During the eleven-day assault, some 1,250 surface-to-air missiles were fired at the incoming B-52s, bringing down fifteen and damaging nearly twenty-five others. The cost was high, but the point was certainly made. North Vietnam quickly resumed peace negotiations, and on 15 January

1973 combat operations in the North were halted. On 27 January 1973 U.S., South Vietnamese, North Vietnamese, and Viet Cong representatives signed the cease-fire agreement in Paris. By 12 February the first wave of American prisoners of war, nearly six hundred in all, were on their way home.

Chapter 31
Ejection

Lieutenant Dennis S. Pike disappeared 23 March 1972, while on a mission just inside Laos. The father of three and a veteran of nearly 175 combat missions, Pike fell victim to an element he couldn't control, engine failure in his A-7E Corsair.

"We were on a mission just south of the DMZ," remembers then Cmdr. Robert Taylor, commanding officer of the *Kitty Hawk*–based VA-192.

Government forces were being overrun by the Viet Cong, and a T-28 with an American pilot and Vietnamese observer also went down. We were on target about forty minutes and finally had to leave. I watched Pike disappear on the way out, and that scene, those ten or fifteen seconds, are embedded in my mind, lived over and over. I was about a mile-and-a-half behind him, saw the smoke come out of his tailpipe, and called him up asking if there were any problems. He replied "Yeah, I've got some oil pressure problems." We were only about twenty miles inside of Laos, and I told him to take a heading toward Da Nang. He rolled out and made the turn from southwest all the way around to the east at five thousand feet. I told him "If you pass three thousand feet and don't have anything left, then out." He replied, "Roger that," followed by an "Uh oh, there goes the engine. Well, see you guys later."

Taylor saw the canopy shatter—"a bunch of glitter in the air which had to be the canopy, and a black object came out. Then I lost it and never picked it up. His wingman saw the object come out, and never picked it up either, and my wingman never saw anything. I do know something left the airplane."

Pike's disappearance had particular significance to Lt. Fred Knee, who on 19 March had gone down under nearly identical circumstances.

Knee, fortunately, had only just left the ship when the engine of his
A-7E failed.

Ted Hill and myself left the ship first that night for a two-man road
recce. I was at turning point two in the rendezvous circle when the
engine failed. I thought there'd been a problem climbing out, not quite
sure if it was night noises or what, but the aircraft just wasn't maintaining
altitude and air speed at the right fuel settings. Whoom, the engine
started shaking and just gave up the ghost. Hill saw a bunch of fire
coming out of the airplane. I tried a relight and nothing but sparks
flew out.

The night was clear, and I headed back toward the ship—descending
without an engine—just to be closer for the ejection. I planned to get
out at 300 knots, thought better of it, and slowed down to about 250.
The ship was at a heading of 360; I went to 330 to be off to the side,
punched out, and was picked up by a helo from the ship.

What struck home the most from this evolution was the Navy training.
I had no other options, and the training just dramatically solidified,
staying crystal clear even after the ejection. Because it was night, I
couldn't see the water, only hear the swishing of the life raft swinging
back and forth. When the raft hit the water, I put my hands on the
koch fittings [harness release snaps] and as soon as my feet hit, released
and cleanly separated from the chute. The LPA [life preserver] inflated
properly, and I rode very high in the water. The water was warm and
comfortable, and I could see the helicopter on its way out and the brightly
lit ship. All in all it was a good experience. I had a flare and threw
that into the life raft, and of course there was the light off the helmet.
The helicopter took an awful long time to get the swimmer in the water.
It flew way forward and dropped a flare, then way back and dropped
another flare, and the whole procedure took a long time. I didn't know
if the [helo] pilot couldn't see me, or what the deal was, but as I was
told later, a hover in the dark of night that close to the water isn't
easy. The swimmer jumped in the water and half-drowned, really more
nervous than I was. The guy had a knife in his mouth, and I thought
he was going to stab me. I just said, "Settle down, I'm okay, I'm
okay," and then he did his job, getting me hooked up and into the
helicopter. Back we went, and what seemed like the entire ship's crew
was waiting, really an exciting sort of time.

I wish I could have done some other things in the cockpit before getting out—read out other information for the tape recording, specifically the oil pressure. For some reason, and I don't understand all the mechanics of it, the accident came down to an understanding of what happened to my oil pressure. I just couldn't remember looking at the oil pressure gauge. I thought it didn't fail, and from that statement Rear Adm. [Damon W.] Cooper decided to up the A-7Es. Four days later Denny Pike went down, and the decision was made to ground the airplane.

The day after the accident, I went over to the *Constellation*, Rear Admiral Cooper's flagship, for a big powwow to discuss the accident. The admiral knew he had an [engine] problem, a spacer problem; and he also knew from intelligence sources something we didn't know— North Vietnam was staging to invade the South. The admiral's questions were very specific, and [he] came to the conclusion, with the pressure of the invasion coming, that the failure of the engine was not a spacer problem in the turbine section—which had been documented as an increasing problem. The accident, according to Cooper's conclusion, was an internal FOD [foreign object damage] problem—a compressor blade breaking apart and fodding the engine. Rear Admiral Cooper assessed the need, he didn't want to ground essentially his entire strike force, and there was uncertainty as to the exact cause. I was very impressed with him; he was a humble man, he seemed to be a gentleman, and probably anybody would have made the same decision.

The death of Denny Pike four days after my accident was tragic because of the decision to continue flying the A-7. Denny was later in his flight than I had been and coming off the target. It's really a sickening feeling to lose a guy like that, but there's also a self-preservation rule that comes into play. We all faced the same threat, and all dealt with the possibility, I may be the one next time. So this self-preservation rule was triggered. Even though you felt sick about the loss, there was something inside of you that said I'm glad it wasn't me. I'm glad it was him, not me. I loved Denny. He was a kind, funny gentleman who kept us in stitches, and a great guy and officer. But no matter, there was that trigger saying, I'm glad it was him. You hardened yourself to that idea.

You did get close to people and a tremendous comradery existed in 192 while I was there. In that 1970–71 cruise, the squadron was very tight knit, very well respected, and nobody was getting hurt. We'd come off four CNO safety awards, two AIRPAC Es; we were the "World

Famous Golden Dragons,'' an institution and a top notch, high morale outfit from top to bottom. From a personal perspective, I was Blue and Gold all the way. The fighting was mostly over the Mu Gia pass [in Laos], and it was a game. We went up North on two occasions, secondary targets out in the forest, not heavily defended but just incursions, I guess, to teach the bad guys a lesson.

The ship came home and something happened in my personal life, I got married. My wife and I had been married maybe a month when the brass moved forward our deployment schedule a month. We came back out, and the atmosphere of the war and squadron had changed. First of all, I jumped out, losing some of my tiger and needing about a month to make the adjustment. Then the North invades the South, and the wing starts getting guys shot down; plus negative events were occurring in the squadron from the JO's perspective. We had some [new] individuals in there, some [squadron] department heads and [a new ship's captain]. More sorties, more sorties for no other purpose than to fly sorties. Guys were getting killed and the morale of the ship and our squadron plummeted. Somehow the magic was lost.

About mid-cruise of the second deployment, I decided that I'm not dedicating my life to this. I'm not a pacifist by any stretch, and I thought I did my duty and did a good job. I was a good pilot, I mean you had to be. But I wasn't into the war the way it was fought. On one occasion, the squadron had a mission into a facility that constructed lighters, the little ships that went out to the merchant ships, loaded off the goods, and snuck back. We rolled in, blew it up, came back, and one of my squadron mates said "Oh, my bombs hung up and they walked right through that village." It just sickened me, and while there probably wasn't anybody in the village anyway, to him it was just great to march a whole bunch of Mk-82 bombs through a little fishing village. I was sick of it; there wasn't a whole lot of sense to it. When we were in a good fight, a good fair fight, boy, I was in there with the best of them. But not when it was just some of this other stuff.

The negativity, stupidity of the war was a real factor in my feelings. We'd launch with 1967 [target] photos, or we'd launch a mini-alpha strike toward a bridge the Air Force knocked down two weeks earlier. Here we flew over the Iron Triangle, Red River Valley, with all these planes exposed to all this mess, get to the bridge, and somebody says it's down. The alternative was "Well guys, let's break up by sections or divisions and go road recce." Another time we launched twenty attack airplanes on a suspected petroleum storage facility, and it's some sleepy fishing village along the river. More than once I'd just pull off, drop my bombs in the river, and say, "This is crazy, this is insane."

Another incident, during the period after Jane Fonda made her impact, involved a squadron pilot hardly dedicated to much of anything. He came back from a hop and in the debrief said, "Well, we blew up this bridge after a recce." The bridge was determined to be a water control device, and this guy found himself in deep, serious trouble. Somebody really threatened to court-martial him; so after that we came back and always debriefed "open storage" no matter what we bombed.

There were missions to be proud of, like the Xong Be Thermal Power Plant. Our operations officer, Mel Munsinger, planned, organized, and led that strike, and it accomplished everything and more. There was deceit: we came in behind Thud Ridge like we were going toward Kep, the MiGs scrambled and came up after us, and the F-4s were lying in wait. Then we circled back and rolled in on the power plant. I was Mel's section leader, and we were in first with 1,000-pound bombs and delayed fuses because the facility was heavily built up. Rolling off the target, with AAA coming at us, SAMs, just a lot of activity, I looked back over my shoulder, and there were sparks of electricity from the first bombs arcing clear across the power plant.

Another effort that stands out was actually the very last mission of the first cruise, a rescue mission, and I, jg Knee, was the division leader. The reason was a squadron concept to get the jgs up to section lead, and we were still on the flight deck when the call came. A little O-1 Bird Dog with an American in the front seat and a VNAF [Vietnamese Air Force representative] in the back seat had gone down, and thousands of bad guys—division or battalion strength—surrounded them. The launch took place at dusk, and our job was to keep the bad guys' heads down long enough for an Air America helicopter to come in and pick up the pilot and VNAF. We carried Mark 82s and Rockeyes, a great anti-personnel cluster bomb; and the enemy had CPU-23s, a vehicle-mounted weapon which fires something like 8,000 rounds a minute with tracers. Vietnam at that point consisted of dropping bombs in the jungle, hoping something might blow up, then heading home. But this mission was war, hand-to-hand, as close as you can get, and for twenty-five minutes we had an airplane at the ground keeping their heads down. Talk about fighting instinct; I rolled in, dropped, and pulled off with the CPU-23 tracers going up right past the cockpit. That stuff could never keep up, and pretty soon your bomb hit and there'd be silence. Nine hundred KBAs [killed by air] were found in the area the next day, the guys were rescued, and we all received DFCs.

Those were good missions, but there weren't many. Most of the time it was hard to see much sense in what you were doing.

The motivation to continue fighting was "it's your duty." You wanted to be a good pilot; you wanted to be a good Navy officer. There was a duty, a sense of duty, you would never let your buddies or squadron down. There was a sense of honor. War without a sense of honor wouldn't work, but there was also the other side. You'd come back to your room after a mission and sit around with the other JOs and drink, complain, and gripe. There were always a very few that wouldn't allow themselves any criticism of anybody. Those guys were treated with an "Oh, get out of here" attitude. I know a lot of the guys, some of the jgs that came in when I was a lieutenant, man, they came into the Navy to get a job with the airlines and didn't need all this. But they did their job; I don't think the war ever impacted anybody's performance, just their attitude. There was just a hundred different things, like the flight schedule. Noon to midnight and midnight to noon, and you'd always be eating eggs in the wardroom. You'd get there for supper time, and it was really breakfast time for the ship crew. Then you'd wake up, go to the wardroom, and it's time to eat eggs again.

When the squadron started flying up North, my attitude hadn't yet changed. Really, I was just trying to get my tiger back up after ejecting. Any Navy pilot who says he wasn't afraid in Vietnam is a liar. You were hanging out there all the time, kept going by this attitude of "it won't happen to me." When it did, or almost happened, that shakes something inside and there's a need to get your tiger developed again. In fact, Dick Kiehl, our skipper, took me back up on the first flight to make sure the lieutenant still had his wits about him.

Our first alpha strike was in April, led by CAG Huntington Hardisty. When he said, "Head'em out," my mouth was full of cotton and the adrenalin was pumping. The runs down South had been nothing, and now we were going into the big time of SAMs and the whole shooting match. There was a month or two when we bombed trains, fresh bridges, targets that were really blowing up, plus MiGs were in the air. The line period was forty-five or fifty days, a lot longer than our previous cruise with two, maybe three missions a day if the spare launched. The brief was nothing more than sit there and watch the tube, then the skipper or whomever you were flying with, he'd look over and say "Fifteen miles and five thousand feet. Any questions?" That was the brief for the entire mission. Initially, there was a sense of hey, we're going to clean up and win this war, but that changed as the tedium of the war went on.

I would love to have a reunion with the guys in the squadron. Those two tours were pretty intense, and there's probably more resident memory from that period of my life than any other period of time. There's a place in my heart for those guys; we were under duress and difficult times together, and we all pulled together. There wasn't any animosity within it all; it was very positive and also very bittersweet. Salt and pepper, if you will. As I get older and reflect, more of the good, positive, and sense of achievement surfaces, and I have to resurrect the reality of the way it really was. But the impressions were indelibly stamped, something I can get out and think about.

Chapter 32
Haiphong Mining

In the early morning hours of 9 May 1972, three A-6 Intruders and six A-7 Corsairs were hurled off the deck of the carrier *Coral Sea*. Commander Roger "Blinkie" Sheets, commander of Air Wing 15, led the A-6 contingent, and Cmdr. Len Giuliani, executive officer of VA-22, the A-7s. The long-discussed mission, code-named POCKET MONEY, took Sheets, Giuliani, and company to Haiphong Harbor, the port through which 85 percent of all shipping traffic entered the country. Each aircraft carried four magnetic-acoustic sea mines, and shortly before 9:00 A.M., the nine aircraft released the mines into the approach to the harbor.

That same day (but actually 8 May because of the twelve-hour time difference between Vietnam and Washington, D.C.), President Nixon addressed the nation. The North Vietnamese "have flatly and arrogantly refused to negotiate an end to the war and bring peace," said Nixon. In response, he announced the mining of Haiphong and all other North Vietnamese ports, the cutting of rail lines and other communication avenues, and the reinstitution of the air war against virtually all military targets. The isolation of North Vietnam had begun.

The new air offensive, LINEBACKER I, officially began on 10 May although Navy carriers had been attacking targets up North for several weeks; two days later the mines in Haiphong were activated, trapping some twenty-six vessels flying foreign flags. Not a single merchant ship would enter or leave any North Vietnamese harbor through the end of 1972.

"There were inklings the bombing was going to reopen, but nobody really knew that," recalls Len Giuliani. "When it did come, I'd say there was real excitement."

We started going North in late April, early May, and for the first month or so, the pace, the defenses, and the action in general were a lot faster than my first trip over there. Compared to when we left in early 1968, the North Vietnamese had rearmed, regrouped, and were ready. There were a lot of bullets and a lot of SAMs. Frankly, my hat is off to the JOs who flew their first combat missions in that kind of environment. Two or three days into the evolution, we lost our CAG, Tom Dunlop, to a SAM in an area of southern North Vietnam, Dong Hoi, that previously had been real quiet.

On May 6, Marvin Wiles, who'd flown three, maybe four or five missions, and I were going to do a day recce, which was very fruitful at that time. In the 1960s I saw maybe one truck moving during the day during two cruises. In early 1972 the trucks were out en masse, and it just didn't stop after the first day. We'd road recce and see trucks all the time, big convoys of trucks, and have a heyday shooting up the trucks in the A-7E.

Marv and I crossed the coast just south of Vinh, a very common navigation point, and I saw a SAM lift-off about ten miles over to the left. I said "Okay Marv, do you have the lift-off?" and he said "I got it." I said "Arm your bombs and let's go get'em," making the decision to bomb the SAM site rather than recce. Marv took up a standard formation some 3,000 to 4,000 feet away.

The smoke had drifted away from the site, so I planned to go in as fast as possible to where I thought the SAM site was, confirm it, pop up, and go bomb it. In the meantime, an Iron Hand, anti-SAM aircraft in the area had picked up the signal and was monitoring the site also. I flew over the site, saw it, popped up, rolled in, and bombed, and as I was pulling off, some three thousand feet off the ground, I rolled over waiting for my bombs to hit. Before they struck, I saw this complete peppering of the whole area, followed about two seconds later by my string of bombs that went right across the upper half of this circular site.

What happened—the Iron Hand guy launched a Shrike that effectively covered the entire site. I had never actually watched a Shrike hit the ground, but this guy put the Shrike right over the radar van, it went off perfectly and spread all these little BBs around, followed by my bombs.

I pulled off to the left and came back to the right, and hearing a couple of tweedle deedle deedles, called Marv and asked if he was in on the target yet. I looked back, and there was an airplane going into the ground. Marv had been hit by a SAM from another site which I'd picked up on my scope but [had] not visually seen.

The difference between a SAM and a bullet was whether you saw the guy shooting. If a SAM was fired and you didn't see it, you were probably dead. If he shot a bullet and you didn't pick it up, he still had to be a good shot, and odds are he wouldn't hit you unless you were being predictable. With a SAM, you could be completely unpredictable, but he's still probably going to hit you unless there was some warning, somebody around to call [your] attention to the lift-off.

To look for Marv, I was faced with a real tough decision of putting my six o'clock to that other SAM site. There was another Shrike on the airplane, so I fired it in that direction, and then went back and started looking around. After what seemed liked three hours—and I guess it was only three minutes—I saw Marv's parachute and followed it down right into a village. He landed right in the middle, and I started getting all kinds of flak and stuff and had to leave.

We never heard from Marv Wiles again, never in all the late breaking news from Hanoi did we hear from him. Nothing about his remains, whether he was alive, dead, or whatever.

I felt bad, and not that it made any difference, but especially since Marv was relatively inexperienced. Here was a typical guy in a high threat environment. I'm sure what happened, he was up at the roll-in point where, no doubt about it, you're vulnerable, especially in a heavy SAM environment. He surely had to have received an indication that SAM site had him locked on or else his gear wasn't working. He never said a word, and had he been locked up, usually there was a call you made, which he didn't make.

A lot of us aren't POWs or dead because of the odds. Sure, there are guys who made mistakes, flying low where they shouldn't have, or who broke basic rules of combat about low pullouts, never dueling with a flak site, or making repeated runs in high threat areas. They broke the rules and spent their time in the motel over there or died. But a lot of them were just guys who got hit in the target area that could have just as easily been somebody else. They were doing everything everybody else was doing, but just didn't make it out.

Chapter 33
Winding Down

June 1972 witnessed the ill-conceived break-in of the Democratic Party's national headquarters at the Watergate apartment and office complex in Washington, D.C., and the beginning of the end for the administration of President Richard Milhous Nixon. June also marked the 266th and final combat hop for Lt. Rusty Scholl.

"My last flight came June 30 with Bill Smith, Len Giuliani, and Don Simmons, by Nam Dinh," relates Scholl. "Giuliani almost got bagged by a SAM, there was something like sixty-plus holes in his airplane, and Smith took him back out to the ship while Don and I went after the SAM site.

"We knocked it out; in fact, they gave me a DFC for it. But you think about it later. Last flight, last combat hop, why did I do it?"

In '71–'72 I was the CAG-15 LSO aboard the *Coral Sea,* flying with the two attack squadrons VA-22 and -94. The CO's philosophies were completely opposite, or more so, the XO's philosophy in VA-22; the CO really didn't run the squadron from a leadership point. He'd sit in the ready room and have cold sweats and call the doctor all the time and ground himself. As the wing LSO, I'd look at his schedule a day ahead of time, see where he was supposed to be, and make sure I was there when he walked in. I'd follow him around like a little puppy because within fifteen minutes, he'd find an excuse to cancel out of his flight, and I'd jump in his spot. He'd look around and say, "Rusty, you doing anything this morning?" And I'd say, "No sir." When he made his one hundredth landing on the ship, probably some three months after the most junior officer made his one hundredth landing, we announced it over the PA system. He was pissed, throwing his helmet across the ready room, screaming, and ranting. At the time, I think I was working close to 175, 200 traps.

But to characterize the difference in squadron philosophies: if you were in North Vietnam, and the SAMs came up, VA-94 would head for the water and 22 for the missile site. VA-94's whole philosophy was to get in there, get back out, and get back safely aboard the ship. [VA-] 22's philosophy was to go in there and see how much havoc could be created. VA-94's skipper, XO, and ops officer, and maybe one other guy were all downed by SAMs, and all four were heading out towards the water at the time.

I flew three, maybe four combat hops with VA-94, and the rest exclusively with 22. [VA-] 94's skipper, Dave Moss, grounded me once for a month from flying his airplanes because I made more than one run on a gun site. He happened to be airborne at the time and heard it. Moss told me you never make multiple runs at an AAA site, that was the stated air wing policy. In a situation like that, the guy on the ground had the better odds next time around because he knew where you were, and what you were going to do. But in that case, I wanted to get that AAA site. Next time out with 94, I'm strafing trucks, and a bullet fired out of the one o'clock position instead of eight o'clock. It went out, ricocheted up into the intake of my airplane, and formed a mound. The bullet, a high explosive round, almost went through, and had it done that, the engine probably would have been shit-canned, and I'd probably have shot myself down. We found the bullet in the intake. My third flight was in a 94 tanker, and coming back I did a flyby of the ship, pulled too many Gs, and twisted the whole refueling pylon.

From then on, all my flying was with VA-22. They were a good squadron; there was an aggressiveness. Take off the number one guy and it was a great squadron. Len Giuliani, the XO, and the CO had completely different philosophies. For the CO, it wasn't as much a fear of combat as it was just getting through it and [being] promoted. Flying around the ship was his avenue to get promoted. He was in 122 as an instructor and never flew there, and was picked up for CO and never flew there. At the time in 1972, I knew Giuliani was having a rough time. And looking back on it, I think he had an extremely rough time because there were two opposite philosophies trying to work together. As the junior man, the number two guy, when everyone in the squadron emulates you, I'm sure it was rough on him.

Len would lead by example; he wouldn't tell you what to do; he'd go out and do it. He's one of those guys who'd say, "Hey, we're going to fly down some well and shoot somebody in the ass," or "we're going to do touch and goes at Haiphong International and drop peace pamphlets." Our response was, "Okay, if you want to go, let's go." We'd follow him to hell; he was that kind of guy.

Certain guys in 94 had that same VA-22 aggressiveness and combativeness, but they also knew there'd be trouble if they did one thing other than drop their bombs and get home.

While out on the line, I never thought about getting bagged. Being young, a go-getter, and gung ho, it didn't enter my mind. I did think about it when I'd come back from liberty, say, Hong Kong or something, and we hadn't flown in a couple of weeks. Then you'd start thinking about fear and dying. But on the line, you might as well forget it.

Losing people hits real close, but not in the fact [that] it could happen to me, just the fact [that] I inventoried the gear of three guys. By inventory, I mean wrap his gear up in bags and stuff, place it in cruise boxes, seal it, and ship the boxes back to the wife. In 1967 Jim Hickerson, my division officer, was shot down, and I can't remember whether I said yes I'll do it, or whatever, but I inventoried the gear. The rule was to leave out anything you were unsure about. For example, a picture of a woman—and she's unknown to you—or letters from someone you don't know. Throw them away; it was better not to have that go home even though it could have been a sister, mother, or whatever. But if you didn't know, throw it away.

We'd make jokes about death, although obviously not while packing some guy's gear. But we'd joke about who got what. Can I have your stereo, or can I have your girlfriend—or I'll tell your wife if she's good looking—and things like that. I found Navy guys, when they got serious, either joked about it, or cried.

I bombed North Vietnam during the '71 stand down, dropping a few bombs on Tiger Island. My wingman, Pat Rounds, and I had six, 1,000-pound bombs each, and we went into Laos or South Vietnam, one of the two. The word came back, there's nothing to hit because the weather is too bad. Right near the DMZ was this patch of rock called Tiger Island, controlled by North Vietnam. I don't think there was anything on it, maybe observers or something. I could see the island up ahead through the overcast, looked at Pat, and switched him over to another frequency. I said, "Hey, have you ever been put in hack before?" "No," he said, "I'm just a wingman." "Okay, fly with me." We turned off the IFF, turned off anything that was radiating, went right down on the water, and came screaming in on this island. I put the pipper on the island, pulled up into the clouds, and the bombs started rolling off in pairs. We came around to look and the bombs are going off boom, boom, boom, boom, right across the island.

The only place I didn't bomb were areas they suspected might be a POW camp. I avoided those places like the plague. But everybody and everything else was fair game. With Air Wing 15, in '72, Don Simmons and I kept trying to get this one dam because there was a big town below it. We figured a cut might start the water.

Simmons dropped mines in Haiphong Harbor and on the way out just strafed the shit out of a Russian freighter. We'd been specifically warned, and knew we could get in trouble, because a Marine officer had been sent home, or severely reprimanded, because he hit a Polish freighter that, I believe, was off-loading coal at Hon Gai. Put a bomb right down the smokestack and the ship sank right there at the pier. On that day, the higher-ups had told us there might possibly be a ship at the pier, and it was a hazy day, late in the afternoon, and the sun was shining. I didn't see it, nobody on the flight saw that ship, and I'm sure the Marine didn't see it either. Hell, over the radio they even said the ship is not at the pier. Boy, there was some deep shit about that.

Anyway, Simmons puts his mines in the water, he's flying out, and here's this Russian freighter. He just blasted it and never stopped. He traps, and the first thing Simmons does is go find the gunnery officer. Hey, load that gun and nothing was shot out of it, right? Right. It's loaded up and not more than a couple of hours later—from the time it took the Russian ship to get hold of Moscow—[Washington, D.C., is] checking to see who shot 20-millimeter. The word goes back the airplanes have been checked and there's been no 20-millimeter shot.

We were also told not to shoot fishing boats. Why don't you shoot fishing boats? The answer is they're not directly involved in the war even though they're bringing food back to the people shooting at you. Well, I shot more fishing boats than you can believe. I've even got motion pictures of shooting fishing boats. Lots of pilots got picked up out of the water by fishing boats when the weather was bad and the helicopters couldn't get down to get them out, and they'd get a reward [from the North Vietnamese] for bringing back a pilot.

Anytime we got off the line and went back to port, it was just standby, mass drinking, and poker playing. Alcohol was tolerated on board the ship, although you couldn't go around drunk on the ship. You couldn't say, yes, it was permissible, because if the officers can have it, then why can't the chiefs? If the chiefs can have it, why can't the first and second classes? And we knew they had it too.

When we went off the line in June of 1972 heading home, we held a great big party in the stateroom area of the Marine A-6 squadron. Guys were posted at the end of the corridors, and nobody except officers could go down the corridors for two complete passageways. The party started that afternoon after the last combat hop, and went on until three or four the next morning. What a fiasco! People were out playing kick the can with beer bottles, Budweiser cans, and guys were so drunk they couldn't stand up or even hold their drinks. When it was all over, the place smelled like a brewery. We managed to get rid of everything but the broken glass, the bottles, and the smell. The beer cans were all stuffed in a bag, holes punched in the sides, and the bag thrown over the side. We just hoped nobody thought it was somebody falling overboard. The booze bottles were left in drawers and thrown out later.

Chapter 34
Bringing the POWs Home

By early summer the driving force for the majority of Yankee Station pilots centered on bringing home the POWs. Certainly the first tour nuggets were interested in piling up the combat missions. But the majority of mid-career and senior aviators, many with three or four combat tours to their credit, wanted only to beat the North Vietnamese into complete submission—which seemed possible as a result of Nixon's isolation program—get their fellow pilots out of the Hanoi prison cells, and head home.

"Whether the war was right or wrong, the motivation in 1972 was to get the POWs back, and the feeling was the only way to get our boys back was to completely devastate North Vietnam," says Scotty Vaught, who flew up North for one month in '72 with VA-94.

Bomb the dikes and drown the country right into the sea, and bomb men, women, and children. Because of all the stories from the ground troops about the women and the children, the way the kids and women would kill, there weren't any good guys. Certainly from the perspective of the women and children, it was the only way to survive; but our perspective said all slanty eyes are bad, so bullshit on don't bomb a school bus since the bus was probably carrying armor anyway.

We wanted to win the war, get the North Vietnamese on the ropes, but I think most importantly, we wanted to get our buddies back. Many of them had been captive for five, six, seven years; they were hurting, and everybody but the rookies had a personal friend that was there, somebody that you knew, somebody you'd flown with. We wanted it over, to get our people back and go back to our nice six-month cruises where we hit all the liberty ports, places we weren't going to but had enjoyed. And we wanted to spend time at home with our wives and families.

I joined VA-94 on board the *Coral Sea* in June, made one line period, and then went home. Flying up North was very important to me. I started teaching kids how to fly for the war in 1965, and I hadn't been there. I spent forty months in the RAG, went out to fly over the South and Laos, and then went back to 122 for another year-and-a-half. When I finally got back to a squadron and went up North, that was very important. I hadn't proven to myself that I could do it yet. I looked forward to the fact I was going up North, but halfway through that line period I figured out what we were bombing, and it didn't make a whole lot of sense. North Vietnam had been bombed so badly; we were sending twenty airplanes to bomb a bridge as big as my driveway, and we were getting shot at. We'd go on day, road recce missions and see nothing, zero. I mean those people had it figured out; the North Vietnamese had the timetables down. They knew we launched every hour-and-a-half, or one [hour] plus forty-five [minutes], whatever it was, and just wouldn't move. And here we are, day in and day out, carrying eight Mk-82 bombs valued at five hundred dollars apiece and putting potholes in potholes.

Initially, I flew wing on lieutenants for at least four or five missions to see what the hell was going on. Experience was vital. The Shrike missions were very important, and I never flew one of those because I never had the experience to work up to that. Some very sharp jgs and lieutenants flew those missions. I became division qualified, and as ops officer of an attack squadron, that would be a normal thing. But you had to prove yourself to get to that point and some people never did. One guy, the senior lieutenant commander in the squadron, never became ops officer because the skipper never had enough confidence in his ability to run the squadron, and/or to fly the missions to give him the job.

In combat, the desire to work hard and hone skills had a lot to do with how good you were. Most everybody had the ability to control their emotions, not to be chicken. But how good you were leading a division, leading an alpha strike, a lot depended on how much effort was put in to developing your skills. Fighter pilots didn't spend the time to be an alpha strike leader; their minds were on air-to-air, shooting down a MiG. The attack pilot's mind was set on leading the alpha strike—ingress, not getting shot at, putting the bombs on target, and getting the hell out. Now certainly it wasn't all black and white; there's a gray area because there were shitty alpha strike leaders who were attack pilots. But again, the bottom line gets down to spending the time instead of watching the movie at night.

There were more poor flight leaders than wingmen, people that didn't take the time to learn the threat. Everybody had little maps, updated daily on where the flak sites were and that type information. Some people wouldn't keep their maps up to date and would take a division or section right over a known flak site and get their asses shot off. Some folks had good reputations, and others not so good. As a result, their division qualification would be taken away. There was no leeway for a JO to say I won't fly with a guy, and it never happened in any of the squadrons that I was with that a JO went to a superior and said "I'm not flying with this guy anymore." But a wingman who knew the lead was heading over a known flak site would say, "Hey lead, such and such is two miles off our nose, let's go to the right about three miles." And the guy would do that; he didn't know what the hell was happening, and he'd be saved the embarrassment.

Some people didn't care. Their attitude was "I'm going into combat, I'm not going to bust my ass, and I'm not going to get killed, and that's all I care about." Other folks, their attitude was "I'm going to lead the alpha strike, no one is going to get killed, and I'm going to spend the time and effort to analyze how we're going in to the target, and how we're going out." They'd check the weather criteria, and have the guts to say [that] the weather is not right, or whatever is not right, we're going back home, and tell CAG and the skipper, "Fuck you very much, I'm not going to lose anybody just to get a sortie count." And yes, there were people who did that.

Going North, there was always a primary and alternate target, and if the weather wasn't right on the primary, you'd head to the alternate. If the alternate wasn't right, then everybody had their road recce missions or whatever. There was big pressure on getting that primary mission, and I didn't realize the pressure that was put on the CAG and skippers from the CARGRU staffs until I was on staff. I guess I must have been some kind of dummy when I was CO because I never perceived that pressure on CAG.

Even after the war was over, the competition between ships remained. This ship flew so many hours, they didn't have any accidents, and we don't care how shitty the weather is, we're going to launch. I never believed in that, and still don't, and I think we've lost a lot of pilots since the war because the feeling from the skipper and CAG, probably coming from staff, was we've got to get those sorties out. The deck's pitching fifteen feet, visibility is half a mile, but we're launching anyway. I figure when the skipper of the ship makes a decision to launch on a shitty night, that's life and death, because there is a good possibility that somebody is not coming back. Certainly the Navy must have a very controlled feeling of what it's trying to do. There must be an image, given to our enemies, that we can launch day or night, foul weather or not. But there has to be a cutoff place somewhere when the intelligent mind says it's not worth the risk of life. That's as true in peacetime as it is in combat. When the skipper or CAG is trying to get that next promotion, and puts other people's lives in jeopardy to get that promotion, that's bullshit.

The first time I led a section, on my wing was a first cruise guy who'd been through the whole nine yards. We flew a road recce, and skipper had taken another section on a RESCAP mission at the same time. Skipper knew when we called feet dry, and he knew when we called feet wet, and the two of us spent something like forty-five minutes looking for a target to hit. When we came back in and in front of me—a lieutenant commander—he chewed this jg's ass out. Just chewed him up and down, and his message was "God dammit, there's nothing out there worth getting shot for, and you know that, but you let this new lieutenant commander take you over the beach and keep you there for forty-five minutes. Now that's fucking dumb."

The point is—the skipper felt this guy had more experience over the North than I did. He'd go along with seniority—i.e., I'm leading the hop—but it was the jg's responsibility to keep me out of trouble. That was the attitude by the time I arrived in June of 1972. There's nothing worth dying for in North Vietnam except the POWs. We'll go ahead and do our alpha strikes, and go pound these guys into the ground, but there's only one reason to lose your life and that's getting our buddies, the POWs, out. My skipper didn't make CAG, and I think one of the reasons he didn't centered on the fact he wasn't pushing the sortie count, wasn't pushing the game. He wasn't playing the game along with the other people, getting promoted because he was a great skipper. His goal when the squadron left on cruise was to bring everybody back. He accomplished it, and I learned from that experience. My primary goal as skipper when I took my squadron was not to lose any pilots or troops, and we accomplished that.

Chapter 35
The Final Years

August 1972 found Bill Shankel spending his eightieth month as a guest of the Democratic Republic of Vietnam. Life had become more bearable, or at least more humane. Freedom, however, was still a half year away. Peace talks between Hanoi and Washington had informally begun in 1967, followed by the start of formal negotiations in Paris the following year. Averill Harriman, Henry Cabot Lodge, and finally Henry Kissinger headed American efforts, which eventually culminated in a January 1973 agreement.

"As a prisoner, what I missed most was the freedom, being able to go to a door, turn the knob and walk through it," notes Shankel.

We enjoy so much freedom in this country. If California doesn't suit your tastes, why not try West Virginia. You can drive through every state between here and there, and if the speed limit is obeyed, nobody will stop you. That's a helluva lot of real estate to just wander around on and not be challenged anywhere, and a concept the gooks could not fathom.

Their level of sophistication wasn't much. I had a debate, or close to a debate, once with Rabbit, and he refused to believe freeways and supermarkets weren't only for the high-ranking government officials. Owning a car or two or three just blew his mind, and Rabbit's version was that not everybody can use cars, not everybody can own them. He just refused to believe it.

Mind games, or more aptly the pursuit of learning, kept Shankel and his fellow POWs occupied as years five, six, and seven of captivity passed by.

I stayed at the Annex until the fall of 1970, moving out to a place about twelve miles from Hanoi. There we would have graduated into a compound situation, but that changed with the raid on Son Tay. We heard the noise, saw the gun flashes and everything else, but didn't know what was going on. The next day no one was allowed out of the rooms except a couple of guys to distribute food and wash the plates. That evening the gooks put us in trucks and took us back to the Hilton complex. About fifty guys were placed in a big room, and it was really funny to walk up and meet some faceless guy you tapped on the wall to for years but had never seen. You've heard the names, gone over their names for five years—and now to meet them!

The atmosphere had changed. The usual room changes took place, but the brutality was over. Some guys were stuck in solitary for getting too salty, but that was all. No irons, and cuffs were only put on loosely. The junior and senior people were for the most part separated, with the senior guys taken off by themselves to another area. They made the rules and regulations, and we talked to them every day by signal and code.

Word of the Paris peace talks came from Hanoi Hannah over the camp radio, but that even stopped after a while because the gooks believed we were getting too much information from her. I felt we were sold out—and my opinion was not the general consensus—when the decision was made to sit down at the table and negotiate. Absolutely nothing was done to even get us POW status and adequate medical treatment. Years after their shootdown, people still had open sores from flak wounds and things like that. The gooks always called us war criminals, not prisoners of war, and five years went by before I got a letter from my mother. I was then allowed to write, but only six lines on a postcard and in seven-plus years I received maybe three letters.

Part of the Code of Conduct says I will keep faith with my government. God, I thought, don't negotiate with the North Vietnamese, just beat them. Don't ask them what to do, tell them. When the bombing was going on, at least we knew something was happening. If the guards were angry and mean, it meant they'd been up all night because of the bombing. That was great. But then the bombing stopped, supposedly to negotiate in Paris upon our behalf. Yet the summers of 1968–69 were the two worst summers ever. The government sold us out, especially senators like Kennedy, McGovern, and Muskie. The really vocal anti-war critics wanted a total pullout from Vietnam, which I interpreted as a "leave the prisoners to fend for themselves" philosophy.

In terms of propaganda, every once in a while the gooks would sit us down and show movies of the demonstrations taking place back home. Most of us thought it was all bullshit. We saw all these people covered with hair walking up and down the streets of San Francisco, and the general thought was "Don't tell us those are average Americans." When I heard people got into a scrap with the National Guard at Kent State and some of them got shot, I thought, Man, that's great. They should have shot more of them. Anybody stupid enough to taunt some guy with a loaded gun, stupid enough to goad another guy with a gun into shooting at you, deserves to get shot.

Most of the ways to pass the time were mind oriented. Where I grew up, people built their own houses, and so I helped a lot of people build homes. My roommate Dave Wheat was an industrial arts major, and he knew exactly how to build a house; plus, he worked for a number of contractors. What the two of us did was get a bunch of broom straws and make floor plans, figuring out how to build houses in various phases. Then we'd contemplate wiring and a three-way switch, where you turn the light on as you come in one door and turn the light off as you go out the door at the other end of the room. Trying to figure out how to wire that would take a couple of days.

In the big rooms, we took ringworm medicine—gentian violet—and made ink, and pieces of bamboo were cut with stolen razor blades to create pens. So with gentian violet and the elephant toilet paper the gooks gave us, we made course outlines, books, and all that. Most people wanted to learn languages, and we ended up having classes in Spanish, German, French, and Russian. The gooks would occasionally have room raids and take all our books away, but we'd just make new ones. I memorized a six-thousand-word French dictionary, really, because there was not a whole lot of intellectual stimuli. We were adept at memorizing names of POWs, and when it came to memorizing, that dictionary posed no problem at all. I could rattle them off, starting at A and going through every word to Z.

At the Annex we were periodically called in to give an English lesson to the gooks. One or two of us would go over and just jerk chains, and I always hated to go over with a guy named Scotty Morgan. My answers were always yes, no, hoping they'd get disgusted and throw me out. But Scotty would start talking to them, telling all the great possessions he owned. They'd ask him, "What do you do with your free time?" Scotty liked to hunt and fish, and he'd tell them all the guns he owned. And they'd ask, "What do you hunt?" and he'd say, "Ducks and gooks." I'd be trying not to laugh, and he just sat there with this North Carolina deadpan expression. Eventually, they did figure out gooks was a derogatory term.

About two hundred of us went to a camp known as Dogpatch near the Chinese border after the bombing started up North again, staying over Christmas and New Year's. We then were loaded up on trucks and brought back outside Hanoi. At that point we knew the war was over; the North Vietnamese had quit, played out all their bullshit, and we were going home. In February the group of us went back to the Hanoi Hilton complex. As the truck crossed the pontoon bridge heading back in, we hiked up the canvas cover and Hanoi was just a mess. We all thought that was pretty neat. At the Hilton, for the first time, we were thrown together as a large group, and that's the first chance I had to talk with Everett Alvarez face-to-face.

I'd known Alvarez before the war; we lived together at the BOQ in Lemoore, and he was everybody's hero because he'd been there the longest, I mean, he'd been a prisoner since August of 1964. The next guy to show up, Bob Shumaker, wasn't shot down until February of 1965. Alvarez was there for fourteen months before I arrived.

The first group of us were released on 12 February [1973]. The sick and injured left; then everybody else by order of shootdown. The only positive factor to being shot down first, you went home first.

Chapter 36
LINEBACKER II

On a day in August eight years earlier, then lieutenant commander John Nicholson had taken part in the first publicly acknowledged combat strike against North Vietnam. Now, as 1972 drew to a close, the Navy captain's assigned task centered on devising a plan to bring the war to a close.

That plan took the form of LINEBACKER II, an unlimited air assault over Hanoi and Haiphong carried out primarily by Air Force B-52 bombers and tactical aircraft, with limited assistance from the Navy's carrier-based squadrons.

The first wave of B-52s struck 18 December, and eleven days later, North Vietnamese officials were more than ready to consider peace negotiations seriously.

Nicholson's role in LINEBACKER II was undoubtedly fitting, for the Oberlin College graduate's naval career had followed the course of the war. From 1964 to 1969 Nicholson deployed five times to Vietnam, the last tour as commanding officer of Attack Squadron 56.

"Arriving back at Lemoore from my CO tour with VA-56, I took over VA-122 in 1970–71," says Nicholson. "From the sense of being in your own environment, I really enjoyed the tour."

My ultimate command was CO of the *Ranger*—there is nothing more awesome than commanding a carrier. But I really enjoyed 122. Morale was high, the squadron was just huge—1,400 enlisted men, 125 pilots, and over 100 airplanes—the A-7E was the number one quality airplane; and the squadron had talent, individuals like Stan Arthur, Dave Carroll, and Mel Munsinger, and the cream of the crop from flight school. Really very exciting in that regard.

I left 122 as a captain and went aboard the *Enterprise* from October 1971 until June 1972 as operations officer. The ship was off Vietnam when I joined the staff, and as ops what I saw were the hops that caused a lot of people to get burned later. These were the unan-

nounced hops, hitting targets in North Vietnam we weren't supposed
to be bombing. The tour was very short, only the nine months,
because they pulled me over to CINCPACFLT staff as air operations.

Based at Pearl Harbor, Hawaii, the CINCPACFLT staff was earnestly
directing the final chapter of America's Vietnam debacle.

As air ops, I saw the war from a different vantage point altogether.
There were twenty-one captains on the staff, and for the first time I
was working with four- and three-star admirals, and a two-star sat in a
hovel right next to me. Really the stratosphere as far as power is concerned.

Up to that point, I'd always been operational, always on the end of
dropping bombs and flying the airplanes. All of a sudden I'm on the
political side, seeing black and being told it's white. For the first time,
I realized the politics involved in the decisions being made, and it turned
me off. I tell you, it turned me off real fast. I'm not a politician, and I
always said I'd stay with the Navy, stay in the Navy, as long as I
enjoyed it. All of a sudden I found myself not really enjoying it. I always believed in honesty, even though it hurt a lot of times, because
you win by being honest. Even a little lie here and there compounds,
and soon someone's in a damn box. I saw boxes being made, and admirals
grappling to get out of them.

The highlight of the tour was my active participation in LINEBACKER
II. One morning, a call came telling me to report to Adm. [Bernard]
Clarey's office. I'm standing rigid in front of this four-star and he says,
"CINCPAC wants you at their headquarters immediately. Take an assis-
tant and get the hell up there, and I want to be briefed on what's going
on when you get back."

I'm taken down into the dungeon, this vault at CINCPAC headquarters,
and in the vault is my Air Force counterpart [from] PACAF. Unlike
the Navy, where you just get to learn the ropes and it's time to move
on, this guy had about six years in the job, and I had great respect for
him. A few minutes later, some big power Air Force type [a general]
came in and said, "Gentlemen, you've been brought in here to end
this war in Vietnam. You're going to stay in this vault and draw up a
contingency plan on how to bring the enemy to his knees and make
them talk to Kissinger in Paris."

The PACAF guy was about ready to retire, and I'm so frustrated the idea has crossed *my* mind, and he said, "Let's do it the way we know it will work." All the AI's were bringing out the dust-covered contingency plans, which called for bombing the dirt footbridges and such, and we said, "Get that garbage out of here." Instead, a map of North Vietnam was taken out, circles drawn around Hanoi and Haiphong and every strategic, military, industrial, and communications target identified. I don't believe either of us thought the plan would sell, but we were enthusiastic about it, giggling and snorting while identifying all these targets and scribbling them on paper. About the third day, this Air Force general reappears and says "Where's the plan?" Our reply was, "We're still working on it," and he says, "I don't have time, give me all your paperwork on what you've got or what you're doing." He put it in a briefcase and left, and back I went to headquarters to brief Admiral Clarey on this contingency plan. Within twenty-four hours the message came back, execute LINEBACKER II. And when I saw the operation of LINEBACKER II, my teeth dropped. Our whole plan was bought, the B-52 strikes and mass tactical air during the daylight hours. It's almost scary when you think about it, how some awesome decisions in this world are made.

The positive aspects of LB II erased some of the frustration I felt, but the frustration really hadn't ended for me. Off goes LB II, and there's a soup bowl over Hanoi and Haiphong. The Navy's sitting out in the gulf not launching any aircraft, maybe a handful of A-6s each night doing an all-weather run. Meanwhile the Air Force is coming out of Thailand during the daylight hours with massive plane formations, dropping on the count and through the clouds.

So as the statistics are going up on the board each morning for the admirals and generals to look at, they're lopsided. The Air Force has all the B-52s and F-105s doing their thing while the Navy has only three or four A-6s going in. The A-7s are sitting on the deck, planes that I would have given my eyeteeth to lead in, and demonstrate the all-weather capability we'd shown in VA-122. But the word from the fleet commander is "No, we can't do that" because the A-7 is not all-weather.

I sat through this entire evolution, sending out little memos like "Hey admiral, notice the statistics, notice the statistics," and nothing was said. LINEBACKER II does its thing, the war ends, and my job is now out of business; there's nothing to do. So the history of LB II is recorded in detail, every bomb, every flight, every flight path, really a monumental task. All these fantastic statistics are put together, and the Air Force came out doing everything, the Navy had only a small role. That really evoked all kinds of emotionalism from the brass, like "Why didn't you tell me this was going on? Why was I not made aware the Navy should have been doing more?" I compiled copies of all my memos, fired them out, and that was the end of that.

Chapter 37
LB II Observer

LINEBACKER II witnessed the most significant aerial assault of the war as over twenty thousand tons of bombs fell on North Vietnam soil within an eleven-day span.

Air Force and Navy tactical aircraft flew some one thousand sorties while the devastating, and truly feared, B-52 Stratofortress left bases in Thailand and Guam to compile 740 missions. In reality, the Navy's aerial role was less than prominent thanks to an overcast ceiling of 3,000 to 6,000 feet over northern North Vietnam. During the entire bombing campaign, just one twelve-hour break in the weather made visual bombing possible.

The first bombs of LINEBACKER II struck the runways and buildings of Hoa Lac Airfield fifteen miles west of Hanoi on 18 December at 7:43 P.M. Before the evening ended, three waves of 129 B-52s hit Hanoi area targets, and three of the massive bombers were brought crashing to earth by SAMs, two aircraft falling over Hanoi and one in Thailand.

Targets in the heavily defended Hanoi and Haiphong area were the primary focus of LINEBACKER II, including rail yards, power plants, communication facilities, air defense radars, docks and shipping facilities, POL storage, ammunition supply areas, and nearby MiG bases.

North Vietnam met the challenge with approximately 1,250 surface-to-air missiles, bringing down fifteen B-52s, including six on 20 December alone. All totaled, SAMs, AAA, and MiG interceptors accounted for the downing of twenty Air Force aircraft and six carrier-based planes. But the message of the campaign—complete military and material isolation—came home to the North Vietnamese loud and clear. And on the final two nights, not one incoming B-52, each carrying over one hundred 500- and 750-pound bombs, was damaged.

The human losses of LINEBACKER II saw, for the U.S., thirty-three crewmen die and another thirty-three captured; the North Vietnamese reported fifteen hundred dead.

While LINEBACKER II was criticized at home and abroad as "unparalleled barbarism," Richard Nixon notes that "our bombing achieved its purpose. . . . Militarily we had shattered North Vietnam's war-making capacity. Politically, we had shattered Hanoi's will to continue the war" (*No More Vietnams*).

Cmdr. Joe Ausley took part in LINEBACKER II, not from the cockpit of a B-52, not from an attack or strike aircraft flying off Yankee Station carriers. He was in his airplane, a RA-5C Vigilante (capable of flying twice the speed of sound), handling electronic countermeasure and photographic duties.

I made eight WestPac cruises, and the most exciting came when LINEBACKER II sent the B-52s north. We were on Yankee Station aboard the *Ranger* flying BDA [bomb damages assessment] and PECM [passive electronic countermeasure] missions. When the B-52s would go north, we'd sit fifteen to twenty miles off the coast, at thirty to thirty-five thousand feet, and pick up all the electronic codes, the various radar signals, and bring it back to the ship for analysis. Really a boring mission.

We liked the BDA mission because the airplane went in very fast, so fast that the F-4s couldn't keep up. Our main concern was the F-4s didn't get too far back and decide we were a MiG. When silhouetted, the RA-5 looks like a very big MiG-21, and there was confusion when the MiGs were flying.

As a rule, RA-5s would go in and get prestrike photography, taking quite a bit of flak and some SAMs too. We'd go back feet wet to some safe spot and orbit, or maybe do a photographic road run down the southern part of North Vietnam; then come back and trail the strike group by five minutes for the BDA. The North Vietnamese knew we were coming, with our arrival timed as the dust settled, and we'd again get the AAA and SAMs.

The backseater, the RAN [reconnaissance attack navigator], ran all the cameras and radar, with balls like you wouldn't believe because these guys never looked down. They closed their window in back to have complete darkness, really a cocoon, except to see flak or stuff in the viewfinder during the day. At night it was total radar and nothing to see out of the viewfinder.

Early on in the war, before the tactics were set and the good ECM equipment came out, the RA-5 mission was very hairy. By the time I got to RA-5s, we had good ECM and good tactics, and the Navy wasn't losing many aircraft. The plane was completely unarmed, and while all of us would have loved to strafe, bomb, or whatever, only the whim of the Navy counted. I definitely was pissed to go from light attack to the RA-5, but there was no choice. I flew A-4s with VA-192 in 1962, at that time tanking F-8s going in below the DMZ and up into Laos with no idea where they were going and not really wanting to know. I went up to Whidbey Island in 1966 and bounced A-3s before going back to sea in 1967 as ordnance and gunnery officer aboard the *Bon Homme Richard,* flying A-4 tanker hops with VA-212.

I really enjoyed flying the A-4; it was a sweetheart of an airplane. An A-5 is more like a Cadillac—the big cockpit, good instrumentation, good lighting, everything the A-4 didn't have initially. The RA-5 was originally called the A3J-1, built to deliver nuclear weapons and drop them on a nail. The system never worked, but even after we became photography recces, the plane still had racks on the wings for nuclear weapons delivery. For years, we had to have wiring checks, and for years it was such a ridiculous thing. The plane carried a lot of gas, and we'd usually launch first to help get the deck clear because it was a big aircraft, and recovered last, supposedly for deck spotting. In reality, there was a fear the plane would break. I didn't feel it was a tough airplane to get aboard the ship; really, it was a very nice airplane and putting fighter and light attack people into the bird was very good for the program.

My combat mission total was 155, 160, not counting the Air Force flights. The RA-5s didn't fly as often as the other aircraft in the wing, partially because we had availability and parts problems at times. In 1972 there were four planes in every squadron and many of the PECM flights weren't over land and didn't count as combat missions. Flying also was scarce when the wing went on an all-alpha strike mode. There'd be two alphas each day, and that's all the RA-5s would fly.

I was up on the initial night of LINEBACKER II on a passive mission. My hop didn't go in, but I counted over one hundred SAMs coming out of Haiphong and Hanoi. Just unreal, and there's nothing so depressing as to see a silhouetted B-52 with its wing on fire going all the way down in a spiral. It was interesting to send the B-52s up North, but even more interesting, we'd go in the next day and not really find that much damage. I think the bombing damaged morale, but the way the

North Vietnamese and Orientals work, they'd have fires and everything out. There'd be no residuals, nothing.

Anytime you were over the beach, the adrenaline flowed. I would say it was not as hairy as the A-4s going in with the Walleyes and such, that was a helluva lot more risky than photo work. But anytime you saw flak the adrenaline pumped, and you never knew what was going to happen over the target. The camera had 140 degrees of field, but you still tried not to jink any more than necessary, making the run as flat and level as possible to get the best photography. You could pull five Gs and such in an A-4 and A-7 to get away from the SAMs, but the RA-5 was such a big airplane, max was three-and-a-half Gs.

There were some interesting missions that were actually dumb at the time. As XO of RVH-5, the skipper and myself, along with two F-4 wingmen, went below a fifteen hundred foot overcast—at 600 to 1,000 feet—and flew just south of the China border, down below the karst towards Haiphong. One plane wasn't enough, because the coverage at that altitude required two airplanes. We got some flak, but there was no way to evade, and we were trying to verify the existence of two God damn Russian-built Komars [PT boats] which carried missiles and were a threat to the carrier. Both were hidden in the karst. We found them, and came out over the point by Haiphong where the lighthouse is, both of us doing about 1.3 mach. I know we must have cracked the walls of that God damn thing.

The word went back to CTF-77, who was in Hong Kong, and the decision made not to strike until he got back. So the strike was delayed for three days, and in the interim, we lose an F-4 chasing another RA-5 to verify the two ships are still there. What was funny about the raid, we hadn't been that far north in a while and everyone thought it was going to be a fun raid. The feeling was somebody might not get back, and there'd be a chance to go in and do the search and rescue bit. When the strike launched, CAG and CARDIV were shaking their heads as to why almost every CO and XO in the air wing flew on the mission.

To me, the attitude in Vietnam was we're doing our job, what the Navy sent us over to do. There was dissatisfaction, going in and bombing POL sites with empty barrels and you know they're empty. Or a MiG is discovered on an airstrip. We'd run over and take pictures, and it's a shell that's been there for years. They'd reinvent the wheel every time we were over there. Tactics were never published, so there were individuals in leadership roles with no combat experience trying to be cowboys and heroes. You nearly had to retrain a lot of the thinking, and that late in the war it was kind of dumb to go over there and do things that were really stupid. But, as a lot of people said, "While it's a shitty war, it's the only one we have."

Chapter 38
CARGRU

Wes McDonald, like many of his contemporaries, spent a good portion of his naval career involved in the events of the Vietnam War.

After his participation as a strike leader in the 1964 Gulf of Tonkin retaliatory mission, he returned a year later to command a carrier air wing. Summer of 1972 found McDonald, then a two-star admiral, taking command of Carrier Group 3 aboard the *Coral Sea*. By December, CARGRU 3 was operating off Yankee Station, and McDonald had a first-hand view of the war's final chapter.

I was out on Yankee Station for the Christmas bombing, the bombing halt, and when the POWs were flown out. During the Christmastime raids, Yankee Station had been moved far enough north so that the B-52s could actually be seen going in. The smoke trails of the SAMs coming up at them were also visible, and every once in a while you might see what was thought to be a B-52 getting hit on the horizon. The sky would light up, there'd be a lot of fire, and the next day the reports would say three B-52s got hit. The reaction would be something like, "oh yeah, I saw that."

My association as one of three CARGRUs out there at the time was [to do] direct planning with the Commander, Task Force 77 [CTF-77], Vice Adm. Hutch Cooper. The action was in many ways hot and heavy, with the air wings flying Iron Hand and night strikes. The A-6s and A-7s were doing all the tasks they were supposed to do, as were the F-4s, flying cover and working against patrol boats up in the Haiphong area.

We were in a continuous planning mode, shifting targets and such, and CTF-77 was on the phone all the time. Really, an alive piece of action compared to what it had been in 1965–66. President Nixon had decided we'd played around long enough—that's my interpretation—and we were no longer going to play around. The only lesson the North Vietnamese could understand was [for us] to dump on them with lots of power, and that was the solution. With the harbor mined, and the bombing of the rails and rail yards, it was obvious from the photography the North Vietnamese weren't going to make it work much longer. Most of the SAMs had been attrited, and the North Vietnamese simply could not get any more.

My role was one of response to the carrier and air wing. I'd been there, I knew what the guys were doing, and it was a coordinated effort among the three carriers. In many ways it was tough for the guys flying, but in other ways it wasn't. The pilots and aircrews were a helluva lot more professional than early in the war, a lot tougher. They were aware of the enemy's capabilities, they knew their own capabilities, and the systems were better. It was pretty well recognized the war was coming to an end, the hope was just to keep from getting any more of our people killed. At the time, I didn't particularly care about their people dying.

When the war ended, there was a tremendous feeling of accomplishment, and then it all went to shit. Our actions were absolutely pathetic; we just pulled in and let it all go, sacrificing a lot of brave people. The South Vietnamese didn't deserve all the criticism received during the war. When we trained them, gave them the proper equipment and stayed with them, they were pretty damn good allies, from what I could gather. I never saw the South Vietnamese in the air because they hardly ever flew up North, but they fought a helluva war against some very ferocious people. For the U.S. to pull in and just walk away knowing full well there was no way for the Vietnamese to sustain themselves without our help is a crime. Ted Kennedy, and people like that, should really face up to it. But they don't, and the country [South Vietnam] is gone.

A highlight was the POW release, and I wanted to go over and see the POWs coming back because I had some good friends who were supposedly coming out. I told somebody my desire to see the POWs come in to Clark, and the word came back that Adm. [Noel] Gayler, [CINCPAC] said [that] no, it can't be done. I thought, you horse's ass, and finally the word came back [that] yes, admiral, you can come but don't try and interfere. Hell, all I wanted was to be there, I wasn't about to interfere. So I sat dutifully in the crowd and Admiral Gayler, when he saw me, invited me to come up and sit with him. As it turned out, I'm not so sure it wasn't his staff giving me all this bullshit.

The POW arrival was terribly emotional. People waving flags, the tears, really one of the most emotional times of my life. I can still remember hearing Jerry Denton say what a privilege it had been and "God Bless America." The moment still brings tears to my heart.

Chapter 39
Homecoming

A select group of individuals observed the LINEBACKER II campaign with more than just a passing interest. For them, the sound of bombs exploding throughout Hanoi was actually the sound of freedom.

Less than two months after the initial bombs from a B-52 struck the capital of North Vietnam, the first of three groups of American prisoners of war had gone home. The first returnees left Hanoi 12 February and by May, the North Vietnamese government had released 591 American POWs, including 138 naval aviators. Among them was Harry Jenkins.

When the B-52s came that first night in December, there was an initial question as to what plane it was. But the bombing went on so long we knew it had to be B-52 attacks which came at night, while tactical air strikes occurred during the day. One time, a bomb exploded right outside the camp wall, a four-foot-thick wall some twenty-feet high separated from our building by a twenty-foot-moat dirt area. A window was above my bunk, and Jim Mulligan said there's a bomb, he'd seen it fall. The bomb went off, blowing our door and roof off, really great. One guy was cheering during the raid, and the gooks beat the hell out of him, failing to see the humor of the situation.

There were occasions to spite the guards, like right after the raid at Son Tay, when the guards were a bit nervous. In the courtyard washing our clothes or exercising, we'd make helicopter gestures. I can't say for sure that bothered them, but they seemed to be a little disturbed that helicopters might come into the yard.

I'm not a big athlete—I played a little basketball in high school and was never very good—but I developed an exercise program over there, everybody did. More than anything else, the purpose of the program was to walk out of the camp when the time came. I was going to last and not let those bastards get to me. You got that attitude after a while, willing to do anything just to spite them. Some, like I said, were funny.

At Alcatraz, I started blowing electrical fuses. While hanging out clothes to dry one day, I noticed an extension cord which stretched across camp to light the rooms on the other side. The two cords joined in the middle, and there were a bunch of loose wires sticking out. So while hanging my clothes, I wrapped the loose wires together. I went back and told Howard Rutledge, through the wall, to hang up his mosquito net before it got dark because the airman-electrician had been out in the yard. The guard came along, turned on the lights, and blew every fuse three or four times before getting the lights to work. The next guard had the same problem, and I could hear people in the camp laughing.

I carried that fun into other camps. In one, the lights in each room were actually a series of lights. If one blew, they all blew. I would bare some wires and put my handcuff pick up there and short them out. Night would come, a few fuses blew, and the camp would be dark all night. The next morning I'd take the pick down before the guards started troubleshooting. They'd just check the lights, find they're working, and wouldn't bother to look for the trouble. Three or four days later I'd do it over again and this would go on and on.

One Sunday afternoon Rutledge and I were listening to the radio. I didn't know much about radios, but remembered a radio was very low voltage. So I broke some wires in the radio speaker, breaking the circuit. The radio line was a common line, and if one speaker went out, they all went out. So I could turn everybody's speaker in the camp off and on. Stockdale was across the camp and because I couldn't think of anything else to do, I tapped out "Hi CAG" by turning this gook music on and off. Stockdale got the message. Certainly these little incidents didn't accomplish a thing, except the feeling you slipped them one.

Of all the tangibles, cold and hunger were the toughest to handle. I got to the point of thinking about food all the time, even dreaming of it. Countless times I dreamed of being in a self-service store, but never able to get to the payout place. I'd have bags full of stuff, then go by the sugar donuts, and boy, they'd look good, and fill another bag. I'd get to the next place, and there'd be brownies, and I'd take out half my donuts and put in brownies. Rutledge told me one night about eating a steak, and he woke up to find he'd chewed the inside of his mouth and could taste the blood while dreaming about eating this steak.

Strangely enough, I didn't think that much about females. I suppose everybody tells his wife the urge for sex is just like hunger—it's a drive—but it's not. I can remember only one erotic dream the whole time I was a POW, and that was about Natalie Wood. I was in the upper bunk of an upper and lower bunk, and Natalie climbed up on the lower bunk to talk to me. She was standing there, and I was leaning over talking to her, and I said "Natalie, do you realize your shorts are so tight they're laying down the crack in your ass?" She said, "I know," and then I woke up. You're either cold, really hurting, or busy communicating, and sex doesn't rear its head when there are other elements much worse. The wives were briefed that a bunch of us would come back homosexuals, and so far as I know, there was not even an intimate moment between any two guys over there.

The B-52 raids came, then stopped so suddenly we knew an agreement had been reached. One day this strange gook came into our camp courtyard, and just kind of hung around. He didn't have anything to do, and he wasn't speaking to anybody. I told Rutledge the North Vietnamese are going to read the peace agreement, and it occurred to me this guy was there to see our reaction. Sure enough, ten minutes later the radio came on and the agreements were read.

The word had been put out by Col. John Flynn, the POW commanding officer, that when the end came, there was to be no display of emotion. After the announcement our camp was silent, absolutely silent. So this guy came over, and he spoke English a little bit, and said, "Did you hear the radio?"

"Yeah, we heard the radio."

"Well, the war is over. You're going to go home."

"Yeah."

"Aren't you happy?"

"Sure, but we've been telling you for seven years we're going home."

The guy just couldn't believe our reaction, and was so frustrated he just turned around and left.

Colonel Flynn had also put out an order that at release time, we would conduct ourselves as officers and go home in a military manner. There would be no discarding of clothes, no obscene gestures, no favors accepted, no flowers, no offers of good will. We would go home in order of shootdown, following any women or civilians, and the sick and wounded. The order called for refusing, or at least resisting, anything other than this.

Flynn asked to see the camp commander after the agreements were read, and this time was allowed to. Flynn told the commander of the direction he'd put out, and unless there was going to be trouble during the release, we were not going home in business suits, but preferred to come home in our prison clothes. The answer was no, that wouldn't be permitted, but that we would not wear coats and ties, nor business suits, and could go home in shootdown order following the civilians and wounded.

There were three releases—and I was on the first—and within three or four people, we knew exactly who would be with what release group. About two weeks before the release, the camp was reorganized by release groups, some of whom I had never met before. We were given virtually free roam of the camp, doors were open, and the opportunity was there to talk with anyone. A lot of activity was taking place in a room on the end, so myself and another guy wandered down there during an exercise period and just walked in. The guards seemed to feel we shouldn't be there, but were unsure as to whether or not to kick us out. We stayed, roaming around a room full of piles of shoes, open collared shirts, windbreaker jackets, belts and pants, our clothes to go home.

A day or two before release, a few guys at a time were brought down to fit for clothes. We were then packed up, and I believe it was either a Sunday or Monday, and taken by bus out to an area near the airport. The buses were open, and the damage around Hanoi pretty visible. The big Paul Doumer Bridge lay in the river and, of course, that was pretty. Buildings were quite damaged, and we all realized Hanoi had taken a few lumps. People along the way were curious—they didn't threaten us or throw rocks, or say a word—and probably were as glad the war was over as we were.

Near the airport, nothing seemed to happen. We were told to stay in a group of buildings, but the head was about a half-block down and guys wandered back and forth. A bunch of tents, Red Cross–like tents, had been set up in an apron area and while we weren't directly at the airport, we knew the airport was close by, because somebody came by and reported a C-141 had landed. Yet nothing happened, we just hung around.

About lunchtime, the gooks brought in some sandwiches and cases of beer. Jim Stockdale, the senior officer of the group, said nobody was to drink the beer. We weren't going to leave with any show of comradery whatsoever. We ate the sandwiches and just drank water.

Finally, buses arrived and drove us out to the airport itself. A C-141 was sitting there, and the first couple of buses unloaded and the guys boarded. The second airplane, my airplane, came in and took right off, not even touching the ground. The immediate consensus was something had been screwed up and the release had fallen through. But the guy circled the field once and came back and landed, and we later found out the agreement had stipulated only one airplane at a time on the ground. In that one trip around the field, the pilot had spoken around the world to President Nixon, who said, "I don't care if there are two on the ground, land." And he did.

An Air Force colonel officially accepted us. He read our names, we stepped out of ranks, met this guy, and shook his hand. A sergeant also came out and helped me to the plane, and nurses were onboard. But the attitude was subdued, almost as if "this could be, but we're not there yet." The airplane took off, and finally, the pilot called up and said, "We're feet wet, over the water," and God that airplane erupted.

Because of the concern about our diets, the only food on the plane was chocolate milk and very bland items. There were no cigarettes, and while the crew gave us theirs, they lasted only five minutes. Because of our experience, recommendations were made for future flights to include spicy foods, drinks, and plenty of cigarettes.

The trip to Clark Air Force Base in the Philippines took some three hours, and nobody was prepared for the reception. We had no indication the POW issue had become so big—the wearing of bracelets or the massive drive to keep our names in front of the public. The North Vietnamese were very conscious of face, and for years the issue of our treatment had been quiet. When that attitude changed with the furor over our treatment, the Vietnamese began to think they had a better chance by treating us humanely.

After landing, our names were called one at a time, and I got off and just thousands of people were there. Some guy screamed "Harry," and I waved but couldn't see who it was. Later I found out the guy was in my wife's high school class and had known me in high school. All of us were assigned an escort officer to handle the debriefing and any personal needs.

Our next stop was the hospital, [where we were] isolated on one of the upper floors. That first night, Robbie Risner called and spoke to the president, and a big pot of thick chocolate milkshakes was brought up. We weren't permitted to leave the hospital, except as a group to go eat in the cafeteria or something of that nature. There was a concern as to what diseases we might have, plus a desire to keep people from bothering us. A bland diet had been planned, but switched to include steaks, desserts, ice cream, and so forth.

A tailor came up and measured us all for uniforms and everyone had to have a watch, so the exchange was opened up for us one night, and the group of us went over about ten o'clock. There must have been about a thousand people standing there to just watch us walk into the exchange wearing our pajamas.

Back home the reaction was unbelievable. Once identified as a POW, you couldn't buy a drink, an airline ticket—everything was gratis. We were wined and dined until it just became tiring.

Eight years after his August 1964 shootdown, Everett Alvarez, Jr., was going home. Home to California; home to his family; and home to friends, such as John Nicholson, who met Alvarez on his arrival in Hawaii. The brief reunion allowed Nicholson the long-awaited opportunity to finally debrief his wingman.

The POWs, on their way home, came through Hickam Air Force Base in Hawaii about 3:00 A.M. for about an hour or so. My wife Evie and I both went to see Alvy arrive, and, God, you couldn't believe the turnout of people. I mean the airport was jammed with flags and people, really just tremendous.

Nobody was supposed to talk to the POWs, but I told my story to this Air Force colonel. "Damn, I've got to see that guy, I've got to see him." He said "I'm not in charge, but I'll tell you what. I'll see the POWs; if he wants to talk, I've got no objection." I said, "That's only fair." He came back and said "Nicholson, come with me," and Evie and I were taken to an all-white room. Just Ev and I in there and one little table with a chair, the most antiseptic room I've ever been in. We waited and waited, and all of a sudden the colonel came in and he had Alvarez with him. He looked at us, we looked at him, and we just ran over and grabbed each other. Then all of a sudden he pushed me back and started to cry, just broke down crying. Soon I was crying, Ev was crying, all of us.

I thought how the hell do you break this ice, so I said "As a wingman, you're unsatisfactory. I've been waiting eight years to debrief that last flight." And he replied, "I'll tell you what, I'll never do it again." That broke it, and we started talking. He told me it was the first time he'd cried, "since I saw you last. I never cried in eight-and-a-half years. I don't know what happened, I just didn't want to cry."

We sat there for the rest of the hour together, and he just absolutely let his heart out. First, he wanted to know where all the VA-144 pilots were who were in on that initial strike. He remembered every pilot, and God I'd forgotten all of them except for two or three. He recalled me saying, "You know what to do," and "all the way down in the parachute thinking, damn it, I *don't* know what to do."

Alvy was in a white uniform, and he looked at all [his] ribbons asking what this one was, how did I get this one. Then from his pocket, he took out a handkerchief just like it was a million dollars. Inside was a Polaroid snapshot of Air Force Colonel Robbie Risner and Alvarez. They were arm in arm, I guess just after repatriation. He said, "I worship the man." Then he folded the handkerchief ever so carefully and put the photo back in his pocket.

Epilogue

The date was 27 January 1973. Lt. Cmdr. Harley Hall, a former Blue Angel pilot, etched his name into the annals of naval aviation history as the last fixed-wing combat loss of the war. Hall's F-4 Phantom went down near the DMZ. Search and rescue found the backseat radar intercept officer. Hall just disappeared.

That same day a cease-fire agreement between North and South Vietnam was signed in Paris, officially ending all American offensive military operations in the North. What began eight-and-a-half years earlier as a Navy retaliatory strike was finally over.

During the course of the conflict, Navy and Air Force aircraft dropped 7.8 million tons of bombs in Southeast Asia, an amount greater than the total tonnage released by all aircraft in all of World War II. More than 4 million tons of bombs fell on South Vietnam, another 1.5 million on Laos, 1 million on North Vietnam, and 500,000 on Cambodia.

Two thousand aviators had been killed and another 1,400 listed as missing in action. Overall, of the 3 million Americans who served in Vietnam, over 58,000 had been killed and another 304,000 wounded.

Provisions of the 27 January cease-fire required the release of all American POWs within two months, in exchange for the clearing of U.S. mines from North Vietnamese waters and U.S. military withdrawal from South Vietnam.

During February and March of 1973, Operation HOMECOMING saw 138 naval aviators released. Thirty-six aviators had died while in captivity, and over 600 naval flight crew personnel were missing and presumed dead.

The goal of American efforts during the war—maintaining an independent South Vietnam—was lost two years later. On 30 April 1975 North Vietnamese tanks rolled into Saigon and through the gates of the presidential palace. Saigon and South Vietnam had fallen to the Communists.

Appendix
Interview List

Capt. Joe Ausley. Spent three weeks in South Vietnam with Air Force as forward air controller in 1967 during ship's company tour on USS *Bon Homme Richard*. As RA-5 pilot, completed Yankee Station cruises aboard *Kitty Hawk* (1969) and *Ranger* (1972–73). President of Ausley Associates, a Washington, D.C., consulting firm.

Capt. Dean Cramer. Completed three combat tours with VA-163 (1967–68) and VA-155 (1972–73), totaling 397 combat missions. Resides in Flint Hill, Virginia, involved with consulting and other endeavors.

Rear Adm. Don "Linn" Felt. Strike operations officer aboard USS *Intrepid* for two combat deployments (1965–66); two combat tours with VA-27 as executive officer (XO)/commanding officer (CO) (1967–69); on the staff of Commander in Chief, Pacific Fleet (CINCPACFLT) as operations officer (1971–72). Resides in Arlington, Virginia.

Capt. Wynn Foster. Commanded VA-163 in July 1966 when his arm was severed by enemy shell. He returned to operational duty in 1968—serving as Carrier Group (CARGRU) operations officer and assistant chief of staff to the commander, First Fleet—before retiring in 1972. He lives in Coronado, California.

Capt. Len Giuliani. Completed three combat cruises with VA-153 (1966–67) and VA-22 (1971–72). Resides in Lemoore, California, employed by a defense contractor.

Capt. Harry Jenkins. Commanded VA-163 when shot down in November 1965. Released in February 1973. Lives in Coronado, California, works for a defense contractor.

Lt. Fred Knee. Completed two combat tours with VA-192 (1970–72). Resides in Lemoore, California, operating his own construction firm.

Lt. Cmdr. Norman Lessard. Flew two combat tours with VA-145

(1966–67). Resides in Winter Park, Florida, working for a defense contractor.

Capt. Dave Leue. Completed two combat tours in 1965–66 as XO-CO of VA-153. A professor at California State University, Fresno, Leue lives in Clovis, California.

Rear Admiral Robert Mandeville. Commanded VA-65 in 1966, the third A-6 squadron to participate in the Vietnam conflict. The Virginia resident is a vice president for Mantech Corp.

Adm. Wesley L. McDonald. As CO of VA-56 led retaliatory strike on North Vietnam in August 1964; served as commander of Air Wing 15 (1965–66), and in December 1972 returned to the Gulf of Tonkin aboard USS *Coral Sea* as commander of CARGRU Three. A resident of Arlington, Virginia, he is active as consultant, speaker, and president of the Association of Naval Aviation.

Capt. Ed McKellar. Served as XO-CO of VA-192 (1966–67), and commander of Air Wing 8 (1970). Director of the San Diego Aerospace Museum.

Capt. John Nicholson. Participated in Gulf of Tonkin retaliatory strike in August, 1964; served as XO-CO of VA-56 during two combat cruises in 1968–69; on the staff of CINCPACFLT as operations officer (1972–73). Resides in Lemoore, California, heading the Sanger High School Navy Junior ROTC program.

Rear Adm. Paul A. Peck. Commanded VA-94 for 1964–65 Vietnam tour and Air Wing 9 on 1968 combat deployment. An attorney, he resides in the San Francisco Bay Area, operating his own business firm.

Cmdr. Rusty Scholl. Completed two tours with VA-147 (1967–69) and another on the staff of Air Wing 15 (1971–72). Resides in Lemoore, California, employed as pilot for Beacon Oil Corp.

Capt. Gary Scoffield. Completed three combat tours, two on the staff of Air Wing 5 aboard the USS *Ticonderoga* (1964–65) and with VA-192 (1966–67). Lives in Alexandria, Virginia, works in the defense industry.

Cmdr. Bill Shankel. Shot down in December 1965 while flying with VA-94. Released in February 1973. A surgeon, Dr. Shankel resides in Laughlin, Nevada.

Capt. Bill Siegel. Flew two combat tours (1967–69) with VA-55. An account executive for Shearson Lehman Hutton, he resides in Lemoore, California.

Cmdr. D. D. Smith. Flew two combat tours with VA-72 (1965–66).

Lives in the Sacramento, California, area, operating his own investment firm.

Cmdr. T. R. Swartz. Completed two combat tours with VA-76 (1967–68), becoming the only A-4 Skyhawk pilot to shoot down a North Vietnamese MiG. Resides in Poway, California, working for a defense contractor.

Capt. Scotty Vaught. Spent three-and-a-half years in VA-122 at Lemoore NAS training A-1 and A-7 pilots for combat, followed by two combat tours with Air Wing 9 (1969–70) and VA-94 in 1972. Resides in Bonita, California, working as a realtor.

Capt. Denis Weichman. Completed five combat tours, including VA-164 (1966–68) and VA-153 (1972–73). Compiled the most fixed-wing combat missions of any naval aviator. Lives in Marietta, Georgia, employed as a Lear jet pilot for a worldwide charter service.

Select Bibliography

BOOKS

Dengler, Dieter. *Escape from Laos*. Novato, CA: Presidio Press, 1979.

Elkins, Marilyn, Editor. *The Heart of a Man, Journal of Frank Elkins*. New York: W. W. Norton and Co., 1973.

Gibson, James William. *The Perfect War*. New York: Atlantic Monthly Press, 1986.

Grant, Zalin. *Over The Beach*. New York: W. W. Norton and Co., 1986.

Karnow, Stanley. *Vietnam, A History*. New York: Viking Press, 1983.

Marolda, Edward J. *Illustrated History of Carrier Operations—The Vietnam War*. New York: Bantam Books, 1987.

Marolda and Fitzgerald. *The U.S. Navy and Vietnam Conflict, Volume II, From Military Assistance to Combat, 1959 to 1965*. Government Printing Office, 1986.

Mersky, Peter B. and Polmar, Norman. *The Naval Air War in Vietnam*. Baltimore, MD: Nautical and Aviation Publishing Company of America, Second Edition, 1986.

Naval Historical Center. *A Short History of the United States Navy and the Southeast Asian Conflict, 1950–1975*. Department of the Navy, 1984.

Nixon, Richard. *No More Vietnams*. New York: Arbor House, 1985.

POW: A Definitive History of the American Prisoner of War Experience in Vietnam, 1964–1973. New York: Reader's Digest Press, 1976.

Sharp, U.S.G. Adm. *Strategy For Defeat, Vietnam In Retrospect*. San Rafael, CA: Presidio Press, 1978.

Sheehan, Neil, et al. *The Pentagon Papers* as published by the *New York Times*. New York: Bantam Books, 1971.

Stockdale, Jim and Sybil. *In Love and War*. New York: Harper and Row, 1984.

Van Dyke, Jon. *North Vietnam's Strategy for Survival*. Palo Alto, CA: Pacific Books, 1972.

ARTICLES

Cagle, Malcom W. "Task Force 77 in Action Off Vietnam." *U.S. Naval Institute Review*. Volume 98 (May 1972): 66ff.
Colvin, John. "Twice Around the World." Reprint from the 1981 Spring Edition of *The Washington Quarterly*.

DATE DUE

GAYLORD		PRINTED IN U.S.A.